The Fine Art *of* RUSSIAN LACQUERED MINIATURES

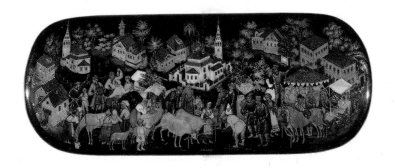

VLADIMIR GULIAYEV

CHRONICLE BOOKS

SAN FRANCISCO

First Published in the United States in 1993 by Chronicle Books.

Produced by Wieser & Wieser, Inc.

Printed in Spain

ISBN 0-8118-0325-2
Library of Congress Cataloging in Publication Data available.

Text by Vladimir Guliayev
Compiled by Liudmila Pirogova, Yelena Doroshenko, and
Olga Serebriakova
Photographs by Dmitry Belous
Translated by Sergei Volynets
Book Design by Alexander Borodin
Cover Design by Laura Lovett and Derek Oyen

Distributed in Canada by
Raincoast Books
112 East Third Avenue
Vancouver, B.C. V5T 1C8

10 9 8 7 6 5 4 3 2 1

Chronicle Books
275 Fifth Street
San Francisco, California 94103

Contents

Fedoskino, Palekh, Mstiora and Kholui are the four renowned centres of the Russian lacquered miniature, a brilliant constellation of traditional folk craftsmanship. Today, the works of Russian miniaturists, remarkable for the refined harmony of forms, loftiness of mood and optimistic representation of reality, have gained truly world-wide reputation.

The Russian lacquered miniature is the marriage of exquisite artistry and impeccable technique of execution. Toying with a small painted box one feels as if warmed by the luminescence of colours that shine through the perfectly polished lacquer coating. Bright cinnabar and emerald verdure, ultramarine and ochre are blended together to create an integrated and colourful pattern permeated with pure golden radiance. A spell-binding effect is produced by the magic play of colours, the filigree traceries, and the clear-cut and well-balanced composition which harmonize with the object's shape and surface. The designs range from very simple patterns to most complex scenes, always suggesting the refined sense of poetry.

The long history of the Russian lacquered miniature has had ups and downs, periods of general recognition alternating with times of disdain. No less complex has been the evolution of styles which, while being largely correlative in the four centres, still remain distinct and inimitable in each of them.

The four centres of the lacquered miniature neighbour upon one another in Middle Russia. The Fedoskino settlement located twenty kilometres north of Moscow is considered to be the mother of them all. In the late eighteenth century workshops supplying lacquer wares made of painted papier-mâché began to spring up in the environs of the settlement thus giving this new craft a start in life.

The narrow band of asphalt traverses the Moscow Ring Highway, makes a gentle curve round the suburban country-houses and reaches the expanse of the Kliazma reservoir. We cross it by a huge bridge before again diving into the copses. Another twenty minutes of ride and we turn right to catch a glimpse of the ledged premises of the Fedoskino Miniature Painting Factory towering above the high bank of the tiny Ucha river.

The road to Palekh passes through the old cities of Vladimir and Suzdal, their unique ancient architectural monuments reminding us of the inspired creative endeavours of the folk artists. The highway connecting Moscow and Palekh runs almost four hundred kilometres through the most picturesque landscape. Long before the journey is over the bell-tower of the Palekh church is visible in the distance. The white shape of the church itself emerges among endless meadows and woods that stretch upon the hills as far as the horizon.

Beyond Palekh the Kholui settlement lies a way off the main road and spreads amply on the banks of the Teza river navigable only by small cutters and boats. Huge crooked willows bend over the river, its banks abundantly covered in grass that creeps like a smooth green carpet.

Today, Mstiora can be reached from the Vladimir–Gorky railway. A merchantile village in the past, it is now a large settlement located among endless flood plains spreading over both sides of the deep and wide Kliazma. Kholui and Mstiora are related not only by the closeness of their territories but also by their inhabitants' age-old engagement in icon-painting.

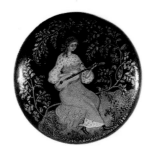

The four landscapes are different, yet comparable, as are the histories associated with each of the four settlements. The lacquered miniature has long been a traditional occupation with the Fedoskino villagers. But Palekh, Mstiora and Kholui, now prized for their miniature paintings that differ in style from the Fedoskino lacquers, before the October Revolution of 1917 ranked among the major centres of icon-painting. In the new situation after the revolution, the antique craft that had flourished for centuries in these parts provided a basis for the emergence of a new form of art. This proved to be more conformable with the realities of our times while still carrying on the traditions of ancient Russian painting and folk crafts.

Lacquer manufacture is known to have existed in Russia back in the early eighteenth century. In 1720–22 ten Russian masters were commissioned by the state to make ninety-four panels, varnished and painted in Chinese style, for Peter the Great's little palace called Monplaisir at Peterhof. However it was not until quite recently that these panels were identified as having been made by Russian craftsmen. For many years the design of wall-panels in Peter's study-room was attributed to Chinese masters. During the Nazi siege of Leningrad in the Second World War many unique interiors of the suburban mansions were ravaged. Only four panels from the Chinese Study survived. Palekh miniaturists, of whom more will be said later, and art historians took up the job of restoring the lost masterpieces. Enormous research work into their history was carried out. Then documents were found testifying that the panels were originally created by the Palekh masters. Furthermore, it was discovered that the panels had been made of lime-wood, more typical for Russia than for China.

It was only natural that in the eighteenth century the first Russian lacquer painters started with imitations of the Chinese lacquer. China is well known as the homeland of fancy lacquer-work that is broadly varied in both style and technique. For many years Chinese lacquers were venerated as the classic model by the Europeans. In the sixteenth and seventeenth centuries Oriental lacquer-work began to spread to Europe from China, Japan, Iran and India. In the late seventeenth and early eighteenth centuries independent lacquer manufactories emerged in the western and eastern parts of Europe.

So far very little is known about the eighteenth-century Russian lacquer painters. A number of this country's major museums hold singular specimens of their works attesting that the Russians were executing ornamental panels, fans, snuff-boxes with painted covers or mounted lockets and many other decorative articles. In the 1760s the Russian masters employed the varnishing technique to burnish the interiors of the palace at Oranienbaum (now the town of Lomonosov near Leningrad).

In the second half of the eighteenth century the lacquering of metal appeared in the Urals. At that time the major metalworks owned by the Demidov family of industrialists was able to provide a natural starting place for the intensive development of lacquered metal manufacture in the region. Thus, Nizhni Tagil, a large industrial centre, supplied all kinds of lacquered and painted metal wares. Painted trays became particularly famous, and having gone through a lengthy and complex evolution, their manufacture has survived till today.

The demand for lacquered goods grew. The customs policy of the Russian government helped the situation. Thus, for example, in the 1780s snuff-boxes, including lacquered ones, were made duty-free.

By the late eighteenth and early nineteenth centuries very many lacquer workshops had emerged in and around Moscow and St. Petersburg. I. Ukhanova, who has carried out a meticulous study of archive materials related to the history of the Russian lacquered miniature, points out that K. Ternberg's writing-paper mill in Oranienbaum District, St. Petersburg Province, had an annual turn-out of as many as 250 dozen fancy lacquer goods. Near St. Petersburg there was a factory owned by K. Tienpon that produced lacquered tin and paper wares. In the early nineteenth century the St. Petersburg factories owned by D. Orlova, a colonel's widow, and by the merchant A. Ekk, as well as three factories in Volhyn Province of the Ukraine, supplied together up to 18,000 dozen articles per year.[1]

---

[1] И.Н. Уханова, *Русские лаки в собрании Эрмитажа*, Л., 1964 с. 11 (I.N. Ukhanova, *Russian Lacquers in the Hermitage Collection*, Leningrad, 1964, p. 11).

Lacquer goods were also supplied by small provincial manufacturers. The period records mention the names of Austen, Bohl, I. Peitz, G. and V. Makarov, I. Zheltkov and many other producers. Information about these enterprises is very scanty and usually confined to the names of their proprietors. Nonetheless it allows us to ascertain that at the turn of the eighteenth and nineteenth centuries the production of lacquer goods was rather wide-spread in Russia.

The factory of P. Korobov holds a very special place in the history of Russian decorative arts. This enterprising merchant set up a factory supplying lacquered peaks for military caps. In Braunschweig, Germany, he studied and assimilated the experiences and basic know-how of the I. G. Stobwasser snuff-box factory, founded in 1763. Upon returning home, in 1798, Korobov started the manufacture of lacquer wares made of painted papier-mâché at the village of Danilkovo near Moscow.

No accurate description is available of Korobov's earliest manufactures. Several museums hold circular papier-mâché snuff-boxes, their covers bearing glued prints of portraits, historical and battle scenes and even geographical maps. These snuff-boxes are traditionally ascribed to the Korobov factory — although in the early nineteenth century such techniques were employed by Korobov's successors and were probably also used by other manufacturers. There are reasons to believe that decorative prints were prefabricated for glueing onto the snuff-box covers.

But why, of all things, snuff-boxes? It should be noted that in the eighteenth and early nineteenth centuries, as virtually all sections of Russian society took to smoking tobacco, they came into immensely wide use. Snuff-boxes were made of all sorts of materials, often expensive — bone (ivory), porcelain, tortoise-shell, mother-of-pearl, silver or even gold, and further embellished with gems and enamelwork. Lacquered snuff-boxes decorated with intricate ornaments swiftly came into vogue. Some of them bore glued prints featuring scenes related to the hottest social and political issues (the 1812 War against Napoleon, for instance), wherefore they were often referred to as "popular newspapers".

The Russian lacquer historian G. Yalovenko has come up with interesting documentary data: "Noteworthily," he writes, "costly as they were, the snuff-boxes stayed in good demand and sold out spectacularly on the home market. Thus in 1804 the output of snuff-boxes totalled 13,429 (there is every reason to assume that the manufacturer concerned was Korobov) out of which 9,094 were sold inside the country. In 1814 Korobov marketed 1,080 dozen snuff-boxes out of which 1,050 dozen were sold. A contemporary wrote that in 1810 home-made snuff-boxes were being marketed in all parts of the state."[1]

Eventually professional artists became more and more engaged in painting on papier-mâché snuff-boxes and thus the art of lacquered miniature came into existence.

By that time there was no lack of skilled miniaturists in Russia. Back in the first half of the eighteenth century miniature portraitists and icon-painters had a good sense of the enamelling technique. In the middle of the century skilful miniaturists made a formidable contribution to the development of porcelain painting at the newly-founded Imperial Porcelain Works in St. Petersburg. In 1779 a special class of miniature painting opened at the Academy of Arts. Many eminent Russian painters were in perfect command of the miniature portrait technique. "Thus", concludes the Soviet art historian S. Temerin, "there is no arguing the fact that the art of lacquered miniature emerged as a continuation and logical development of the experiences of the Russian national school accumulated by several generations of folk enamel painters, miniature porcelain designers and miniature portraitists. The special methods of painting on black-lacquered and smoothly polished papier-mâché surface were assimilated by Russian masters who had a wealth of experience in painting on other materials".[1]

The Lukutin family who took the business after P. Korobov made a major contribution to the development of lacquer painting. At some point between 1817 and 1819 the factory passed to Korobov's son-in-law Piotr Lukutin who introduced advanced technologies and appreciably expanded the manufacture. Korobov employed twenty-eight craftsmen in 1804 and thirty in 1812 while under Lukutin, in the 1840s and up to the 1860s, the number reached sixty.[2] Korobov employed both Russian and German masters, the latter recruited from Braunschweig. Lukutin invited no foreigners and managed with serfs and free-lance Russian painters. He set up a special school for training young craftsmen and issued grants for the best apprentices to study at the famous Stroganov school. Thus Lukutin made sure that his personnel comprised virtuoso craftsmen capable of executing the finest miniature work.

He notably expanded the range of products to include diversely shaped snuff-boxes (round, oval, rectangular, square, high and low), cigarette-cases,

[1] Г. В. Яловенко, *Федоскино*, М., 1959, с. 9 (G. V. Yalovenko, *Fedoskino*, Moscow, 1959, p. 9).

[1] *Русское декоративное искусство*, т. 3, М., 1965, с. 250 (*Russian Decorative Art*, vol. 3, M., 1965, p. 250).
[2] Yalovenko, *op. cit.*, p. 10.

traveller's tea-glasses made in different sizes so that one was insertable into another, tea-caddies with painted sides and cover, and caskets for needle-work and knick-knacks. The factory also supplied specimens of desk-sets, ornamental plates and other utensils. From 1818 many articles of the factory bore the monogram of its owner, and in 1828 Lukutin was entitled to mark his high-quality products with the Russian state emblem — a sign of the nation-wide recognition of his factory's handicraft goods. Thence the term "Lukutin lacquer" gained common currency in both literature and colloquial language.

Between 1843 and 1863, when the factory was jointly owned by Piotr Lukutin and his son Alexander, and later, when Piotr Lukutin died and Alexander (1818–1888) became the sole proprietor, the business ran spectacularly turning out ever more varied goods and gaining access to foreign markets after a series of successful showings at various trade and industrial exhibitions.

A couple of workshops owned by the Vishniakov family — the emancipated serfs of Count Sheremetev — existed next to the Lukutin factory. Eventually these manufacturers worked out a new

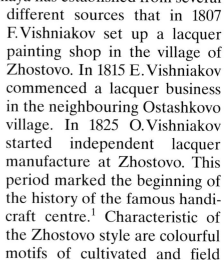

and distinctive style of lacquer painting that, in the twentieth century, proved to be crucial for the separation of the Moscow suburban lacquered miniature into an independent art form.

One of the leading Soviet experts in Russian folk arts I. Boguslavskaya has established from several different sources that in 1807 F. Vishniakov set up a lacquer painting shop in the village of Zhostovo. In 1815 E. Vishniakov commenced a lacquer business in the neighbouring Ostashkovo village. In 1825 O. Vishniakov started independent lacquer manufacture at Zhostovo. This period marked the beginning of the history of the famous handicraft centre.[1] Characteristic of the Zhostovo style are colourful motifs of cultivated and field flowers arranged in bouquets or spread in curlicue garlands. However, in the Vishniakovs' time this was by no means the sole existing pictorial style. Both the Vishniakov and Lukutin works supplied varied and diversely decorated utility articles made of papier-mâché.

Before reviewing the forms and contents of nineteenth-century lacquered miniatures a brief comment is required on the lacquer technology.

[1] И.Я. Богуславская, Б.В. Графов, *Искусство Жостова*, Л., 1979 с. 5, 6 (I. Ya. Boguslavskaya, B. V. Grafov, *The Art of Zhostovo*, Leningrad, 1979, pp. 5,6).

Basically the methods of painting on lacquer have not changed, although individual craft processes have been updated and new brands of varnish, dyes and other materials become available.

The blank is made of cardboard sheets wound tightly on the mould, sized under pressure and boiled in linseed oil, whereupon it is ready for joinery. The bottom and cover are applied to the blank, then it is multiply dried in a hot furnace at a temperature of 100°C. It is then primed, padded and ground. The *modus operandi* goes back to the eighteenth- and nineteenth-century miniatures: the painter consecutively applies several coatings of paint to achieve greater profusion of colours. At both the Lukutin and Vishniakov factories the miniatures were made in oils. Drying under high temperature appreciably changed the colour tonality compelling the painter to allow for these alterations by selecting the colour very carefully. With all the coatings dried and varnished, the surface of the object underwent lengthy and thorough polishing. Often it was ornamented with inlaid mother-of-pearl patterns set on a metal background of gold leaves or silver plating. In the latter case the application of translucent colours permitted the glowing ground to shine through and beautifully enrich the overall colouration. Articles incorporating inlaid mother-of-pearl designs were particularly fascinating. Quite often the craftsmen used the iridescent surfaces of these insets to achieve beautiful decorative effects of snow, water or mist.

More often than not the object was coloured in black to provide a lovely background for the polychromatic painting. Even stronger decorative effect was imparted to the lacquer object by bright cinnabar, usually applied to the varnished inner surface. The effect was that of the hot red radiance that seemed to illuminate the inside of an elegant black papier-mâché casket, box or powder-case. The combination of the richly nuanced painting, glimmering black ground and deep red inner surface made for the harmony of colours which is a mark of a truly fine art-work.

Apart from narrative paintings, both old and modern masters have made good use of other pictorial styles. Thus, the papier-mâché objects were patterned in tortoise-shell, ivory, birch-bark or jewelled motifs while the inner surfaces bore mahogany or tortoise-shell designs. In the past white foil insets were applied, predominantly to embellish tea-caddies assuming that a vessel plated with thin metal better preserved the flavour of tea.

Two types of decorative design had the widest currency: *zierovka* (derived from the German verb *zieren* meaning to "beautify") and "tartan". The *zierovka* designs were made by applying paint to a thin coating of tin or any other shining metal glued on the surface of the object. Next the pattern was scratched on the metal whereupon the surface was varnished in the conventional manner. The scratched lines took on a gold-like colouring and were sometimes tinted in different hues to intensify the decorative effect.

The "tartan" style, like that of the Scottish cloth, consisted of a geometrical pattern shaped like a polychromatic network. Russian lacquers decorated in this style varied broadly in terms of colours, rhythm and complexity.

An extraordinary decorative effect was achieved by the use of the so-called "filigree" method. The filigree technique (from the Italian *filigrana*) was used in metalwork to produce open-work or fine designs soldered onto the metal base. This term of metalwork was used to define the specific method of lacquer ornamentation. The craft process was as follows: multitudes of minute details made into different sizes and shapes — "petals", "commas", "snow-flakes", "points" — were carved off the metal using a special small die. The details were arranged in a pattern and glued on the wet varnish coating of a papier-mâché object. The effect was that of very fine inlaid metalwork on papier-mâché. The "filigree" method came into wide use at the Lukutin factory in the second quarter of the nineteenth century.

For quite some time the Russian miniaturists were extensively borrowing scenes and themes from the Western arts. However, Lukutin was swift to bring his designs in line with the tastes of all sections of the Russian society — thereby appreciably diversifying both subjects and styles. Thus the high-class clientele (nobility and wealthy merchants), both in and out of Russia, were supplied with costly articles of labour-intensive manufacture. Copies from Western paintings and from works by the most prominent Russian artists predominated through the work — mythological, historical and genre scenes as well as landscapes, still lifes and portraits of popular figures. One of the leading Soviet art historians of the 1920s and '30s Anatoly Bakushinsky wrote in this connection: "Lukutin's copies followed the same range of styles as the period's great art and therefore reflected the influence of classicism, romanticism, the advent of realism as well as the complicated mutual struggle between them."[1]

Cheaper goods of less elaborate design were supplied for the lower-middle class, petty merchants and clerks. The designs featured town and country scenes, and ethnographic types. Copies from paintings were made without such great precision. The copies were naturally not made from the original paintings but from reproductions,

[1] А.В. Бакушинский, *Исследования и статьи*, М., 1981, с. 269 (A.V. Bakushinsky, *Studies and Articles*, Moscow, 1981, p. 269).

drawings and prints. However, the selection of works by the masters was carried out very carefully and these were seldom exactly reproduced. The miniaturist using a composition created by another artist, reworked it to some degree basing his formal principles on the design of domestic objects as works of decorative art. The degree of divergence from the original picture depended on the quality of the surface, size and designation of the utensil. Components were added, taken away or the picture was reshaped completely. A miniature composition does not always allow the identification of the original from which it was copied. However, when it does, it is usually very clear that the original composition was used by the artist merely as a starting point for elaborating his own, independent solution.

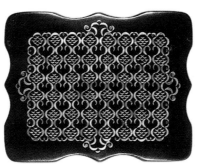

The Russian *troika* scenes have, since Lukutin's time until the present moment, been in great favour with miniaturists. These scenes provide a good illustration for the above argument. For instance, quite a few compositions were based on one and the same lithograph by the nineteenth-century Russian romantic painter Alexander Orlovsky, an artist of turbulent spirit. For all the romanticist conventionality of this lithograph showing a courier who rushes along in a *troika*, it features a number of concrete details. Thus the courier is seen hurrying through a Russian village, past huts and milestones, carrying the royal dispatch. Under the paint brush of Lukutin's artists the image of the *troika* underwent numerous transformations: becoming the dashing gallop of hussars, the festive ride of village youth, or the impetuous journey of a couple of sweet-hearts. Changes introduced by the miniaturists amounted to the elimination of many concrete details: removing huts, fences and milestones from the background, altering the number of figures, changing clothes worn by fares and the coachman, tightening the curve of the horses' necks, sharpening the turn of their heads. The purpose of imparting greater dynamism to the scene, disposing of the characteristic details of the landscape, changing the characters was to generalize the message and raise the picture to the level of a symbol.

Since olden times *troikas* meant more to the Russians than just vehicles. Riding on a *troika* was always a festive occasion, an exciting and memorable event. A *troika* personified the vast expanses of Russia, the endless journeys through the country and the excitement of a jolly gallop. More than one generation of the Russian lacquered miniaturists elaborated the so-called "winter" and "summer" *troika* scenes to express the generosity and fortitude of the Russian character. These scenes recall the famous passage from Gogol's *Dead Souls*: "Eh, thou troika, thou that art a bird. Who conceived thee? Methinks 'tis only among a spirited folk that thou couldst have come into being... Ah, these steeds, these steeds, what steeds they are! Are there whirlwinds perched upon your manes? Is there a sensitive ear, alert as a flame, in your every fibre? Ye have caught the familiar song coming down to you from above, and all as one, and all in the same instant, ye have strained your brazen chests and almost without touching earth with your hoofs, ye have become all

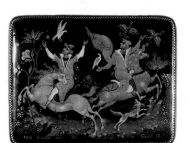

transformed into straight lines cleaving to the air, and the troika tears along, all inspired by God!" Another motif immensely popular with the Russian lacquer miniaturists was the tea-party. The Russians became accustomed to drinking tea in the seventeenth and especially in the eighteenth centuries. A tea-party signified a communal rest after a long and difficult journey, after a hard day's work, a jolly gathering of relatives, friends or just chance companions. There is always some solemnity inherent in tea-parties, especially if the table is decorated with a big singing *samovar* of shining polished copper and nickel. Such an atmosphere was favourable to leisurely and heartfelt intercourse. The miniaturists intensively exploited and endlessly varied this scene in their compositions. At the Lukutin factory there were several teams of skilled miniature painters whose specialities were *troika* or tea-party scenes.

In the nineteenth century lacquered miniatures showing the sights of Russia's old capital Moscow, especially the Kremlin, the new capital St. Petersburg and scenes based on the national history or elaborating the patriotic themes, became very fashionable. A characteristic example of the Chinese style that was in great vogue in the first half of the nineteenth century is *The Noble Family* painting on a casket cover (pl. 2).

By the middle of the nineteenth century major changes in public consciousness and the dissemination of democratic ideas stimulated greater interest in motifs borrowed from folk life, particularly that of the countryside. With this miniatures became noticeably more realistic than before. The miniaturists manifested a keen observation and an ability to capture and reproduce characteristic details, expressive gestures and typical appearances.

At the same time the peasant life was much idealized and made to look more joyful and untroubled than it was in actuality. This can be naturally explained. Such treatment is partly defined by the laws of this form of art: the lacquered miniature is in itself poetical. And in addition this was in accordance with the desires of the consumers. When snuffboxes began to fall out of fashion in the 1860s and the demand for them gradually declined, Lukutin effectively accommodated the buyers' requests by boosting the output of fancy needlework caskets, cigarette-cases, tea-caddies, Easter eggs, purse plates, album covers and many other goods. Buyers were mainly townsfolk, especially the middle-class merchants, petty bourgeois and gentry who seemed to be quite happy with both the subjects and artistry.

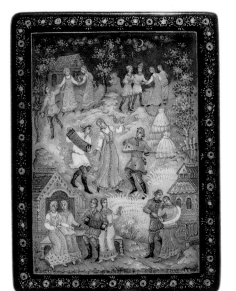

The peasant scenes were sentimental, touched by humour and bringing out the painter's mixed feeling of affection and condescension for his characters. Such were the immensely popular "Ukrainian scenes". The Ukraine always fascinated artists with its spectacular customs, ardent dances, colourful national dresses that seemed to be both like and unlike the Russian clothes, just as the two Slavic cultures are generally similar and yet distinct. The Ukrainian mode of life offered a broad scope for a painter's creative imagination by seeming familiar and at the same time more exotic and festive than his habitual environment.

With a good deal of affection blended with melancholy or humour the painters treated the much favoured "rendez-vous" and "farewell" scenes. Usually such scenes were set near a well, by a wattle-fence, in fields or forests and suggested a sense of simple family joys. Haymaking, reaping and threshing were shown as light, enjoyable and playful labours, the characters invariably wearing colourful festive clothes. Only with the advent of critical realism in the 1870s and '80s, with its keen awareness of social vices, the lacquered miniature began to show the social contrasts of life.

The styles and aesthetics followed by the Lukutin and Vishniakov miniatures were dissimilar in some respects. The former stood out by their elaborate designs and refined and austere colouring (although the factory's mass-manufactured cheap articles were often executed in a more simple manner). A number of art historians observe a close affinity between the Vishniakov miniatures and peasant art, pointing out that both are characterized by a disposition for ornamental effect. In contrast to the amazingly versatile configurations, elegant plasticity and perfect harmony of the miniature with the form of the object featured by the Lukutin articles, the Vishniakov goods looked crude and unsophisticated, the paintings sometimes appearing as pictures just superimposed on the varnished surface. Nonetheless the Vishniakov miniatures were fascinating in their own way as

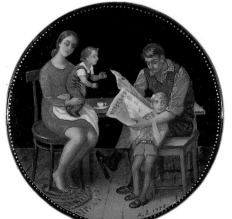

are the ingenuous peasant distaffs or earthenware toys. In its time, the Vishniakov factory supplied buyers outside the high-class elite — wealthy peasants, low middle-class and petty merchants. Now, however, these articles are not rated as inferior to the Lukutin goods and are always a desired acquisition for any art museum or amateur collector.
The 1870s saw a growing interest in national history in the various circles of Russian society. Paint-

ers, sculptors and graphic artists working on a large scale probed with awe and fascination deep into the heroic and tragic past of the Russian people. The result was massive, somewhat theatrical, "loquacious" multi-character canvases, outwardly impressive but psychologically superficial and lacking genuine insight into the history. The lacquered miniature, always more or less related to the professional art of the cities, could not avoid the impact of the new aesthetic trends. The miniature copies from easel paintings featured minute elaboration of intricate patterns decorating lavish gold-embroidered attire. A good example is the copy of Konstantin Makovsky's *Boyaryshnia* (a courtier's unmarried daughter) made by one of Lukutin's best miniaturists – Dmitry Krylov, whose accomplishments in the craft earned him the title of "Honorary Citizen of Russia". The miniature (pl. 25) minutely reproduces the texture of the velvet *sarafan* worn by the lovely young girl, the pattern of the golden needlework and the lustre of the pearls. At present the attitudes towards works of this kind vary between praising the miniaturist for his masterful handling of a complicated artistic task and scorning him for being far-fetched, excessively sugary and historically flimsy.

The late nineteenth and early twentieth centuries were hard times for the lacquer centres near Moscow. Largely relying on hand-manufacture and employing the labour of skilled painters, joiners, varnishers and polishers, the lacquer factories were hard put to compete against the swiftly growing design industry. Many miniaturists degenerated into ordinary copyists imparting no creativity to their work. N. Lukutin (1853–1902), the last in the family of manufacturers, is known to have said: "This business is running at a loss. The only reason I am still in it is to carry on the family tradition and honour the memories of my father and grandfather." He was a public figure and an enlightened patron of arts — with a major collection of Russian porcelain. However, he managed the factory carelessly and probably quite inexpertly. Two years after his death the factory closed down and the craftsmen went different ways — some getting jobs at the Vishniakov factory in the neighbouring village of Ostashkovo.

However, this was not the end of the story of the Lukutin miniature. At the end of the last century workshops producing lacquered papier-mâché and metal wares sprang up abundantly in more than ten villages around the Lukutin enterprise.

Experts estimate that besides the Lukutins and Vishniakovs there were at least 40 small manufacturers employing over 170 workers. In fact when Lukutin's business ceased, quite a few skilled painters found themselves out of work, although they wished to keep on with their craft. Fortunately they received backing from local intellectuals. L. Derzhavina, a teacher at the Fedoskino school, studied the legal procedure for starting a producers' cooperative society and suggested that the unemployed painters should appeal to the Moscow provincial council.

It should be clarified at this point that after the abolition of serfage in Russia in 1861 local governments were instituted in a number of provinces. Their powers were limited, yet when progressive liberals had the majority on the councils they dealt quite successfully with local matters of education and health care. The provincial councils also implemented measures to improve the performance of farms and provided support for handicraftsmen who were failing to withstand competition with large-scale manufacture. The councils extended varied organizational aid to the cooperative societies. It was mainly due to the local councils that many domestic crafts in Russia were preserved and the unique craft centres, including those of the lacquered miniature, did not die out.

Fedoskino

After much trouble a cooperative society under the official name of "Fedoskino Labour Artel of Former Employees of the Lukutin Factory" was inaugurated at the members' constituent meeting held at the Fedoskino village school in May 1910. Thus the small village of Fedoskino having long merged with Lukutin's Danilkovo went down in the history of Russian art. Mikhail Chizhov, a well-known Fedoskino miniaturist, cites L. Derzhavina's account of setting up the cooperative society: "It was quite a job to stir individual peasants who were unaccustomed to collective work. They found it hard to comprehend how they could run a complex enterprise all by themselves, how one of their own kind could be entrusted with managing all the works. How could the head of the collective be controlled? How could sufficient funds be raised to obtain equipment, materials and instruments?"[1]

The very first goods produced by the Fedoskino cooperative were acquired by the Moscow Provincial Museum. The museum had been founded back in 1885 by the Moscow Province Council and essentially acted as a methods centre extending all kinds of assistance to the handicraft artists. The museum's support for the Fedoskino works had considerable significance and before too long the cooperative commanded a ready sale of its products. Fedoskino miniatures were successfully dem-

onstrated at major exhibitions in various Russian cities. The miniature workshops failing to meet competition with them began to close one after the other.

The establishment of the Fedoskino cooperative society that cultivated and carried on the artistic traditions of the Russian lacquer-work was of crucial significance. However, in the conditions of pre-revolutionary Russia the handicraft businesses were predominantly governed by the rule of chance and heavily relied on such factors as the market situation or the support of patrons. The Fedoskino cooperative was unlikely to last long under the onset of large-scale manufacturers who swamped the market with banal but cheap goods. The preservation of the Fedoskino trade as well as of many other unique handicraft centres against total extinction could be ensured only on the basis of a radical renewal of the entire social, economic and political situation. The way for such a renewal was paved by the victory of the October Socialist Revolution of 1917.

From the very outset Soviet power took care to preserve and develop the folk arts as part of its more general policy of preserving and turning to good account the cultural values of the past. Lenin repeatedly emphasized the vital importance of this task for the development of new socialist culture. The problem was also touched upon in many state-

[1] М. С. Чижов, *Среди миниатюристов. Записки федоскинского мастера*, Л., 1982, с. 52, 53 (M. S. Chizhov, *With the Miniaturists: Notes of a Fedoskino Artist*, Leningrad, 1982, pp. 52,53).

ments and articles by the People's Commissar for Education Anatoly Lunacharsky. One of the most enlightened persons of his time, Lunacharsky made a formidable personal contribution to the development of the new culture. He believed that folk arts, with their impeccable styles, refined forms and profuse means of expression elaborated in the course of many centuries, could provide fertile soil for the growth of this new culture. Lunacharsky called for thorough theoretical study and practical implementation of the task of safeguarding handicrafts against the onset of factory-made products. The future of mankind must be joyful, he argued, and it is art that brings joy to the people while industrial manufacture suppresses individual creativity. Lunacharsky was among the most passionate adherents of this fundamental aesthetic postulate of the 1920s. On the other hand, he never ceased emphasizing the importance of the internationalist principles, the policy of internationalism and the cultural rapprochement of nations. In the communist future, he reasoned, elements of national cultures will complement and enrich one another.

The seventy years of steady progress in the area of folk arts under socialism has been ensured by the consistent policy of safeguarding the cultural values of the past and adapting them to the new social requirements. However, in the first years after the revolution the development of handicraft businesses was hampered by the general economic set-back.

The country's national economy was much sapped by the First World War and the Civil War. The handicraft trades including the lacquered miniature were also badly affected by the wars. With the

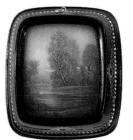

conditions of general economic collapse in the earliest years of Soviet power the lacquered miniature centres around Moscow found themselves hard pressed for both materials and market.

The Soviet government implemented a series of measures to support the handicraft trades. Even in the turmoil of the Civil War a special decree was issued by the government granting handicraftsmen a whole series of privileges. In addition the decree actually listed some handicraft trades specializing in the production of works of art: pottery, jewellery, embroidery, toy-making and also painting — for which were intended various kinds of studios. All privileges were extended to these trades.

There are materials in the archives testifying that in August 1920 the Fedoskino cooperative consisted of twenty-three members and employed thirteen workmen and three apprentices. In 1924 there were thirty painters and five apprentices. The expansion of the business was subsidized by the state. Thus, in 1927 the Moscow Council issued a special long-term grant of 500,000 roubles for the cooperative societies to acquire mechanical equipment. More than 3,000 roubles out of this sum were allotted to the Fedoskino enterprise. A broad variety of services was rendered to the handicraft artists by the Handicrafts Museum, which had then become a state institution. The museum provided guidance to the new aesthetic ideas, offered specific recommendations as to the choice of themes and even suggested models for reproduction. For instance, Afanasy Kulikov, an artist working for the museum, offered his canvas *Radio in the Village* to the Fedoskino

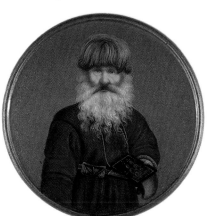

painters to make miniature copies from it. In 1926 one of the Fedoskino miniaturists designed a painted casket, its cover reproducing Kulikov's canvas (pl. 29). The scene is set in a peasant hut. An old peasant listens in amazement and rapture to something quite unheard of in the retarded village — a radio broadcast. The faces of the old peasant women and the young lad at the table are mixtures of curiosity and doubt. Only a gallant, ruddy Red Army man, who has apparently seen much of the world in his young life, shows no surprise and is merely glad that a new life has come to his village. The miniature bears a touch of good-natured humour and recreates the style of the cheap popular prints (*lubok*) that had wide currency in Russia in the seventeenth to the twentieth centuries. These prints were separate sheets printed from wooden blocks and characterized by pictorial laconicism, clear-cut and simple composition, conventionalized figures and a humorous or satirical representation of the subject. *Radio in the Village* and other works by Kulikov, an educated professional artist, are indicative of his familiarity with the *lubok* style. However, in the 1920s the Fedoskino painters found his manner rather confusing and hard to imitate and hence *Radio in the Village* was reproduced just once. Decades passed before this particular style became established in the art of the Fedoskino lacquered miniature and in the design of painted trays manufactured in the neighbouring Zhostovo village. Evidently Kulikov was slightly ahead of his time. Still he laid foundations for the development of a whole new trend of decorative folk art. In addition, the miniature *Radio in the Village* exemplifies the characteristic manner of presenting the changes that were occuring in the Russian village after the revolution.

Generally, in the 1920s the Fedoskino artists were carrying on the traditions of the Lukutin and Vishniakov lacquer-work. Quite a few members of the cooperative had experience of working for one or other of the factories and were well acquainted with the methods and styles of the traditional Russian lacquered miniature that had taken shape in the course of a whole century. Apart from cultivating these traditions, craftsmen of the older generation imparted their own artistic sensibilities to the miniature paintings. The result of intensive experimentation combined with the rational utilization of the Lukutin and Vishniakov experiences was the emergence, over the years, of the distinctive Fedoskino style of miniature painting.

The boundaries of this style were flexible enough to allow for individual aesthetic pursuits and free choice of themes. In the 1920s and '30s the more gifted artists went beyond directly copying the old Lukutin miniatures and easel paintings and began to elaborate independent compositions. Thus, Nikolai Petrov's landscapes witness to his immense professional skill and high artistic culture. Ivan Semionov and Alexei Kruglikov proved able to work in many genres, their miniatures invariably demonstrating good use of all the Fedoskino ornamentation techniques. Nikolai Tsybin's endless variations of the *troika* scene argued for the artist's ability to achieve superb virtuosity within the framework of one and the same theme.

Alexei Leznov moved to Fedoskino from Zhostovo where he had applied the methods of lacquered miniatures to design ornamental trays in patterns of flower bouquets and fruits brought to life by colourful butterflies and exotic birds. As he changed over to pure miniature, he readjusted accordingly to achieve finer detailing and more austere, elaborate colouring.

Neither the Lukutin factory, nor the Fedoskino cooperative after it, confined themselves exclusively to papier-mâché paintings. The designs included the afore-mentioned *zierovka* and "tartan" as well as the "filigree", "tortoise-shell" and other inherited or reconstructed decorative styles.

Note to the plates: All the details are reproduced in natural size

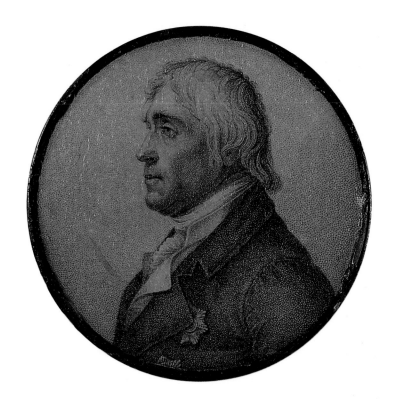

1 P. Korobov Factory
Snuff-box: *Portrait of an Unknown Person.*
Early 19th century

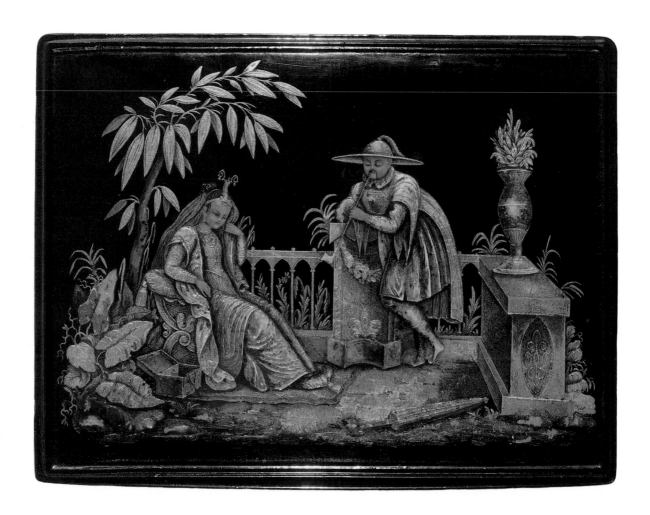

2   P. Lukutin Factory
Casket: *The Noble Family.* 1820s–1830s

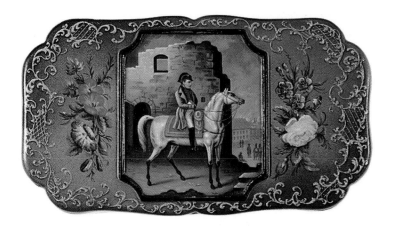

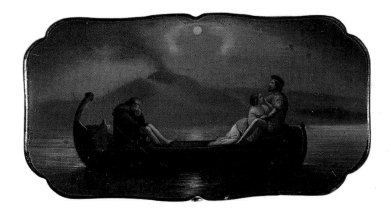

3 P. and A. Lukutin Factory
Snuff-box: *Napoleon in Burning Moscow.*
1843–63

4 P. and A. Lukutin Factory
Snuff-box: *Sweet-hearts in a Boat.*
1843–63

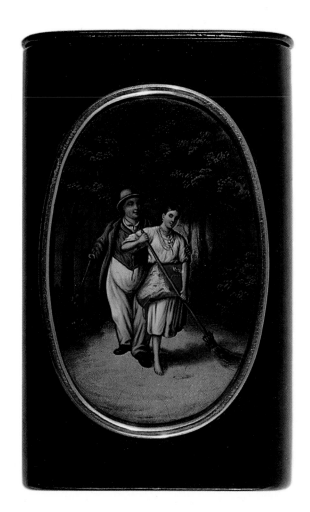

5   A. Lukutin Factory
Cigarette-case: *Courting a Woman*.
1863–88

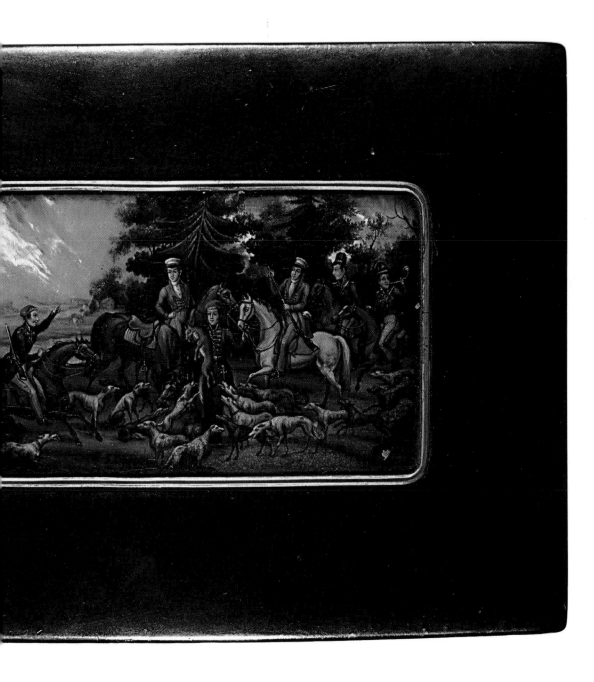

6   A. Lukutin Factory
Casket: *Fox-hunt.*
1820s–1830s

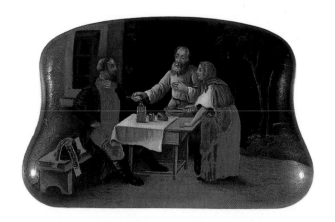

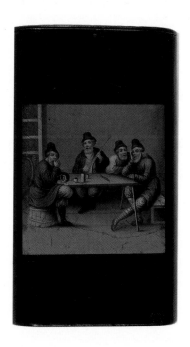

7   A. Lukutin Factory
Purse cover: *Demyan's Fish-soup.*
1863–88

8   P. and A. Lukutin Factory
Cigarette-case: *Peasants in a Pot-house.*
1843–63

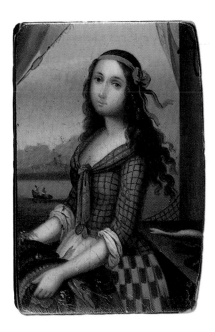 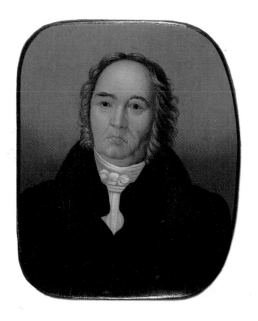

9   P. and A. Lukutin Factory
Snuff-box: *Portrait of a Fisher-woman.*
1843–63

10   P. and A. Lukutin Factory
Purse cover: *Portrait of Ivan Krylov.*
1843–63

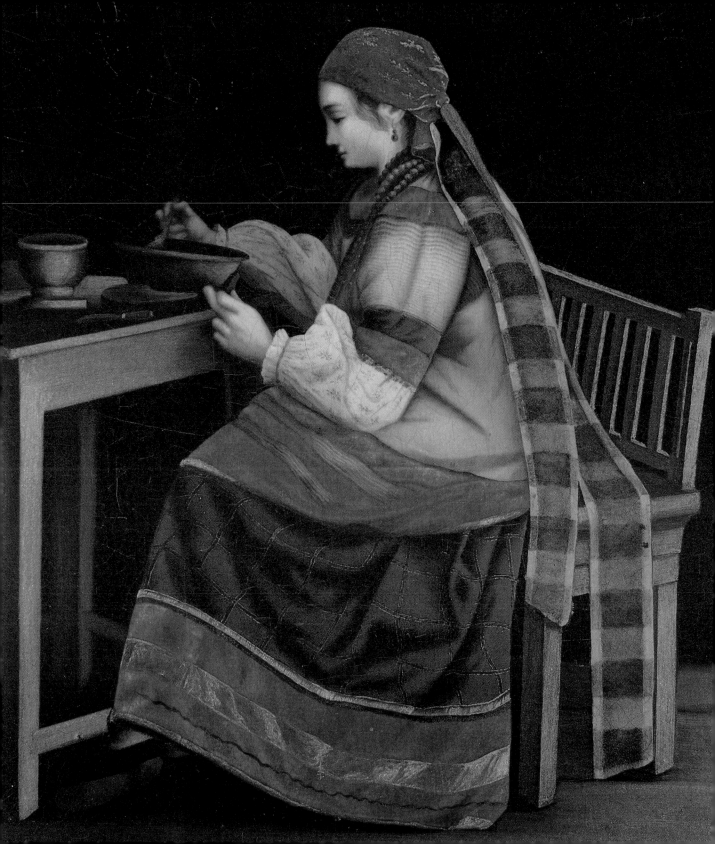

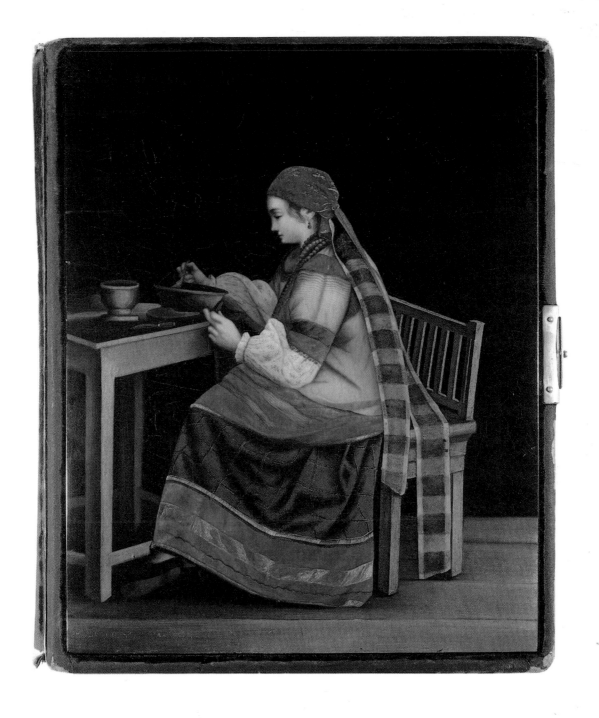

11 A. Lukutin Factory
Photograph album. 1863–88. Detail

12 A. Lukutin Factory
Photograph album. 1863–88

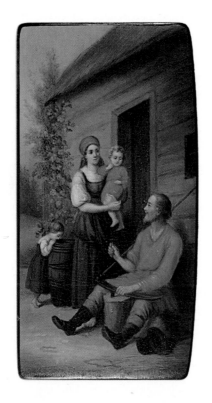

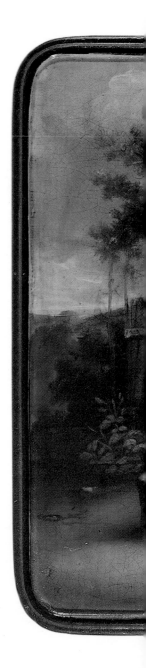

13   P. and A. Lukutin Factory
Snuff-box: *A Peasant Whetting His Scythe.*
1843–63

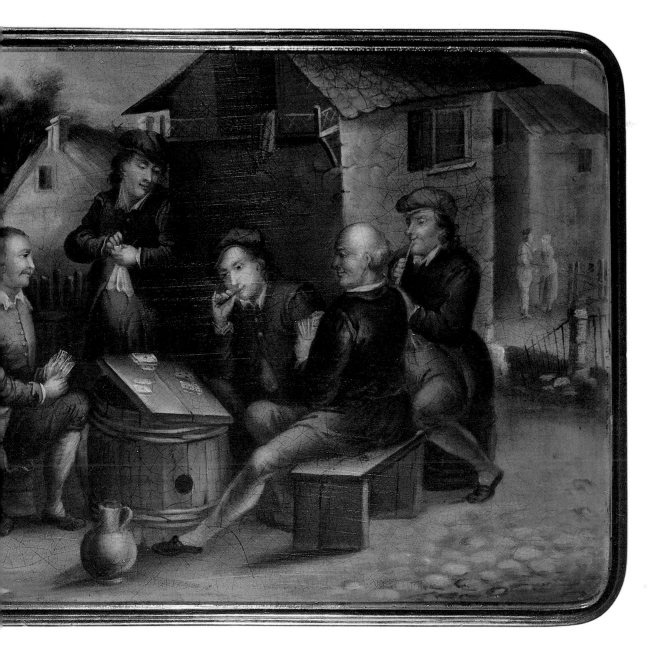

14   P. and A. Lukutin Factory
Cigar-box: *A Game of Piquet*. 1843–63

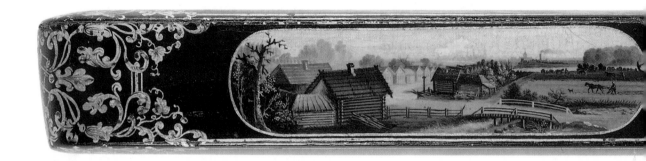

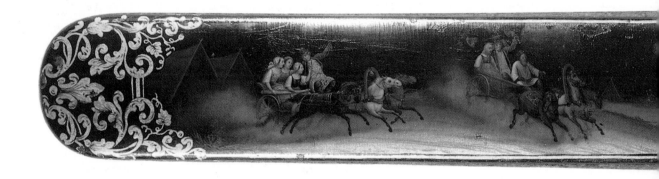

15, 16   A. Lukutin Factory
Pencil-case: *The Village of Fedoskino*
and *Troikas.* 1843–88

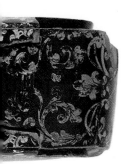

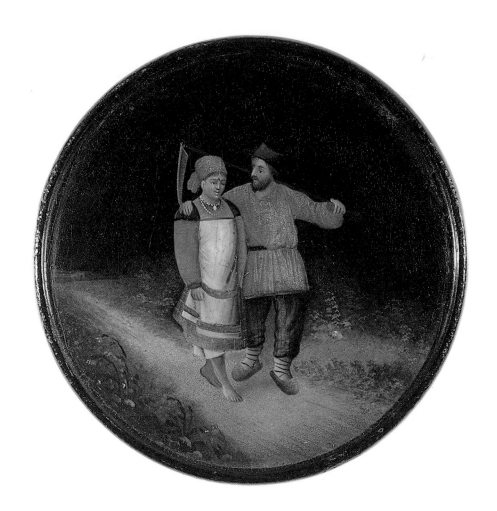

17   The Vishniakov Workshop
Round casket: *Peasants on the Way Home
from Haymaking.* Late 19th century

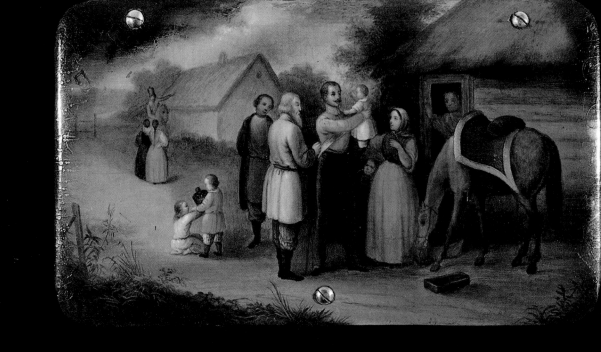

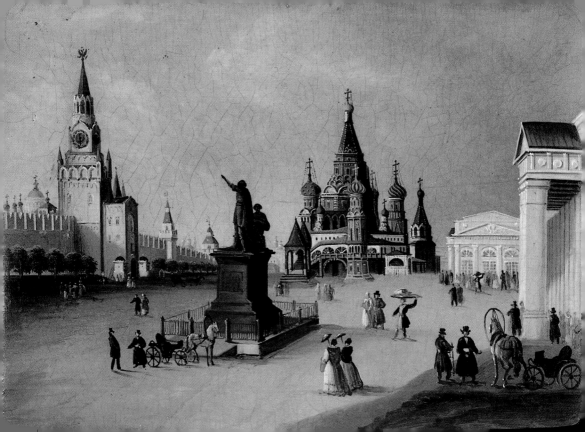

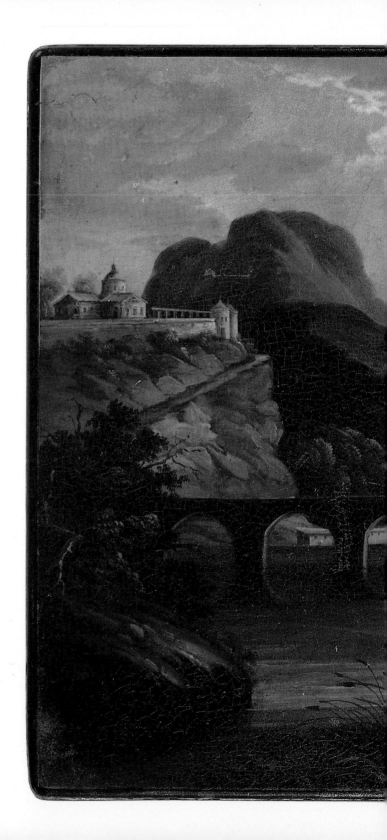

←
18 P. and A. Lukutin Factory
Cigarette-case: *Coming on Leave.* 1843–63

←
19 P. and A. Lukutin Factory
Casket: *Red Square.* 1843–63

20 P. and A. Lukutin Factory
Casket: *Morning.* 1843–63

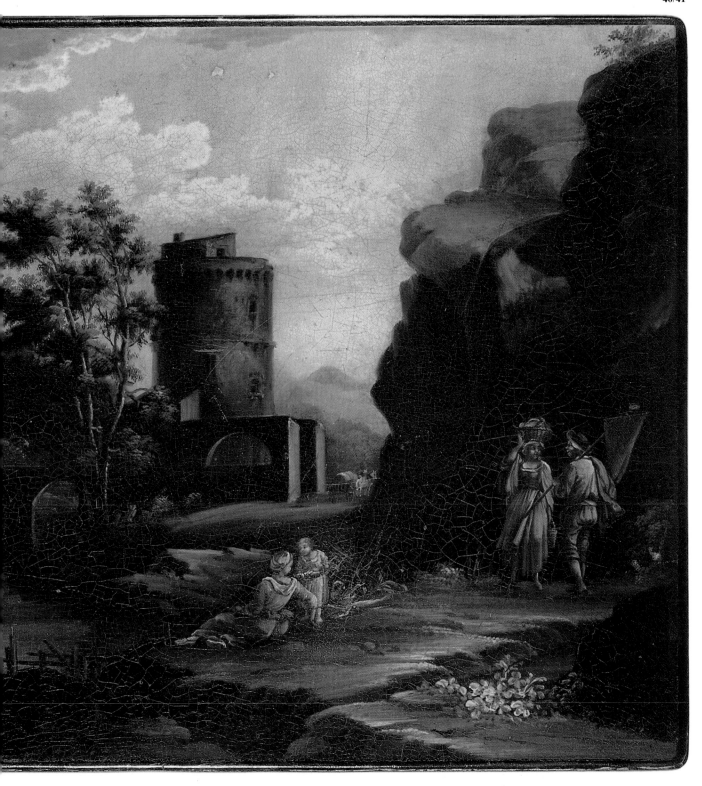

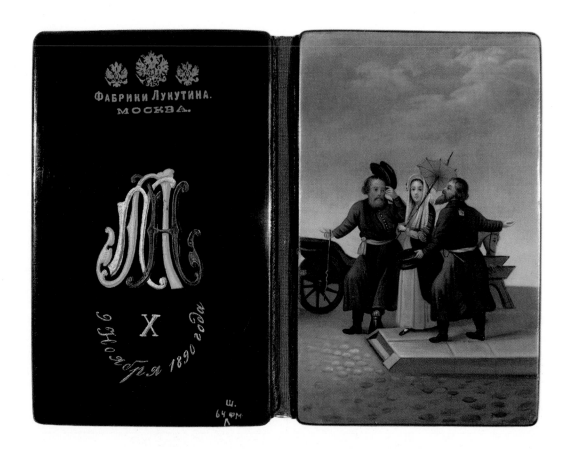

21   N. Lukutin Factory
Menu cover: *A Lady and Two Coachmen*.
1888–1904

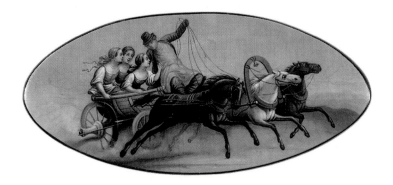

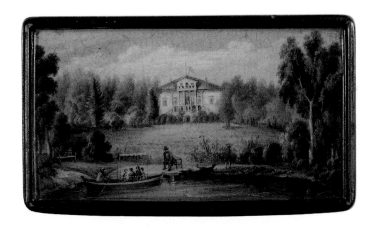

22 P. and A. Lukutin Factory
Snuff-box: *A Summer Troika*. 1843–63

23 P. and A. Lukutin Factory
Snuff-box: *The Danilkovo Estate*. 1843–63

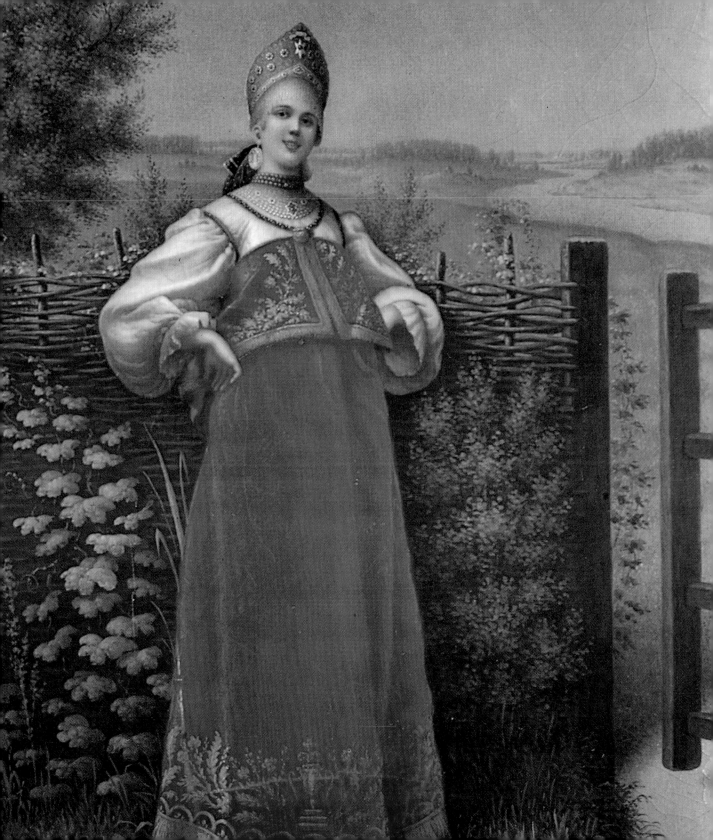

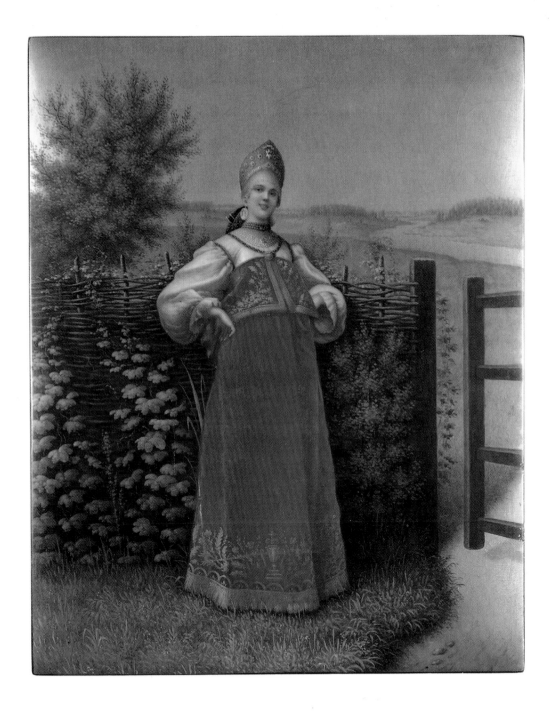

24 Dmitry Krylov
Panel: *Boyaryshnia at the Wattle-fence.*
Late 19th century. Detail

25 Dmitry Krylov
Panel: *Boyaryshnia at the Wattle-fence.*
Late 19th century

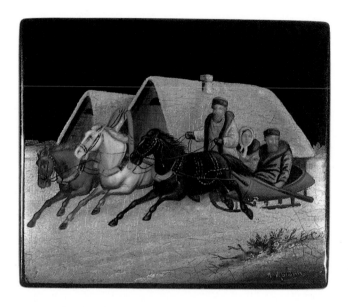

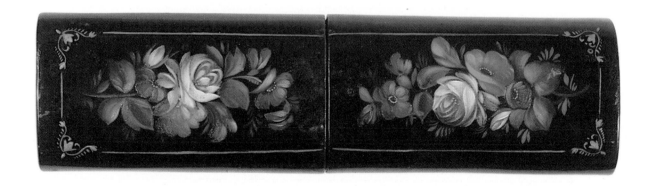

26 Nikolai Tsybin
Casket: *A Winter Troika*. 1932

27 Alexei Leznov
Pencil-case: *Flowers*. 1944

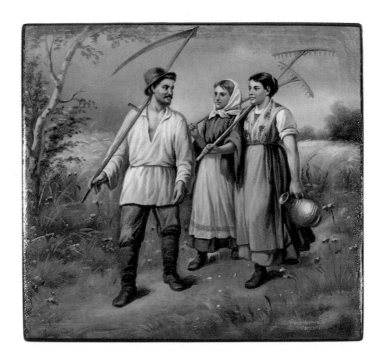

28   Mikhail Popenov
Casket: *Haymaking Season.* 1947

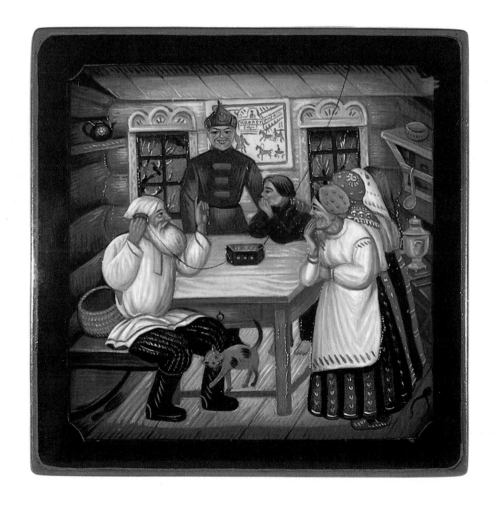

29   Afanasy Kulikov
Casket: *Radio in the Village*. 1920s

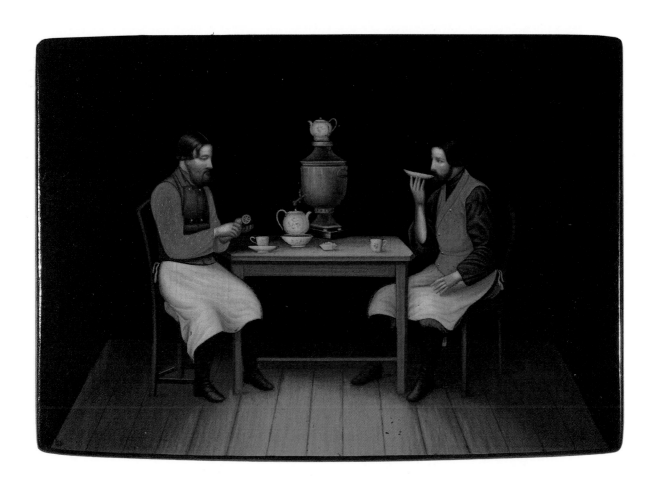

30 Vasily Lavrov
Casket: *Drinking Tea.* 1935

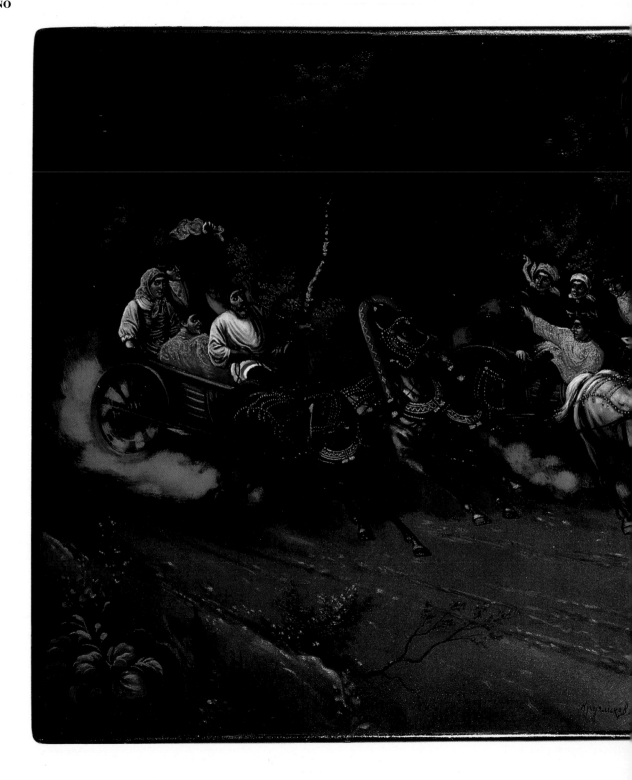

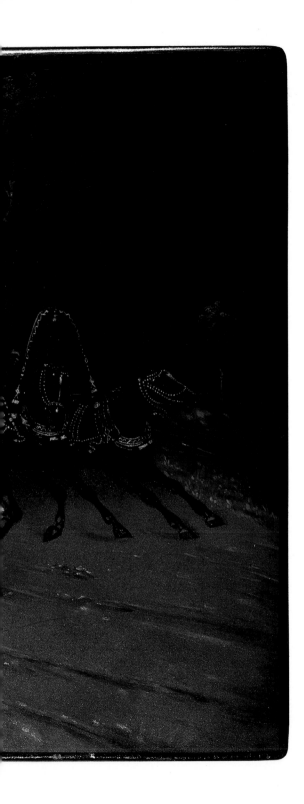

31   Alexei Kruglikov
Casket: *Summer Troikas.* 1943

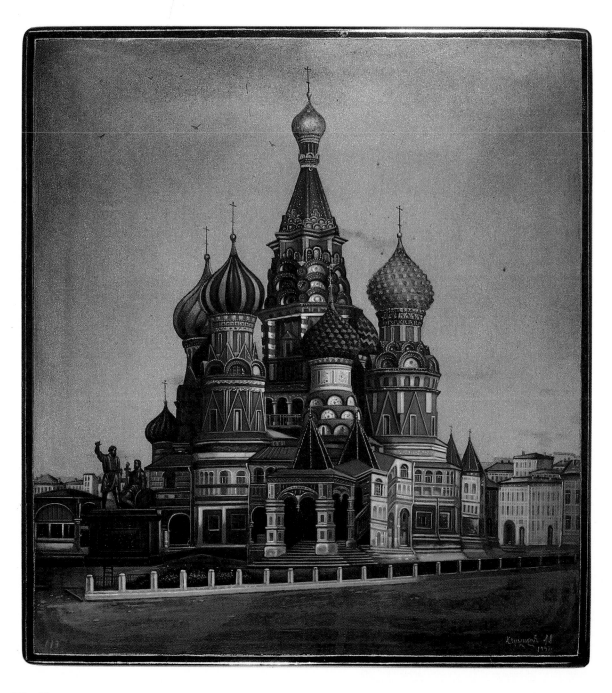

32   Alexei Kruglikov
Casket: *St. Basil's Cathedral.* 1943

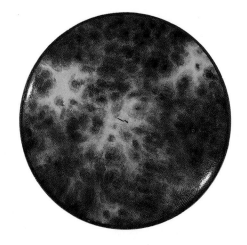

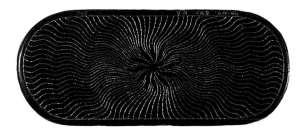

33 Mikhail Chizhov
Round casket. "Tortoise-shell" technique.
1960s

34 Vasily Korsakov
Decorative box. *Zierovka* technique. 1964

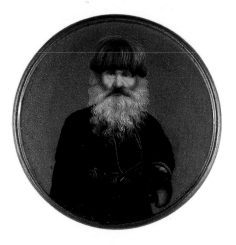

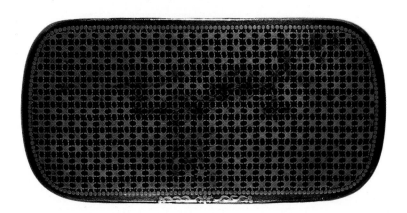

35 N. Lukutin Factory
Round box: *Portrait of an Old Man.*
1888–1904

36 P. and A. Lukutin Factory
Snuff-box decorated with "filigree"
ornament. 1843–63

37 The Vishniakovs Workshop
Tea-caddy: *Lunching Children.*
Late 19th century

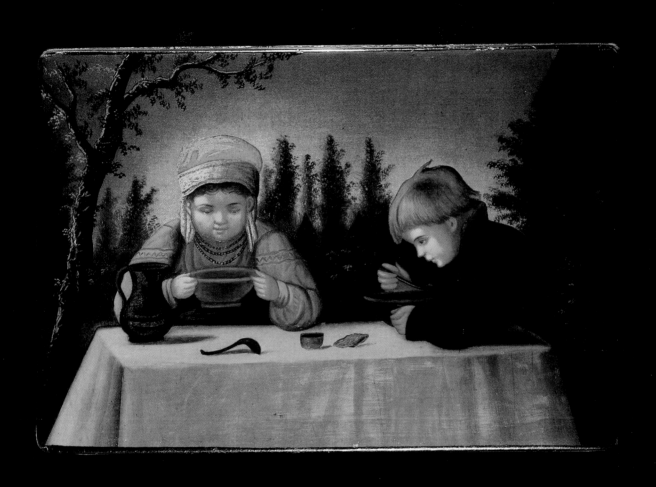

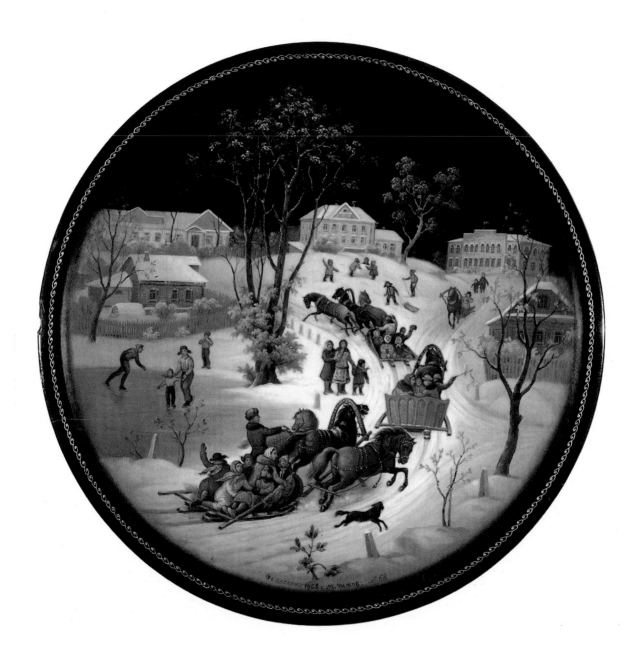

38   Mikhail Chizhov
Round casket: *Russian Winter Festival
in Fedoskino.* 1968

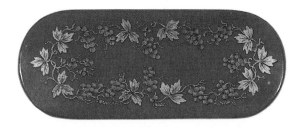

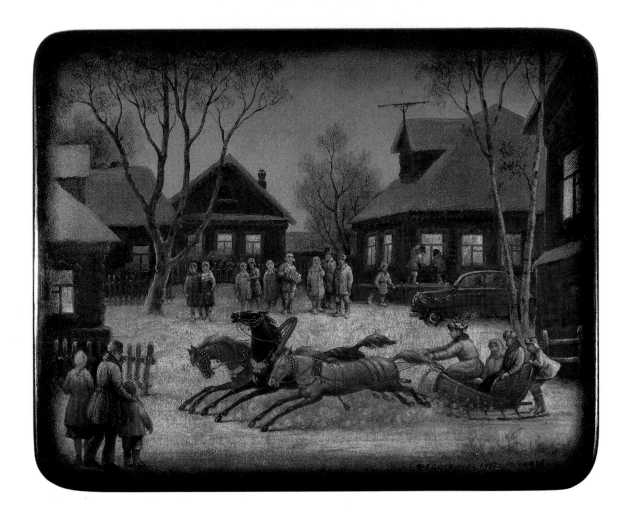

39 Mikhail Chizhov
Decorative box. 1960s

40 Mikhail Chizhov
Casket: *Evening in the Country.* 1972

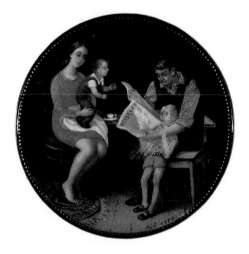

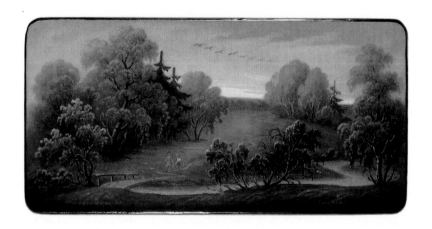

41   Victor Antonov
Round casket: *The Family.* 1977

42   Mikhail Korniyenko
Casket: *Moscow Suburb.* 1978

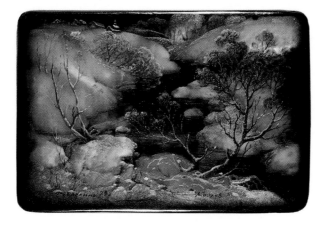

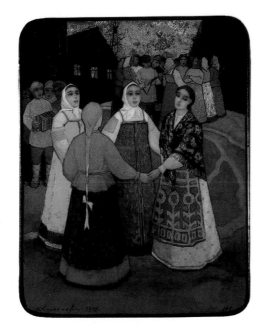

43   Alexander Kozlov
Decorative box: *March*. 1979

44 Yuri Karapayev
Casket: *The Northern Song*. 1970

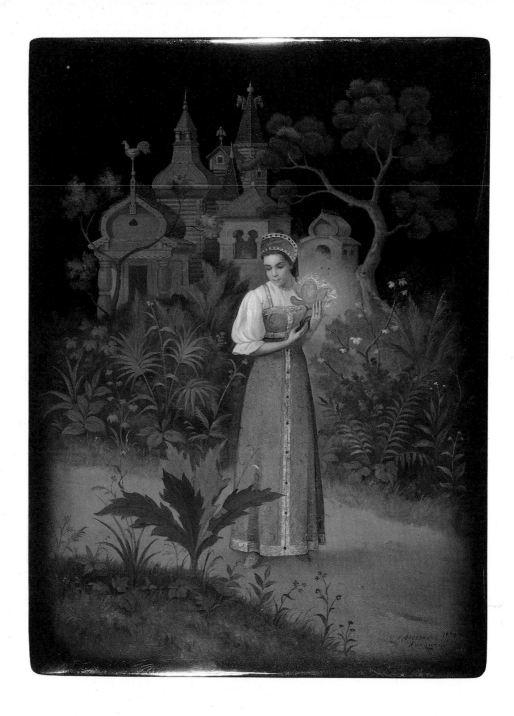

45   Victor Lipitsky
Casket: *The Scarlet Flower.* 1979

46   Victor Lipitsky
Casket: *The Scarlet Flower.* 1979. Detail

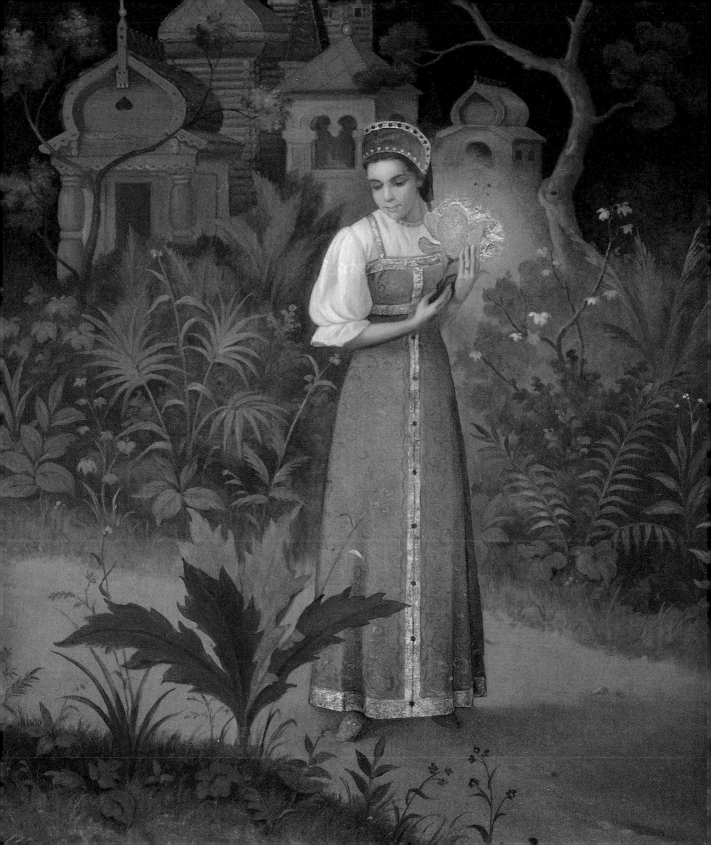

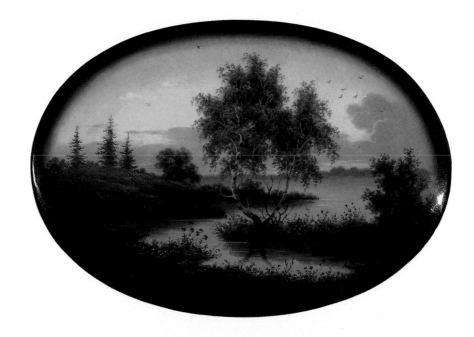

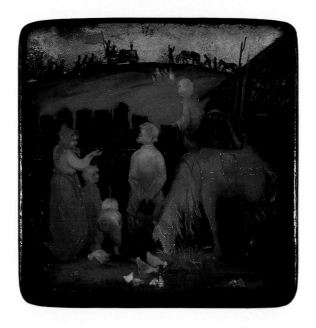

47 Sergei P. Rogatov
Oval casket: *Birch-tree*. 1960s

48 Gennady Larishev
Casket: *A Seredniak (Peasant of Average
Means)*. 1968

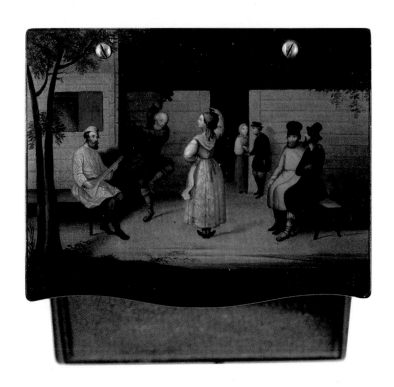

49   A. Lukutin Factory
Match-box: *A Peasant Dance.* 1863–88

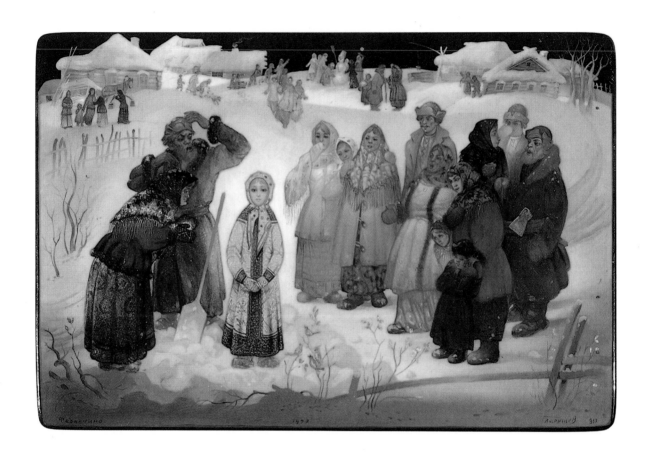

50 Gennady Larishev
Casket: *Snow-maiden.* 1977

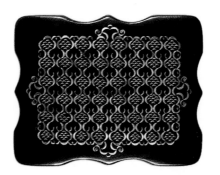

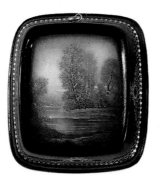
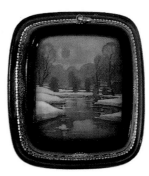

51 Sergei Monashov
Decorative box: *Maids' Room*. 1970s

52 Oleg Kurzov
Set of pendants: *Seasons*. 1970s

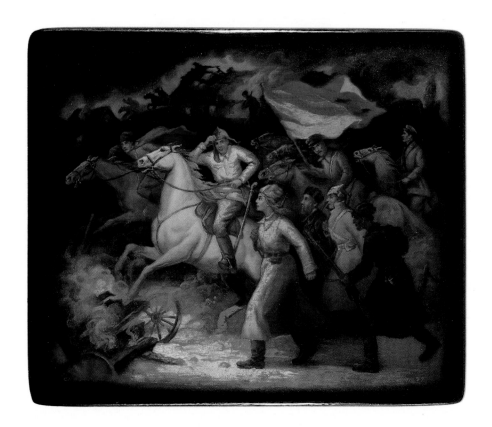

53   Gennady Skripunov
Casket: *Kakhovka*. 1977

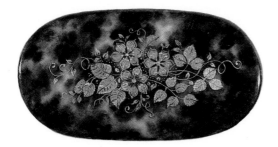
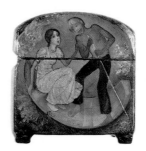

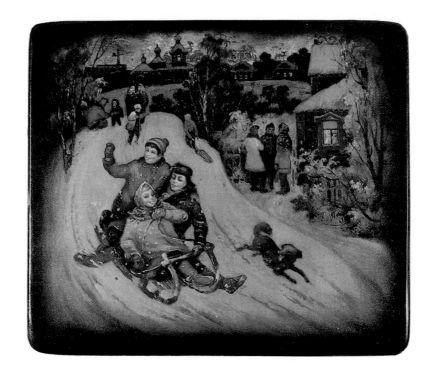

54 Lydia Stroganova
Decorative box. "Tortoise-shell"
technique. 1980

55 Viacheslav Sviatchenkov
Decorative box: *In the Boat*. 1981

56 Alexander Tolstov
Casket: *Winter in the Country*. 1974

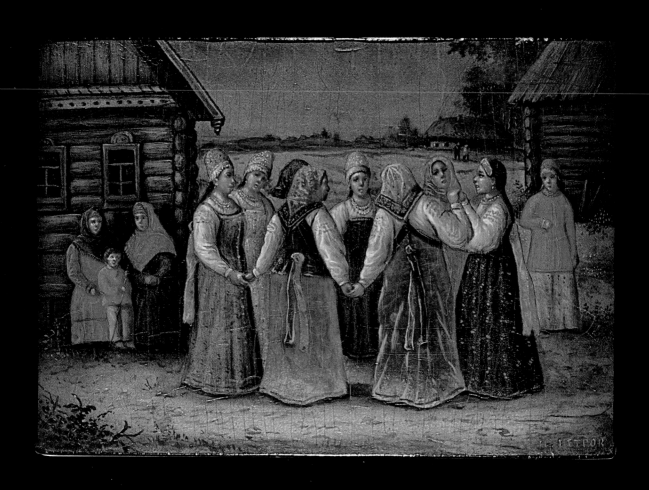

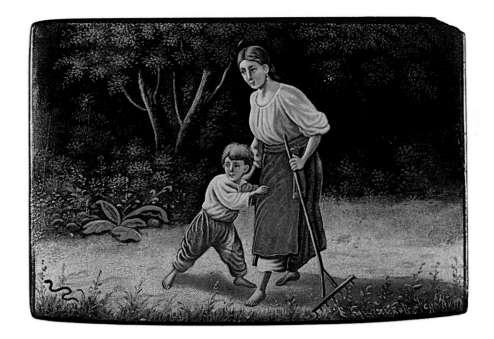

57   Nikolai Petrov
Casket: *Round-dance.* 1925

58   Vasily Kruglikov
Casket: *Scared by Snake.* 1930s

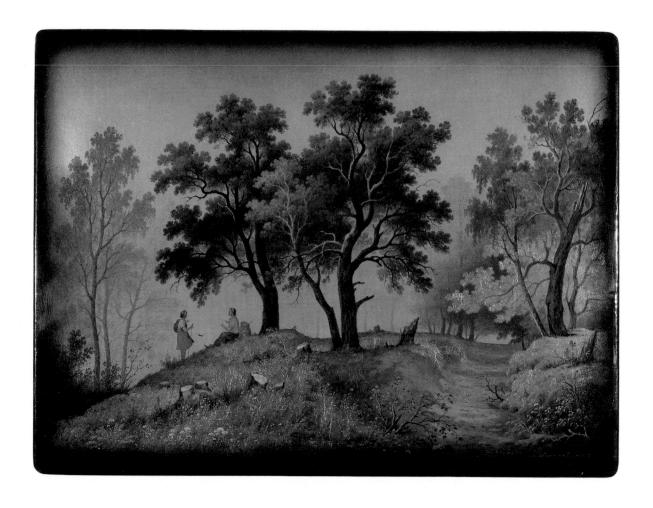

59   Ivan Strakhov
Casket: *The Tourist Routes.* 1972

60   Ivan Strakhov
Casket: *The Tourist Routes.* 1972. Detail

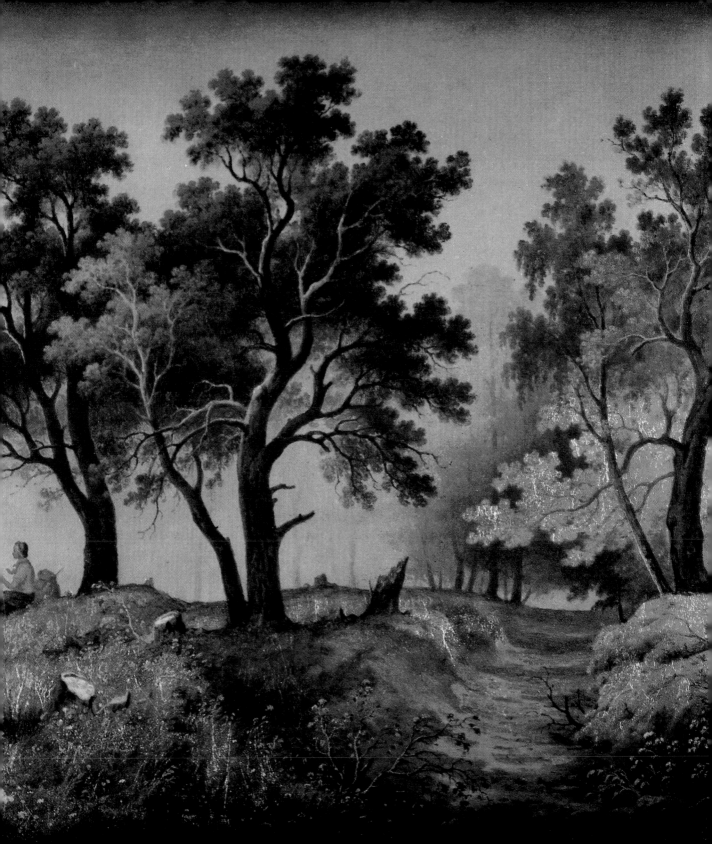

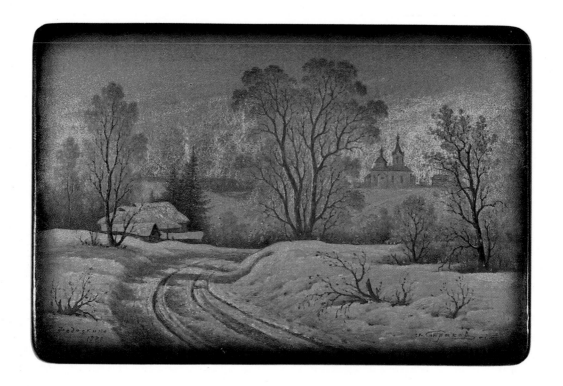

61   Ivan Strakhov
Casket: *Winter in Fedoskino.* 1977

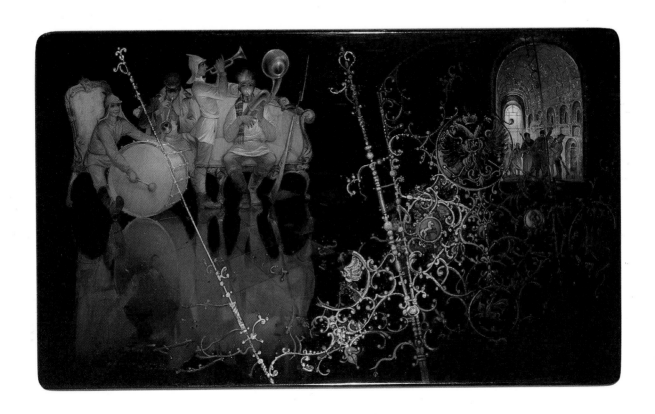

62 Sergei Kozlov
Casket: *The New Marches.* 1981

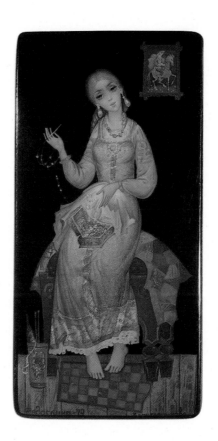

63   Yelena Khomutinnikova
Decorative box: *Katiusha*. 1979

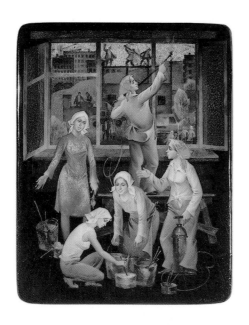

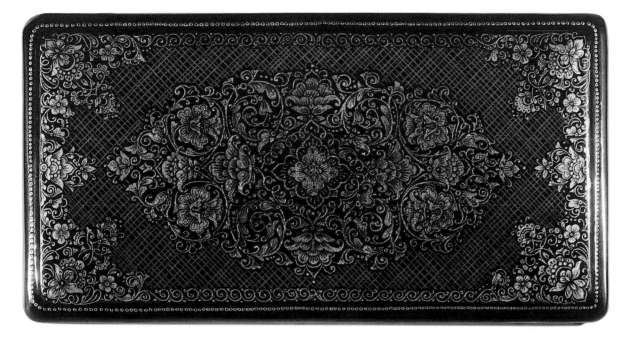

64 Sergei Chistov
Decorative box: *Construction Workers.* 1978

65 Yuri Gusev
Casket: *Russian Ornament.* 1980

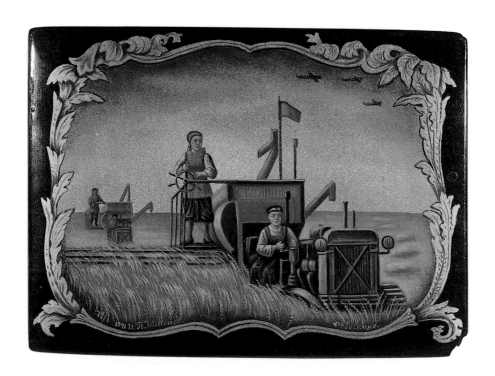

66   Ivan Platonov
Tea-caddy. 1945

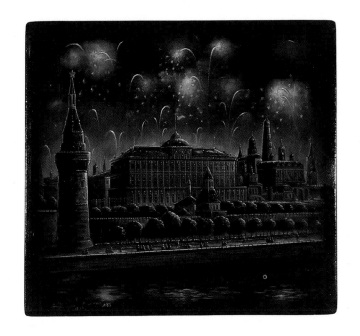

67 Ivan Semionov
Casket: *The Salute.* 1944

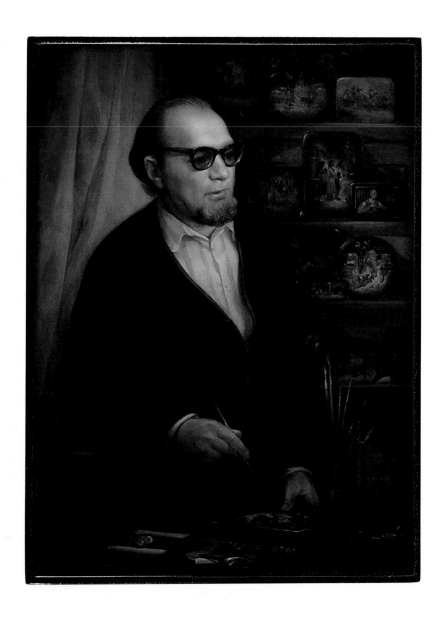

68 Nikolai Soloninkin
Panel: *Portrait of Mikhail Chizhov.* 1984

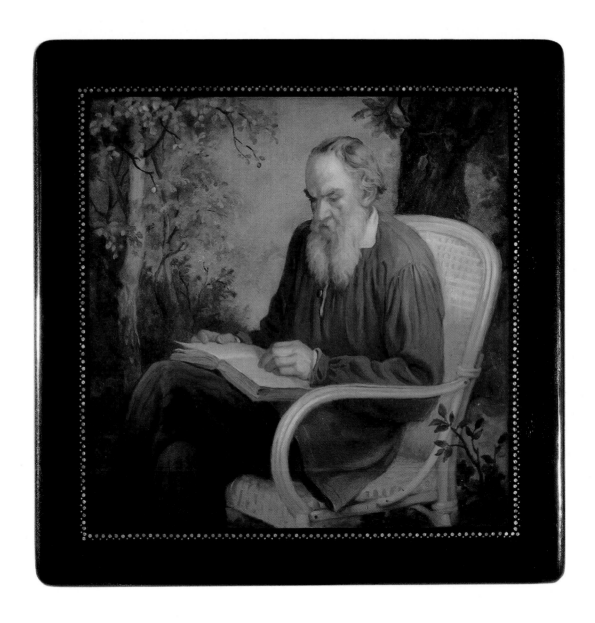

69   Victor Lipitsky
Casket: *Leo Tolstoy.* 1985

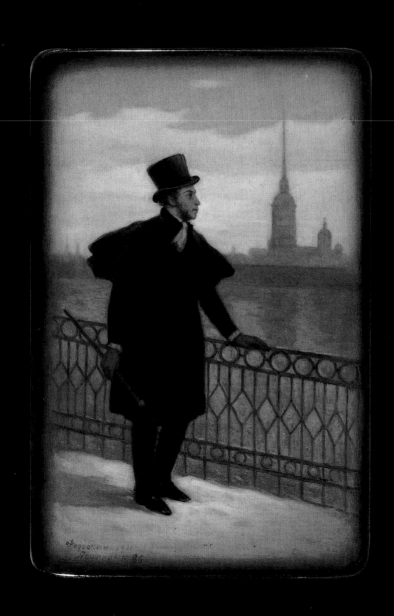

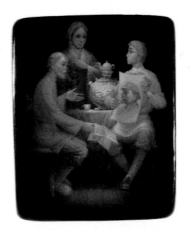

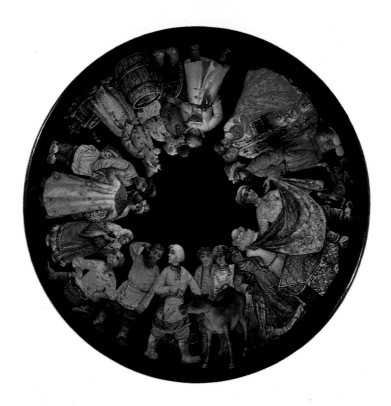

70   Mikhail Pashinin
Decorative box: *Alexander Pushkin*. 1971

71   Anatoly Kuznetsov
Decorative box: *A Story of Lenin*. 1980s

72   Sergei Rogatov
Round casket: *The Fair*. 1979

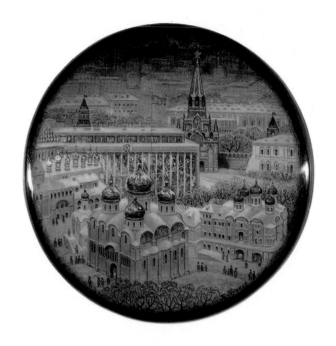

73   Piotr Puchkov
Round casket: *The Kremlin Ornaments*. 1978

Palekh

After the revolution, the Fedoskino artists did not have to explore an entirely new field of decorative arts. Due to this the traditions existing in this trade up to the moment of the revolution were not broken with and the artists preserved the former techniques and fundaments of style. In contrast, the icon-painters of Palekh, Mstiora and Kholui had to adapt and find an outlet for their creativity in lacquered miniatures. In order to understand the sources of miniature painting in these centres, it is necessary to cast a glance at their long histories.

Palekh is one of the oldest centres of icon-painting in European Russia. In the tenth to the thirteenth centuries it was part of the Vladimir-Suzdal principality, the major state formation of medieval Russia and the birth-place of a unique style of ancient Russian art. A twelfth-century chronicle reports with satisfaction on the accomplishments of the Suzdal icon-painters at the local church. The Byzantine tradition that had provided the basis for the Russian style of icon-painting was given an original interpretation in the works of the local painters who renounced austerity in favour of serenity, gentleness and restrained harmony.

In the sixteenth and seventeenth centuries the art of icon-painting spread broadly across the Vladimir-Suzdal territory. Much like the royal workshops in Moscow the centres of icon-painting were founded in monasteries, though townsfolk, peasants and the less affluent clergy worked at home helped by members of their families. The art of icon-painting was studied at that time in Suzdal, Vladimir, Murom, Shuya as well as other towns and villages, including Palekh, Mstiora and Kholui. However, as manufacturing began to be concentrated in large cities, first and foremost in Moscow, traditional art centres started to decay. Only in Palekh, Mstiora and Kholui did the masters maintain their craft. Historians ascribe this survival to the particularly large number of painters, the strong artistic tradition and the masters' own interest in their work. Also of great significance were the regular orders for icons from the Trinity–St. Sergius Monastery, the renowned bulwark of the Russian Orthodox Church. Another influential factor was the rather limited farming practices in the three villages, making it so that the residents could not possibly live by working the land alone. In fact the Kholui villagers did not even possess plots of arable land and were probably the first to engage in icon-painting.

The fame of Palekh, Mstiora and Kholui spread far beyond their boundaries. This is evident from the following curious fact. Goethe in a conversation with the Duchess of Saxen, Weimar and Eisenach, the daughter of the Russian Emperor Paul I, expressed a wish to receive information about icon-painting in the Suzdal area. Notes were prepared for him, as were two Palekh and two Kholui icons.

The Palekh style of icon-painting emerged in the seventeenth century and fully matured in the eighteenth. At its core were the Novgorod and Stroganov styles. The former originated in the north-west of Russia, in the city of Novgorod, its characteristic features being monumental imagery combined with laconicism and pictorial simplicity. The other style named after the millionaire merchant family, the Stroganovs, who had set up a school of icon-painting in the northern town of Solvychegodsk, is distinguished by its intricate composition, minute elaboration of details and profuse ornamentation. The Palekh artists learned the aesthetics and techniques inherent in both schools and blended them into a single, distinctive style which became that of the Palekh icons.

In the last decade of the nineteenth century Palekh was a relatively small town with just one big street. Its population was mostly icon-painters who also ran small peasant farms and grew rye, oats, flax and clover. The veteran Palekh painter Nikolai Zinovyev recalls: "In the 1890s icon-painting shops were scattered all over the town. I have very clear memories of some of these shops, their painters and proprietors. Quite a few masters regarded icon-painting only as a source of subsis-tence for their families. Others treated it as an art, thoroughly studied the ancient styles and techniques and generally loved the work they engaged in. Similarly, among the proprietors there were those who ruthlessly exploited the craftsmen with the only purpose to rake in profits, and those who looked after their painters well and helped the ultimate realization of their talents. In particular, they paid the best artists generously, encouraged the cultivation of the long-standing traditions, were accurate with commissions and brought up new kinds of work."[1] The expensive Palekh icons executed by complex techniques became the most well-known.

Icon-painting had long been based on the division of labour. The work process involved several operations performed by separate workmen. Thus the joiner provided the board. The primer was applied by another worker. A gilder laid the gilt ground and some details. One artist painted the saint's attire, the landscape and the architecture while another painted the faces and all the naked parts of the body. Yet another workman applied the drying oil. Even in the making of cheap icons that involved fewer operations the same division of labour was used — this was reflected in the quality of the work and kept the painter within strict limits.

Icon-painters often executed monumental frescoes in churches throughout Russia and also took

---

[1] Н.М. Зиновьев, *История Палеха*, 2-е изд., Л., 1974, с. 17 (N.M. Zinovyev, *The History of Palekh,* 2nd ed., Leningrad, 1974, p. 17).

part in various rehabilitation projects. For example, shortly before the First World War a group of sixty icon-painters participated in the restoration project for the Moscow Kremlin's Assumption Cathedral in the course of which seventeenth-century murals were discovered.

In the late nineteenth and early twentieth centuries the art of icon-painting swiftly fell into decay. Cheap and low-quality articles prevailed as a natural reaction to the market being swamped with factory-made, printed or stamped foil icons. On top of this the antique tradition of icon-painting began to vanish with the advent of the realistic style and all efforts to revitalize it proved futile. It was very obvious that the ancient art had all but had its day. After the revolution the demand for icons slumped disastrously. In the '20s their manufacture still continued but only reached some ten to fifteen percent of the pre-revolutionary level and even that due mainly to the cheap types of icons. The brilliant artists had to look for other jobs and even give up painting completely.

The icon-painters of Palekh were among the first in the trade to readjust themselves to making

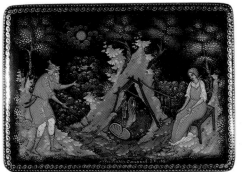

painted papier-mâché goods and in so doing borrowed heavily from the Fedoskino techniques. The result was a radical renewal of the old art of icon-painting and the emergence of a vast field for the application of the painters' skills. In the expert hands of former icon-painters cheap materials were transformed into unique works of art that were made in a distinctive style, consonant with the new aesthetic demands and at the same time following tradition. To be sure, all this did not miraculously happen in a moment but was the result of enormous and daring efforts on the part of the former icon-painters.

The search for an appropriate organizational structure and suitable language of expression was long and painful. At the outset the artists of Palekh, Mstiora and Kholui tried to paint on wood and other customary stock and regulate the sale of goods, painters set up cooperative societies.

These cooperative societies enjoyed all-round support from the Soviet authorities who regarded their activities as a form of public self-government. The Programme adopted by the seventh Congress of the Russian Communist Party (Bolsheviks) in March 1919 defined the party's policy for the handicraft businesses as favourable and supportive. In practice this meant extensive placement of state orders, provision of materials and fuel, and financial support for the cooperatives.

The emergence of cooperative societies was the immediate result of this state policy. Thus, the Palekh Wood-painting Society, comprising thirty members, was set up in 1919. The name of this early cooperative society shows the artists' desire to pursue innovative objectives and explore an entirely new field of decorative art where traditional style could become the basis for working out art forms, consonant with the spirit of the times. The artists and the state were equally interested in preventing the waste of the huge potential contained in the ancient art. And so the age-old expressive language of icon-painting began to be radically reshaped.

The newly-founded cooperative of former icon-painters began to produce painted wooden, metal and, less often, earthenware goods. At the outset the results were anything but inspiring. The objects looked dull, were not very useful in daily life and lacked the sense of poetry that always marks a genuine work of folk art. All the same, to make use of the traditional style of icon-painting for the elaboration of themes drawn from folk songs, na-

tional history and peasant life seemed a very fruitful idea.

At last, in 1922, a hitherto unknown Palekh painter Ivan Golikov, later joined by his colleague Ivan Vakurov, began to experiment with papier-mâché painting in a workshop in Moscow owned by a well-known icon connoisseur A. Glazunov. The idea received the approval of art historians and museum experts. An associate of the former Handicrafts Museum related to the author: "One day in the early '20s A. Glazunov dropped in at the museum. After I had showed him around the exhibition he stopped at the display case containing the Lukutin and Fedoskino papier-mâché ware. 'We must give it a try,' Glazunov said. Later he arrived with his son-in-law Ivan Golikov, an odd peasant type wearing felt boots. We discussed prospects for starting the manufacture and sale of painted papier-mâché goods..."

Golikov conducted his first experiment with a papier-mâché cuvette in Glazunov's workshop. First he filed the edges and obtained the plate on which he painted a hunting scene in gold. Seeing the good results the Handicrafts Museum gave the Palekh artists a half-finished Fedoskino papier-mâché casket. There followed a major order for the 1923 National Agricultural Exhibition. This order was executed simultaneously at Glazunov's workshop and in Palekh itself. The results exceeded all expectations and the panel was awarded a first-grade diploma of the exhibition.

From the beginning the outstanding folk art historian Anatoly Bakushinsky gave inestimable assistance to the Palekh artists. This highly educated scholar, encyclopaedically knowledgeable about the world of arts was also well informed about all the subtleties of the local school of icon-painting. His collaboration provided members of the newly-founded cooperatives with vital guidance through the complex and often controversial styles the art of icon-painting had followed at different stages of its evolution. It was Bakushinsky who suggested that the Palekh artists should give up the degenerating style of the latest period and turn to the late eighteenth and early nineteenth centuries, when Palekh icons had stood out sharply against the common ground due to their outstanding artistic qualities. The idea was to revitalize the best elements of the old style, moulding them into the new aesthetic values.

The foundation of the Ancient Painting Cooperative Society by seven Palekh artists (Alexander Kotukhin, Ivan Golikov, Ivan Markichev, Ivan Bakanov, Ivan Zubkov, Vladimir Kotukhin, Alexander Zubkov) in December 1924 became a historical landmark in Russian decorative and applied arts. With it began the organized and systematic elaboration of secular themes by former icon-painters who had assimilated the previously unfamiliar technique of lacquered miniature painting. This qualitative leap was followed by a long process of maturation. After some time the technology of preparation and production of papier-mâché was taken from Fedoskino and the Palekh artists started their own manufacture of semi-finished goods. Unlike the Fedoskino masters who used oil paints, the former icon-painters preferred the egg tempera that they were more used to. This accounts for the distinct colouring of the Palekh articles and sets them apart from the Fedoskino wares.

Already in his lifetime Ivan Golikov had the reputation of Palekh's finest miniaturist. He was also referred to as an artist born of the revolution. Previously an unknown craftsman performing routine operations in a painting shop, under the new conditions he revealed to the utmost his outstanding talent.

Ivan Golikov was born in 1886 (early 1887 according to the New Style) and lived a hard and fascinating life. He came from a family of a peasant icon-painter in Palekh. His father failed to make ends meet with his work, the family was dragging a wretched existence and the six children knew poverty and starvation. At the age of ten the future artist was apprenticed to the "king of icon-painting", N. Safonov. However, Golikov never completed his training and instead moved to Moscow where he got a job at an icon-painting workshop run by a group of Palekh artists. Later he also worked in St. Petersburg. Life in the capitals was quite instructive for Golikov who paid regular visits to museums and even attended evening classes at the Industrial Art School. He travelled throughout Russia with teams of Palekh artists painting churches and monasteries. During the war he fought on the front-line, got shell-shocked and served as regimental cook and book binder. Even so, wherever he was, he never stopped painting.

After the revolution Golikov painted a three-metre poster for a soldiers' meeting. They say when the poster, showing a soldier and a peasant, was carried to the meeting, the peasants passing by took off their hats and crossed themselves because, for all its revolutionary content, the poster was executed in the unmistakable Palekh style of icon-painting.

When Golikov returned to Palekh he found all the painting shops gone. After working for some time as set designer with provincial theatre companies, he again went to Moscow where, together with A. Glazunov, he conducted a series of successful experiments with painting on papier-mâché. Returning again to Palekh, he swiftly established himself as the town's leading miniaturist. As soon as he gained freedom from the strict conventional limits of an icon-painter (in the past his job was painting garments and landscapes while faces and hands were executed by someone else), it became very obvious that in his person Palekh had obtained a mature, distinctive and spirited artist.

Over the first two decades of existence of the Palekh lacquered miniature two tendencies distinctly revealed themselves within the framework of a single pictorial style. One showed a bent for romanticism and expressionism while the other remained more down-to-earth and realistic.

Golikov was a passionate and irrepressible romantic. His favourite subject was the duel of horsemen. The bodies of men and horses, interlaced in tight knots, created an infinitely dynamic all-over decorative pattern, expressive of strength, courage and valour. A recurring motif of Golikov's miniatures were dashing, skyward-bound *troikas*, the horses of which were given swan-like, curved necks and seemed not to be galloping but flying in a vortex.

Fundamental to Golikov's manner was the Stroganov style of icon-painting, from which came his compositional dynamism, brightness of colour, minute elaboration of figures and dresses, generous use of silver and gold, and heightened ornamentality. Golikov noticeably enriched the traditional style by imparting his observations from life to the compositions. Nikolai Zinovyev thus recalls his comrade in art: "He was in the habit of taking long walks through fields and forests early in the morning, taking in various shapes of tree-leaves, the lustre of dew-drops shot with silver or gold from the sun. He picked wild flowers and when at home laid them out in different combinations on his working table, looking for appropriate colour solutions for his future compositions. For hours on end could he watch horses galloping downhill, noting every movement. Masterly application of the traditional techniques allowed him to always reproduce these observations vividly and cogently."[1]

Dmitry Butorin's life in art followed much the same pattern. He was among those artists who knew both the realistic method and the traditional Palekh style. His manner of figure drawing followed the old rules: first came the naked body reproduced with anatomical precision, then the clothes were added. Not unlike Golikov, Butorin attributed great importance to the gold and silver finishing of a miniature which added particular elegance and nobility to the whole picture.

Ivan Bakanov stood out as an excellent icon-painter before the revolution, specializing in monumental paintings for churches. As a miniaturist he retained the monumental serenity, steadiness as well as gentle colouration. Conventionalized as they are, Bakanov's miniatures are not entirely devoid of realism.

One of the most astonishing Palekh artists of the older generation, Aristarkh Dydykin joined the cooperative society in 1926. His manner of painting is very individual, sharp and potent, featuring a wealth of humour and acute characterization. Nikolai Zinovyev joined the cooperative in 1927, i.e. shortly after its foundation. He lived the long, pure and serene life of a wise man and genuine thinker. In 1978 the national artistic community broadly marked the 90th birthday of this venerable master and teacher who had educated more than one generation of painters. His manner of painting was distinctly realistic and down-to-earth, rejecting abstract symbol as alien. He always readily responded to the topical issues of his time, showing a bent for subjects with a

---

[1] Zinovyev, *op. cit.*, p. 75.

broad historical content. His painting of a writing-set, *History of the Earth* (pl. 149), executed in 1930, is quite illustrative of this. It recreates the evolution of life on the earth from the emergence of the planet to the rise of man, the labourer and the thinker. The very choice of the subject of this complex work is significant as it had been previously viewed as lying beyond the powers of the art of miniature. The painter effectively coped with wide-ranging compositional problems by allocating meaningful pictures on diversely shaped and often quite inexpressive objects and masterfully blending them into an integral artistic entity. This work exemplifies the artist's conscientious approach to the choice of theme as well as the painterly side of his art.

The Palekh miniatures were swiftly gaining reputation. In 1925 they were successfully shown at the International Exhibition in Paris and later continued to carry off prizes at various overseas shows. The cooperative grew fast and by the end of 1930 employed twenty-three painters, two joiners, two polishers and three office-workers. In the late '20s the government allocated 10,000 roubles for the cooperative to set up a system of apprenticeship. In 1930 there were eighteen apprentices including four girls, thus setting a precedent for women to take up work as miniaturists.

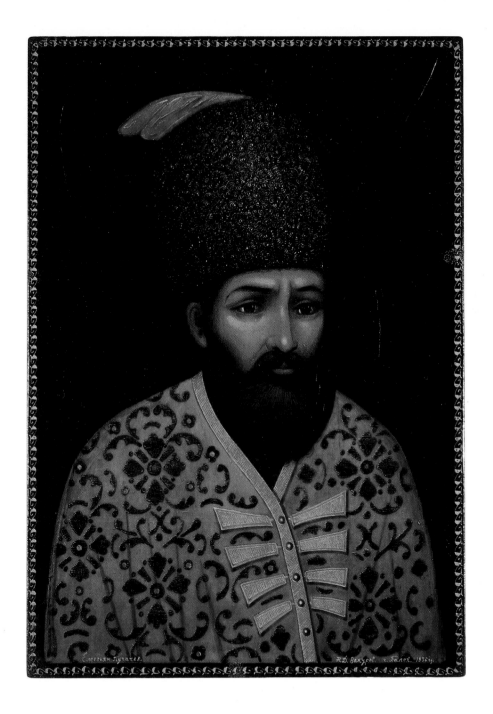

74   Nikolai Vakurov
Panel: *Yemelyan Pugachov.* 1936

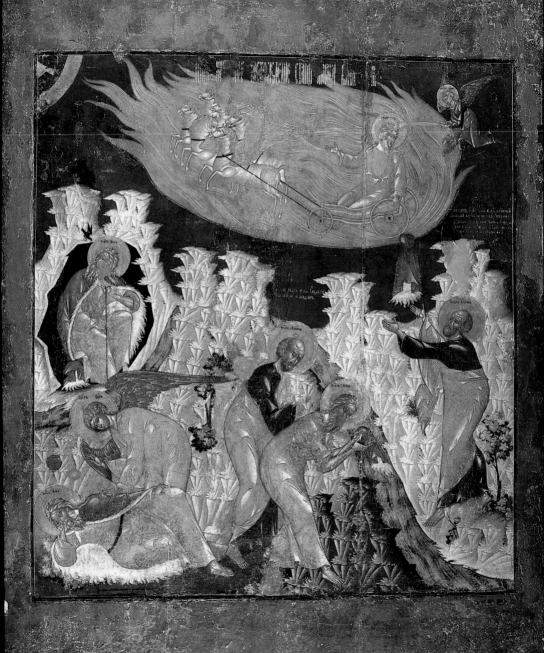

Ηλαγγ҃ʌᴏ ҃ зхотᴀꙗстᴠᴎ҃ архꙗᴄᴛраᴛᴎ Ηᴧамᴎхаᴎлᴀᴦᴏᴏᴀᴦᴏᴩᴎᴀᴎᴎ Стᴀᴨᴏᴧᴎᴀ ҃ ᴠᴏᴦᴎ ᴄᴀ Ηᴀ ᴨ ᴏᴇ ᴨ ᴎᴛ ᴎ ᴦᴀ ᴄᴀ ᴨ ᴎᴛ ᴎ ᴛᴀ ᴨᴏᴎᴦᴀᴛᴎ ᴄᴏᴀᴩᴎᴎᴎᴠᴀ
ᴦᴏᴏᴇᴄᴀᴛᴎᴎᴎᴨᴩᴀᴦᴏᴧᴎᴨᴏᴦᴏᴧᴎᴎ ᴎᴎᴇᴀ ᴄᴧᴨᴏᴩᴎᴨᴧᴀᴛᴎᴎᴨᴎᴎᴎᴧᴎ Ηᴎᴧᴎ ҃ ҃ᴎᴎᴨᴎᴎᴠᴀ ᴄ ᴨᴧᴠᴎᴎᴛᴀᴎᴎᴄᴛᴀᴨᴎᴎ Ηᴀᴎᴄᴇᴆᴀᴦᴏᴎ ᴨᴩᴏ
ᴄᴨᴀᴨᴦᴩᴀᴎᴏᴨᴀ Πᴏᴎ ᴄᴛ ᴎ ᴎ ᴀ ᴄᴦᴧᴀ ᴎ ᴇ ᴎ ᴏ ᴦ ᴀ ᴎ ᴀ ᴦ ᴎ Κᴀᴎᴎᴎᴎ ᴀ ᴦ ᴎ Πᴇ ᴧ ᴀ ᴎ ᴎ ᴇ ᴎ ᴎ ᴎ ᴎ ᴦ ᴎᴎ ᴎ ᴎ ᴎ ᴎ ᴦ ᴎ ᴎ
ᴇ ᴦ ᴎ ᴎ ᴎ ᴎ Πᴏᴎᴎ ᴎ ᴇᴎᴎ ᴎ ᴎ ᴀ ᴦᴎᴧᴎ ᴎ ᴄᴀ ᴎ ᴎ ᴏ ᴎ ᴎ ᴨ ᴎ ᴎ ᴎ ᴎ ᴎ ᴎ ᴎ ᴎ ᴎ ᴎ ᴎ ᴀ ᴎ ᴎ ᴎ ᴎ ᴎᴎᴎ ᴎ ᴎ ᴎ
ᴎ ᴦ ᴎ ᴦ ᴎᴀ ᴦ ᴎ ᴎ ᴦ ᴎ ᴎ ᴎ ᴎ ᴎ ᴎ ᴎ ᴎ ᴎ ᴎ ᴎ ᴦ

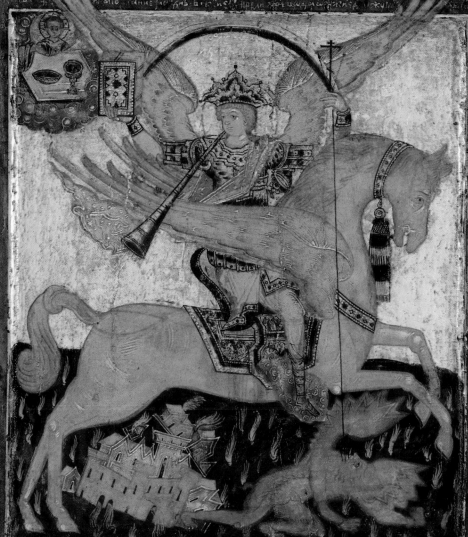

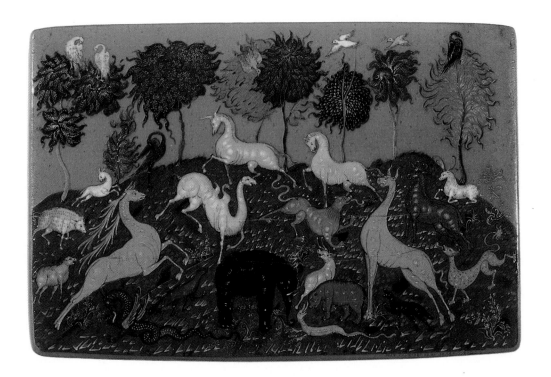

←
75 Icon: *The Fiery Ascent of the
Prophet Elijah.* Early 18th century

←
76 Icon: *The Archangel Michael
the Voivode.* First half
of the 17th century. Detail

77 Ivan Golikov
Casket: *The Beasts.* 1925

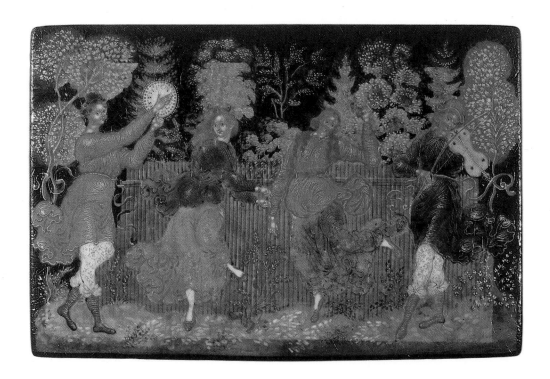

78   Ivan Golikov
Casket: *The Dance.* 1925

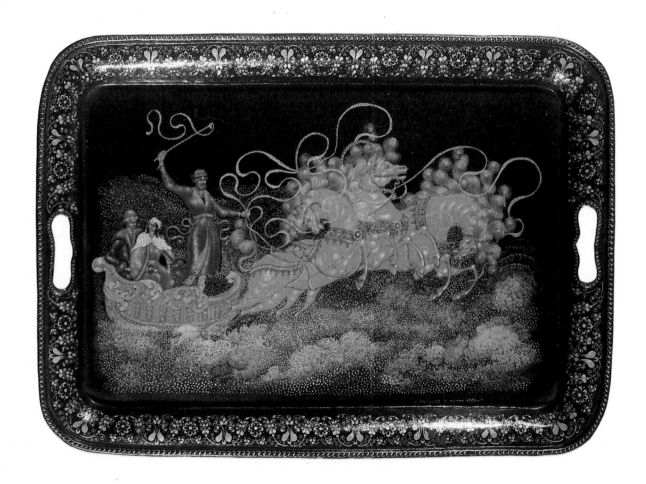

79 Ivan Golikov
Tray: *Troika.* 1926

80 Ivan Golikov
Tray: *Troika.* 1926. Detail

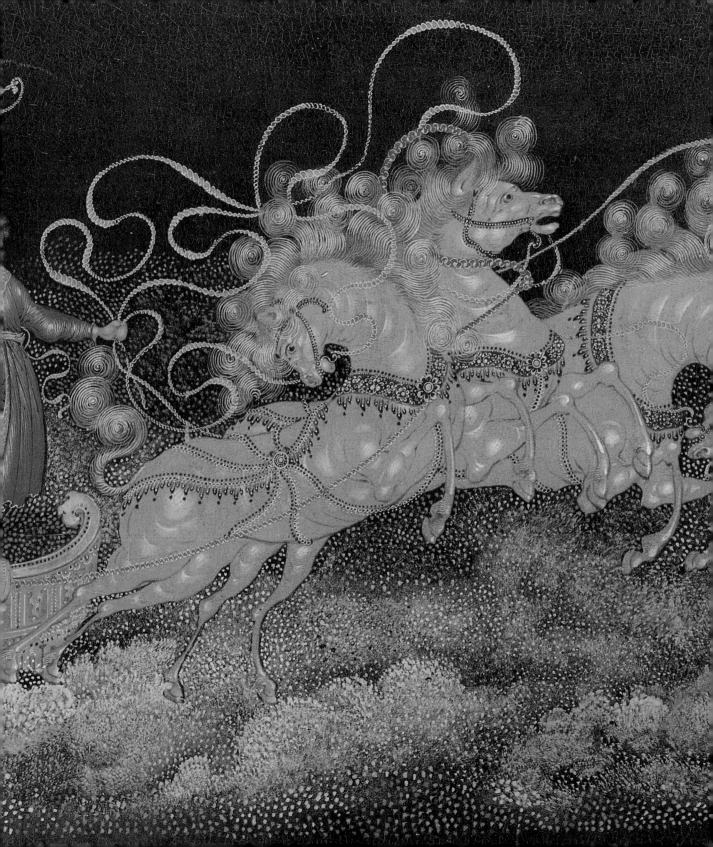

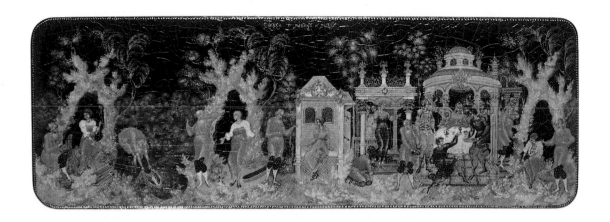

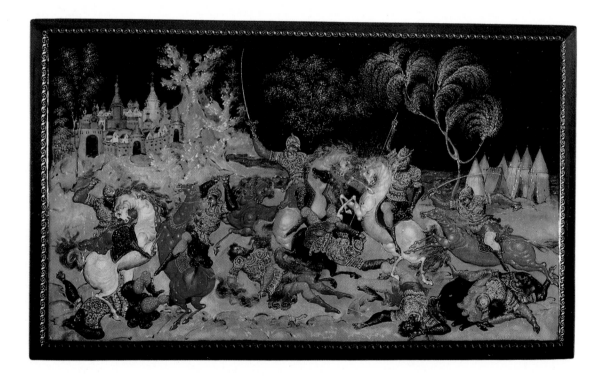

81 Ivan Golikov
Casket: *The Tale of the Fisherman
and the Golden Fish*. 1927

82 Ivan Golikov
Panel: *The Battle*. 1927

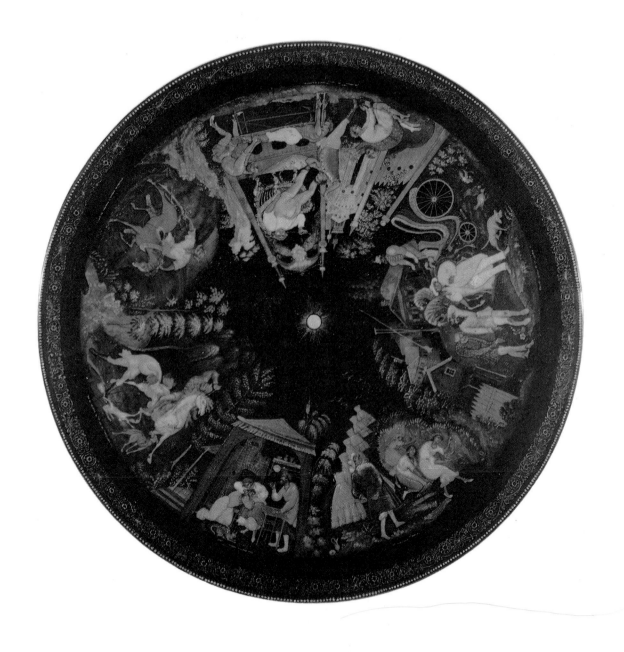

83 Pavel Bazhenov
Decorative plate: *The Corvée.* 1932

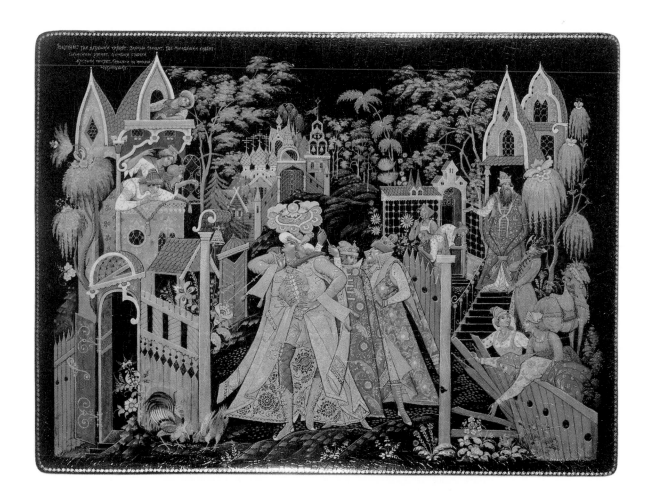

84   Pavel Bazhenov
Casket: *Churila Plenkovich*. 1934

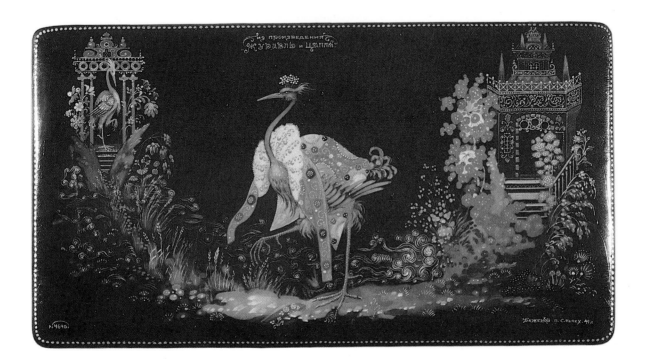

85   Pavel Bazhenov
Casket: *The Crane and the Heron.* 1941

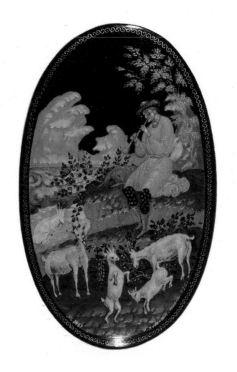

86   Ivan Zubkov
Oval box: *Herdsman's Pastime.* 1926

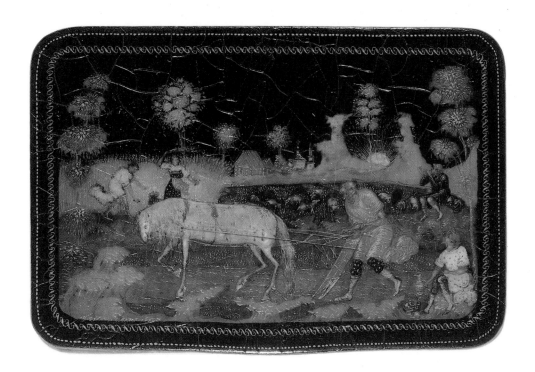

87 Ivan Zubkov
Cigarette-case: *The Ploughman*. 1926

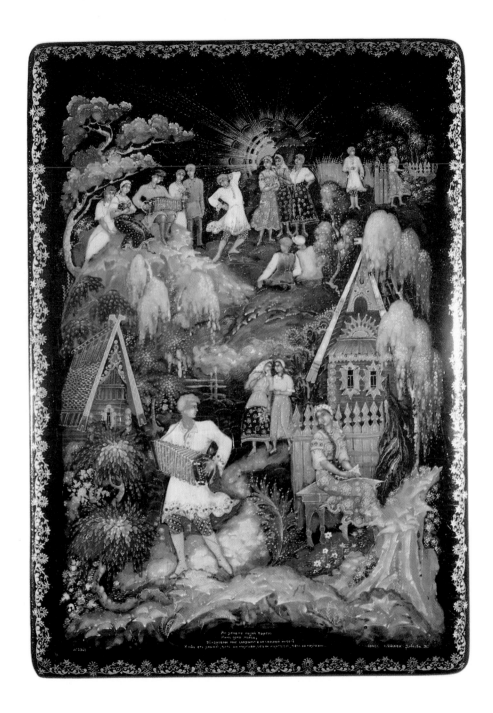

88   Tamara Zubkova
Casket: *"What's on his mind?"* 1946

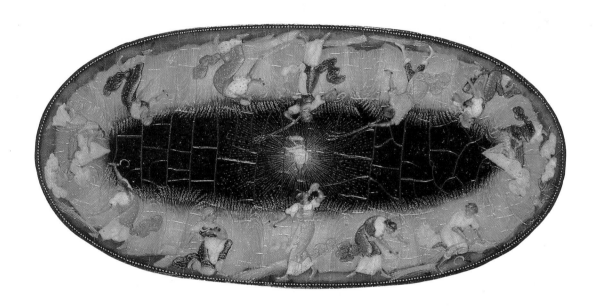

89   Ivan Zubkov
Oval casket: *Harvesting*. 1929

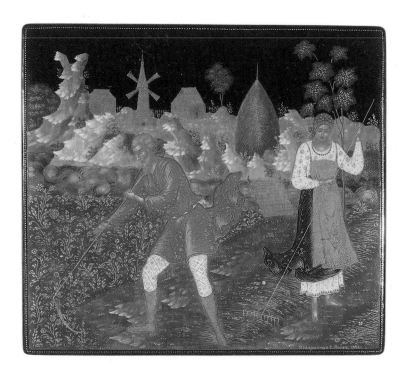

90 Ivan Markichev
Casket: *Haymaking.* 1926

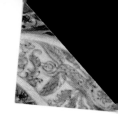

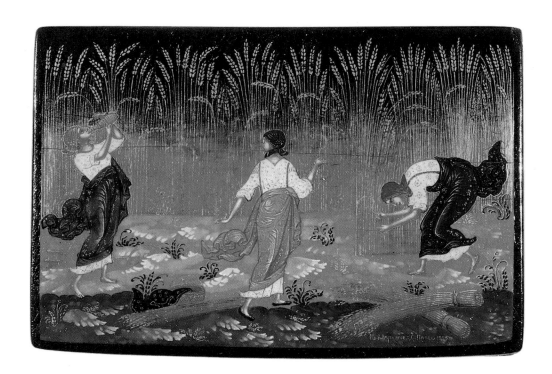

91   Ivan Markichev
Casket: *Harvesting.* 1925

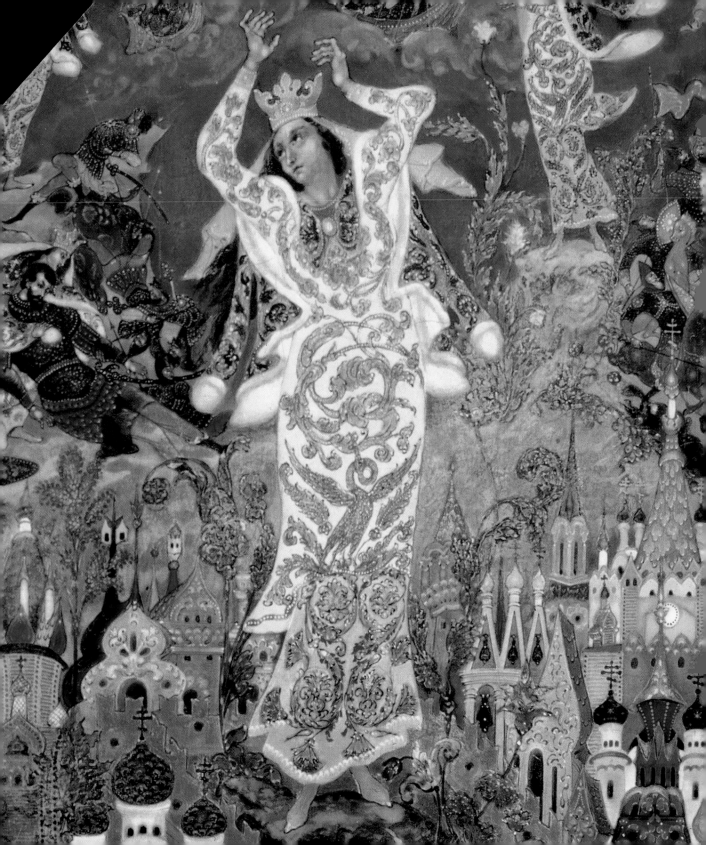

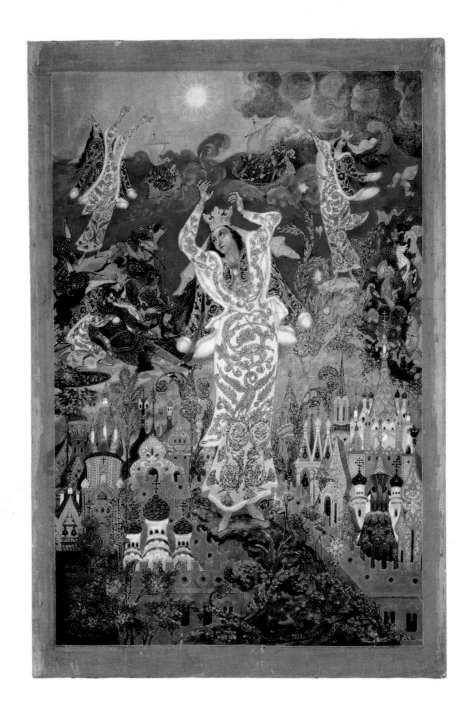

92 Ivan Golikov
Panel: *Yaroslavna Weeping*. 1933. Detail

93 Ivan Golikov
Panel: *Yaroslavna Weeping*. 1933

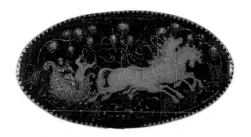

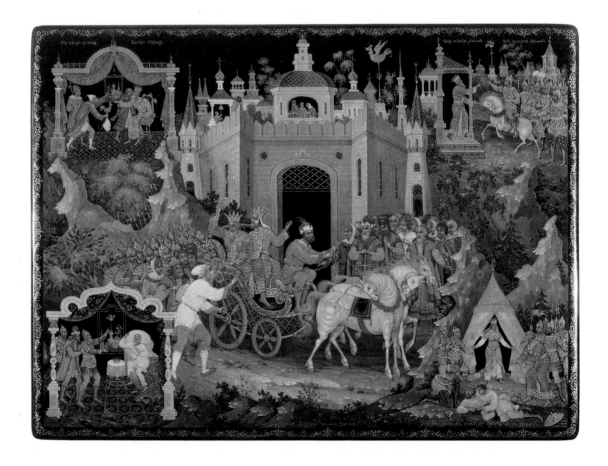

94 Vladimir Kotukhin
Brooch: *Troika*. 1929

95 Alexander Kotukhin
Casket: *Pushkin's Fairy-tales*. 1939

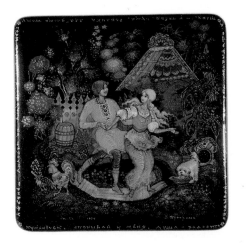

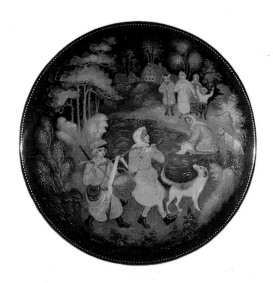

96   Stanislav Butorin
Decorative box: *"Hey, crony, why don't
you come in?"* 1974

97   Stanislav Butorin
Round casket: *The Sun Pantry.* 1978

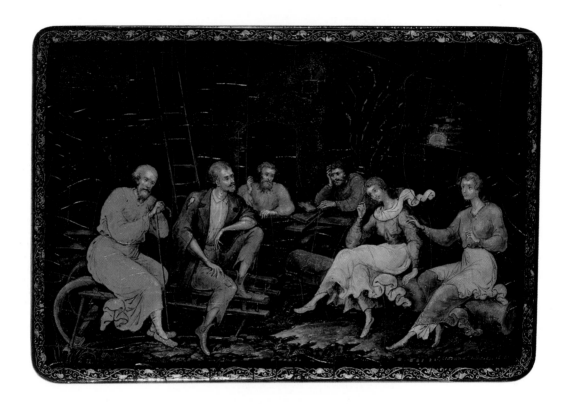

98   Sergei Solonin
Casket: *The Lower Depths.* 1932

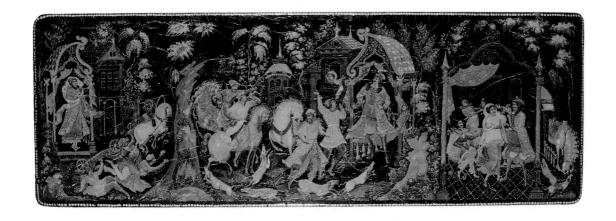

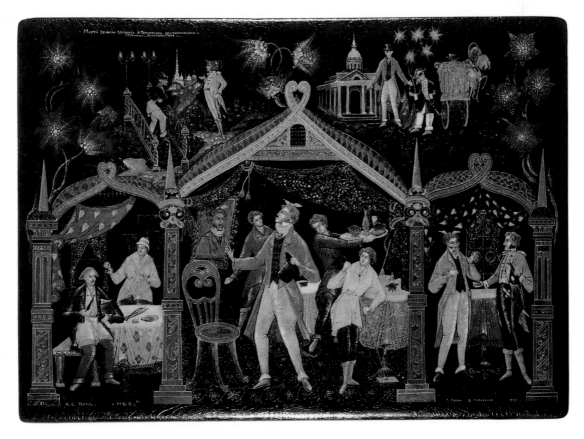

99   Dmitry Turin
Casket: *Count Nulin.* 1934

100   Vasily Salabanov
Casket: *The Nose.* 1935

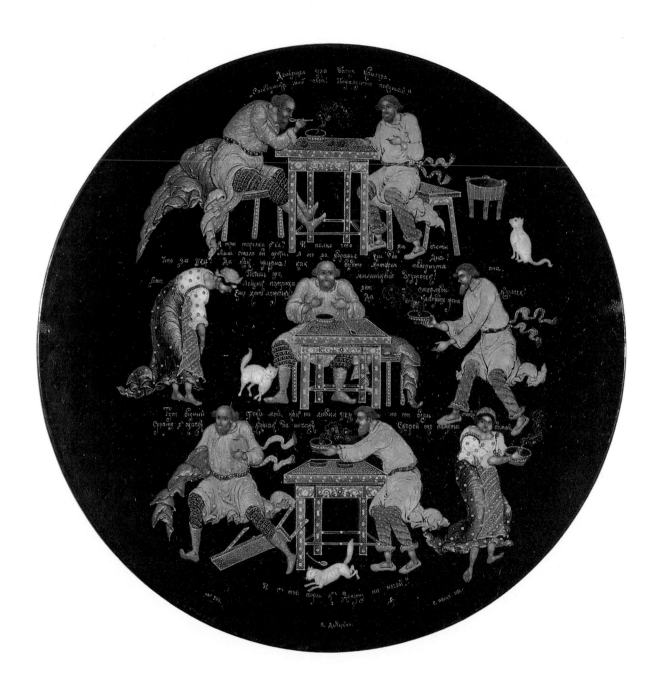

101   Aristarkh Dydykin
Decorative plate: *Demyan's Fish-soup*. 1931

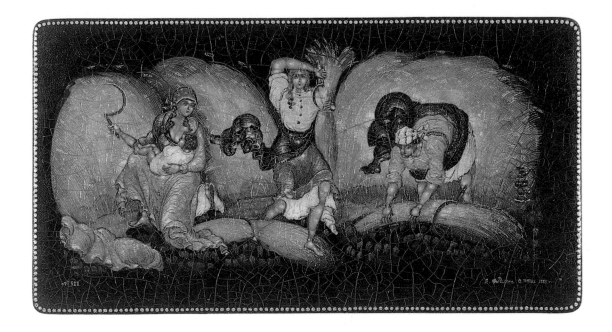

102   Aristarkh Dydykin
Casket: *The Reapers.* 1933

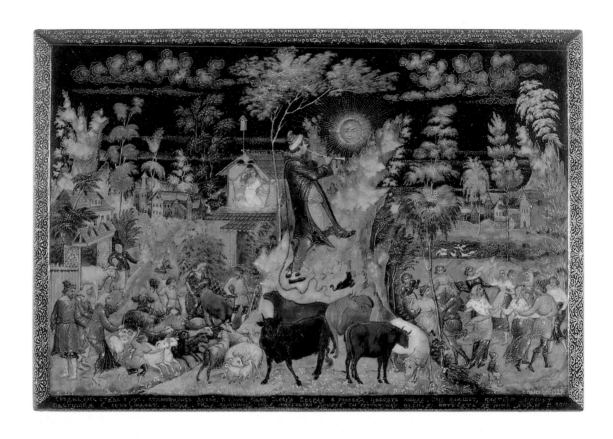

103   Ivan Bakanov
Panel: *Morning in the Country.* 1929

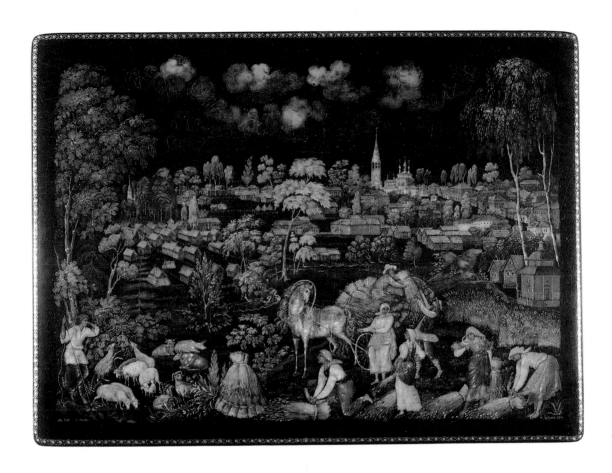

104 Ivan Bakanov
Casket: *Palekh*. 1934

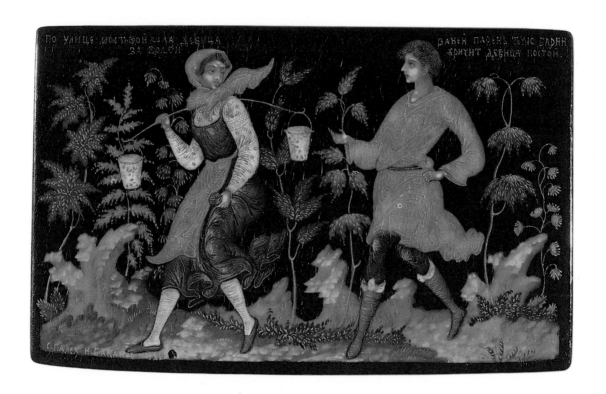

105   Ivan Bakanov
Casket: *By the Roadway.* 1934

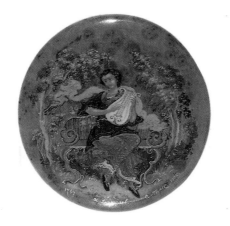

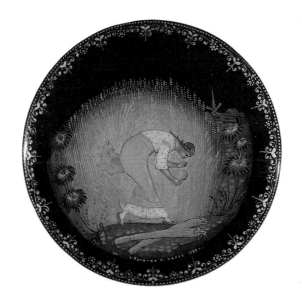

106 Ivan Dorofeyev
Powder-case: *Leisure-time.* 1936

107 Alexei Vatagin
Powder-case: *The Reaper.* 1932

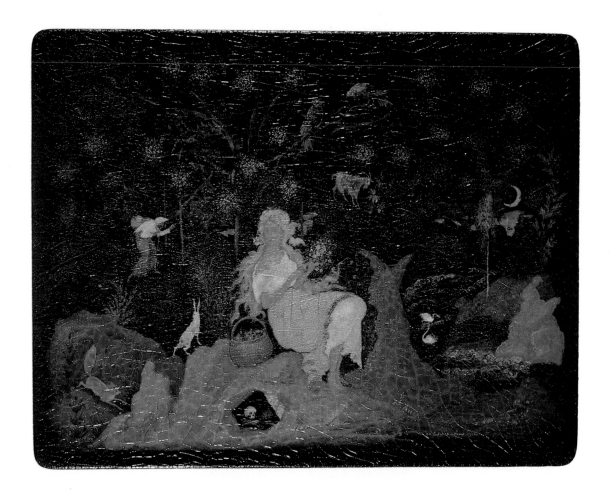

108 Ivan Vakurov
Casket: *The Forest Tale.* 1932

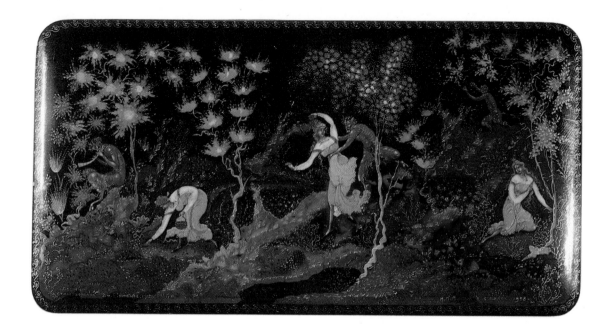

109   Ivan Vakurov
Casket: *The Wood Goblin.* 1928

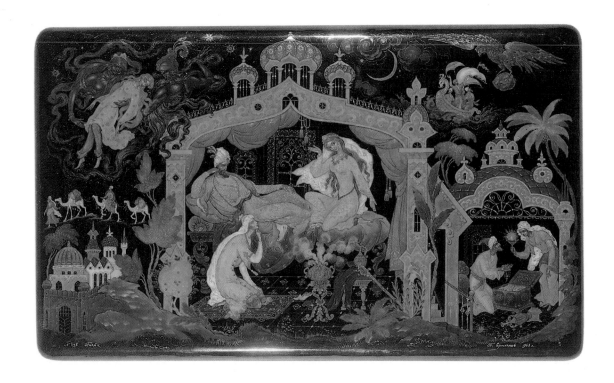

110   Boris Yermolayev
Casket: *The Arabian Tales.* 1968

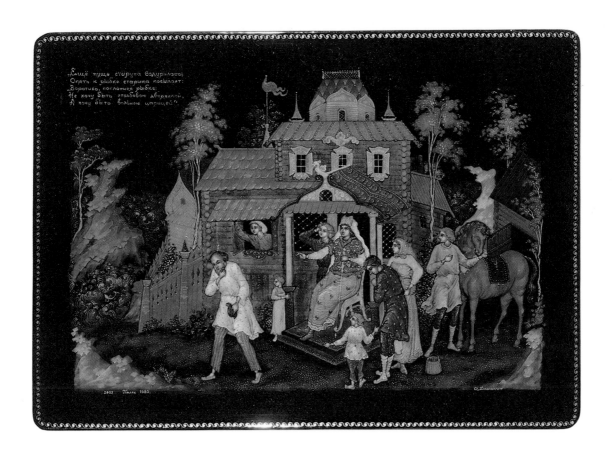

111   Alexander Doshlygin
Casket: *The Tale of the Fisherman
and the Golden Fish*. 1980

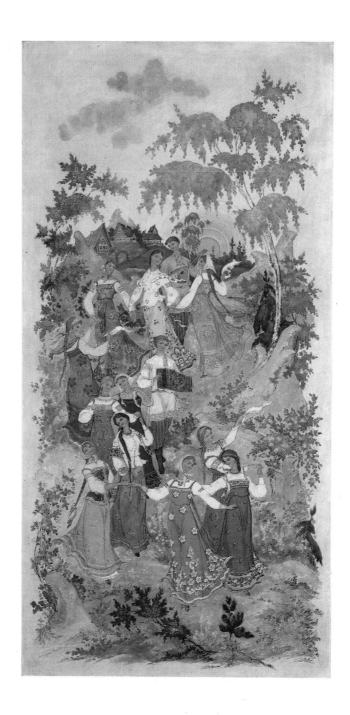

112   Anna Kotukhina
Panel: *Birch-tree*. 1956

113   Anna Kotukhina
Panel: *Birch-tree*. 1956. Detail

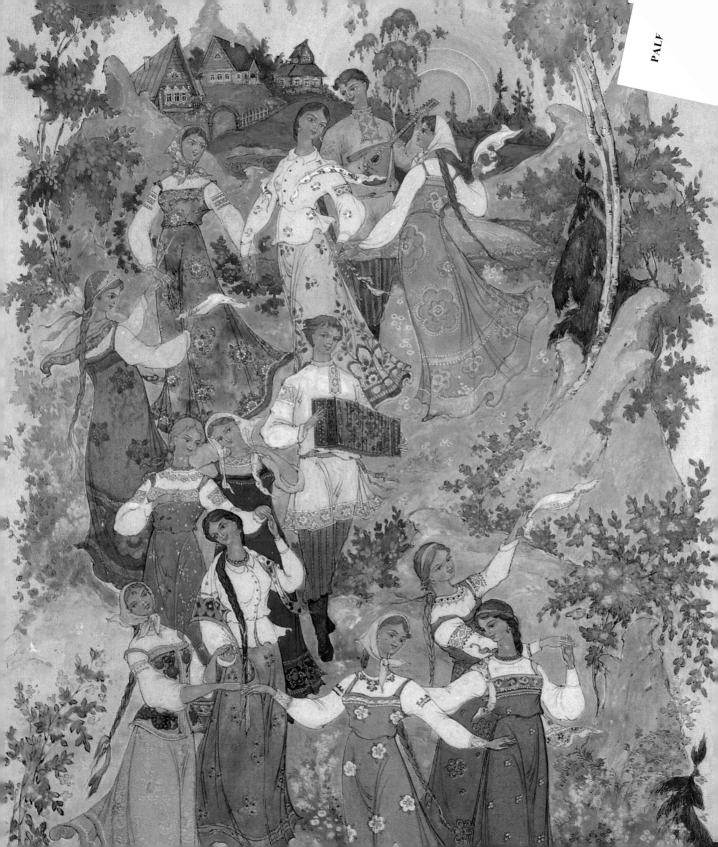

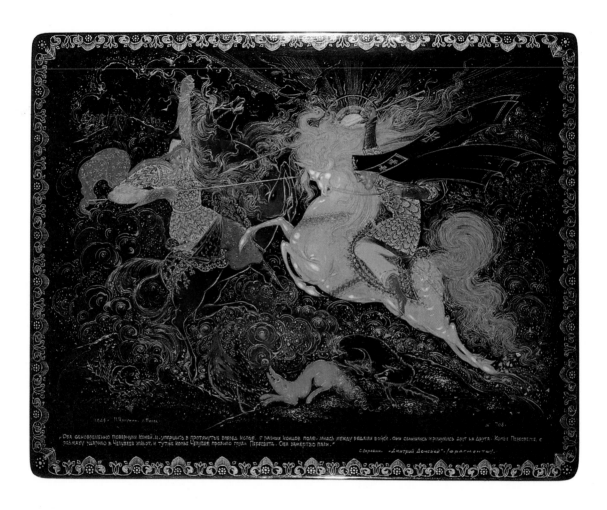

114 Pavel Chalunin
Casket: *Peresvet Fighting Chelubei.* 1945

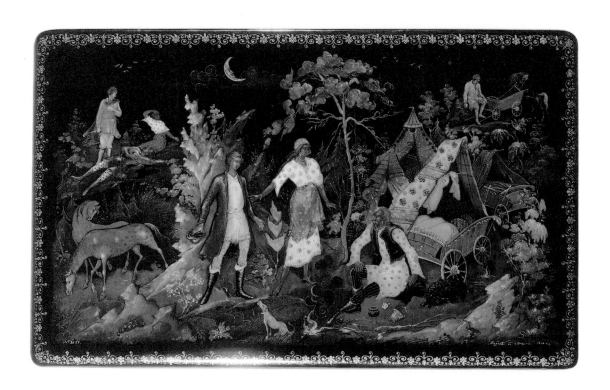

115 Grigory Bureyev
Casket: *The Gypsies.* 1946

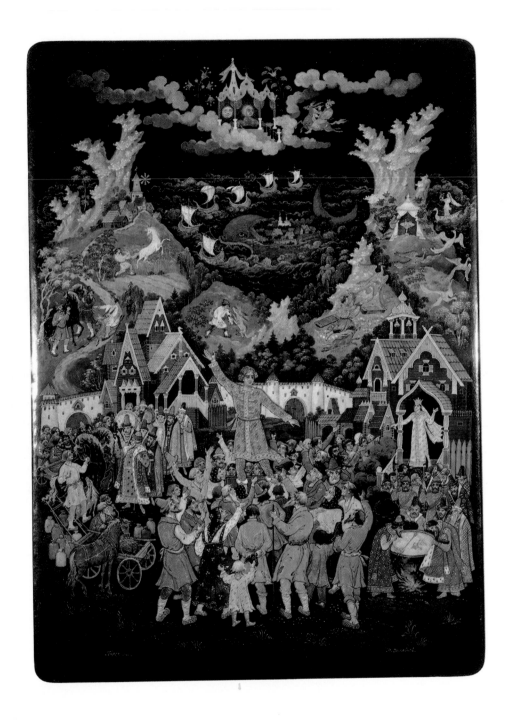

116 Nikolai Zinovyev
Casket: *The Little Hunch-backed Horse.* 1967

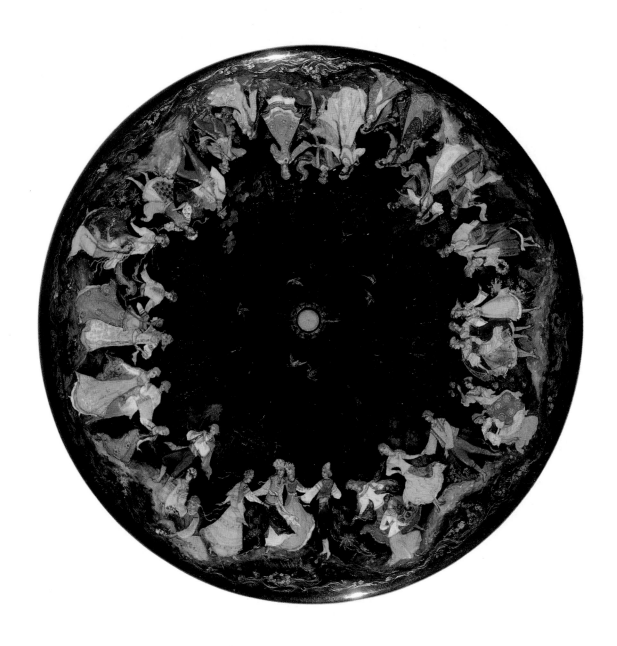

117 Kaleria Kukuliyeva
Round casket: *The Garland of the Danube*.
1967

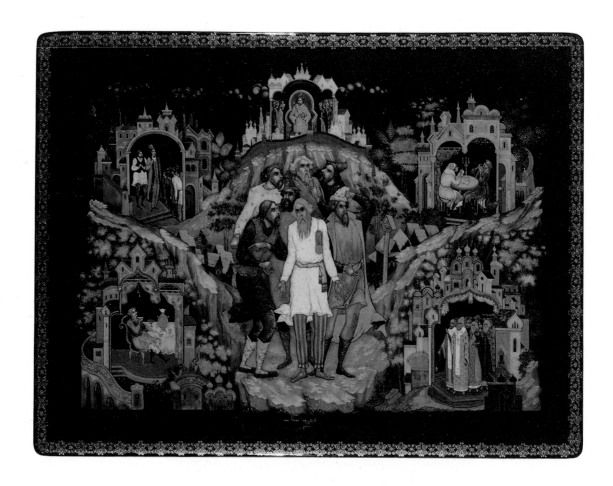

118   Oleg An
Casket: *Seven Muzhiks.* 1979

119   Oleg An
Casket: *Seven Muzhiks.* 1979. Detail

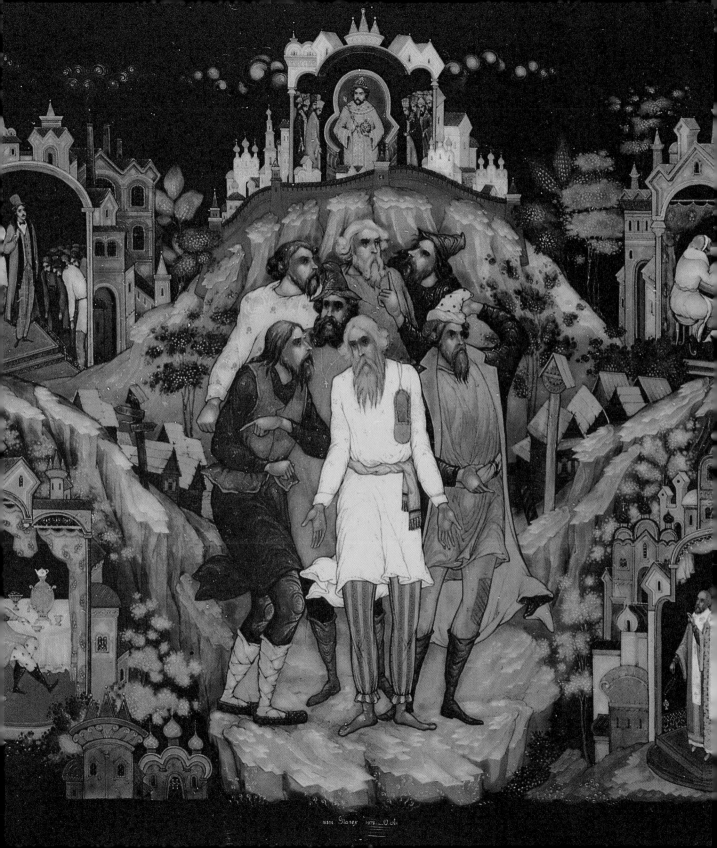

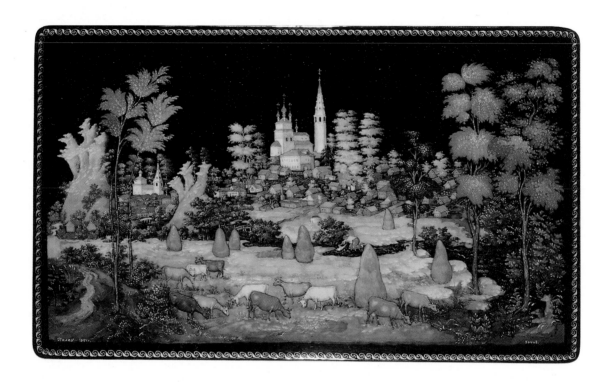

120   Vadim Zotov
Casket: *Autumn*. 1984

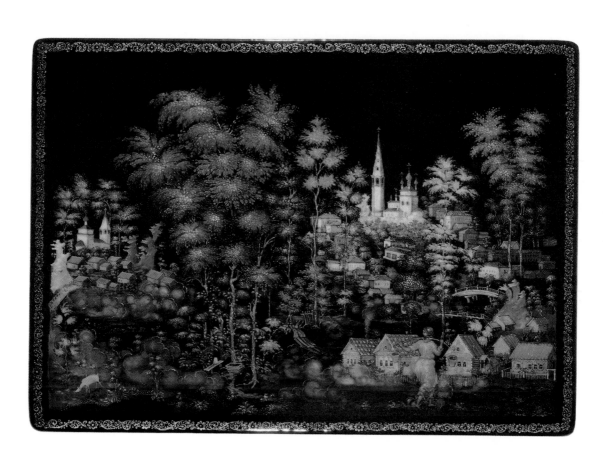

121   Vadim Zotov
Casket: *Morning*. 1984

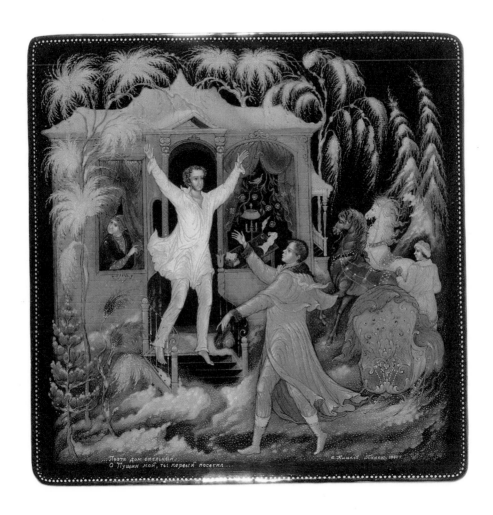

122 Alexander Klipov
Casket: *Alexander Pushkin Meets
Ivan Pushchin*. 1984

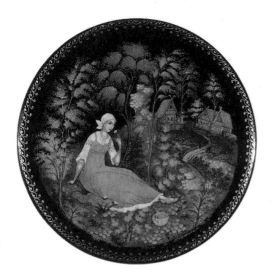

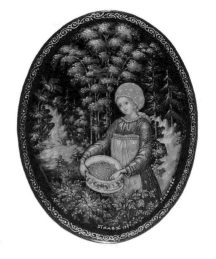

123 Tatyana Andriyashkina
Powder-case: *In the Wood*. 1984

124 Irina Livanova
Portmanteau: *Picking Berries*. 1984

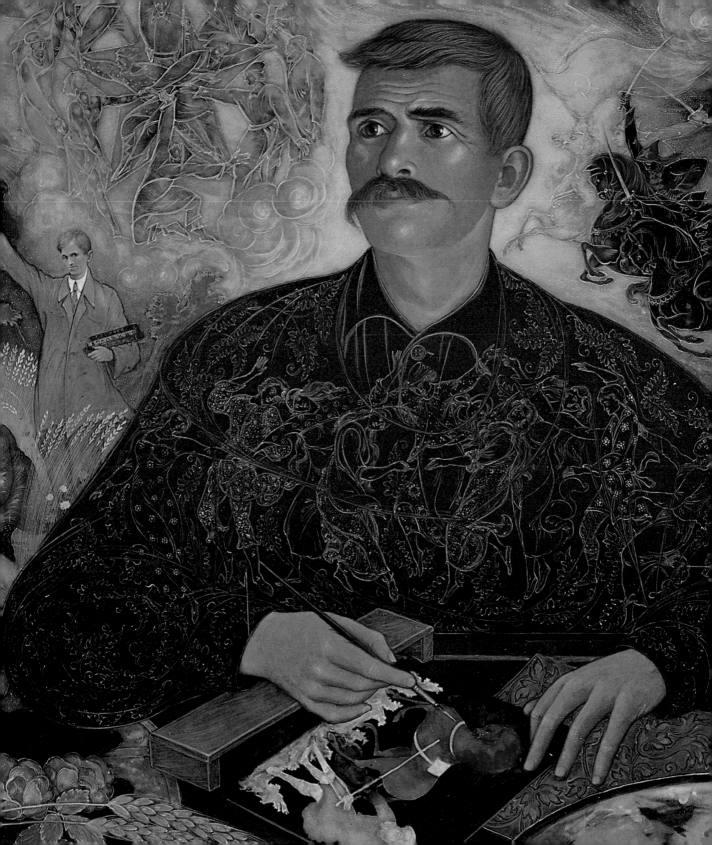

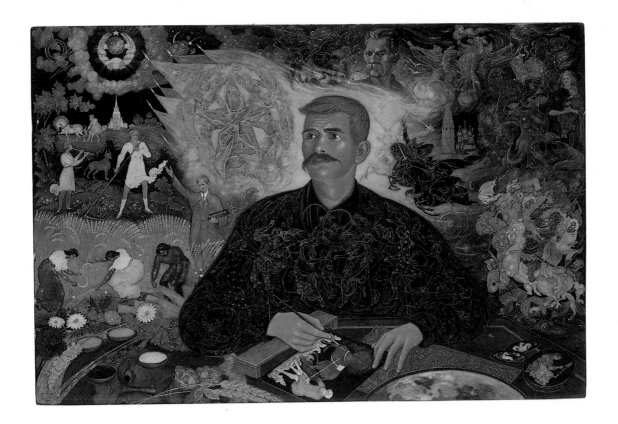

125   Grigory Melnikov
Panel: *Ivan Golikov.* 1967. Detail

126   Grigory Melnikov
Panel: *Ivan Golikov.* 1967

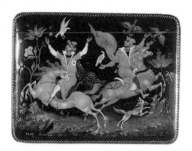

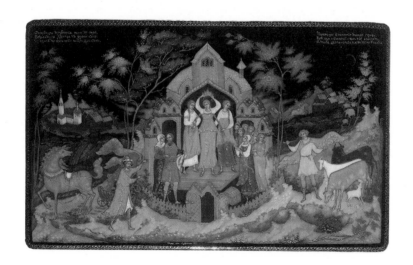

127 Nikolai Gribov
Casket: *The Hunt.* 1981

128 Olga Subbotina
Casket: *The Trumpet Blared.* 1984

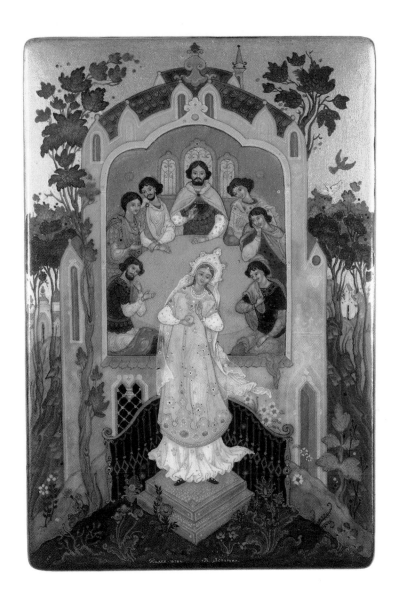

129 Nikolai Lopatin
Casket: *The Tale of the Dead Princess.*
1979

→ 130 Valentin Khodov
Decorative plate: *Summer.* 1980

→ 131 Gennady Kochetov
Casket: *Noon.* 1984

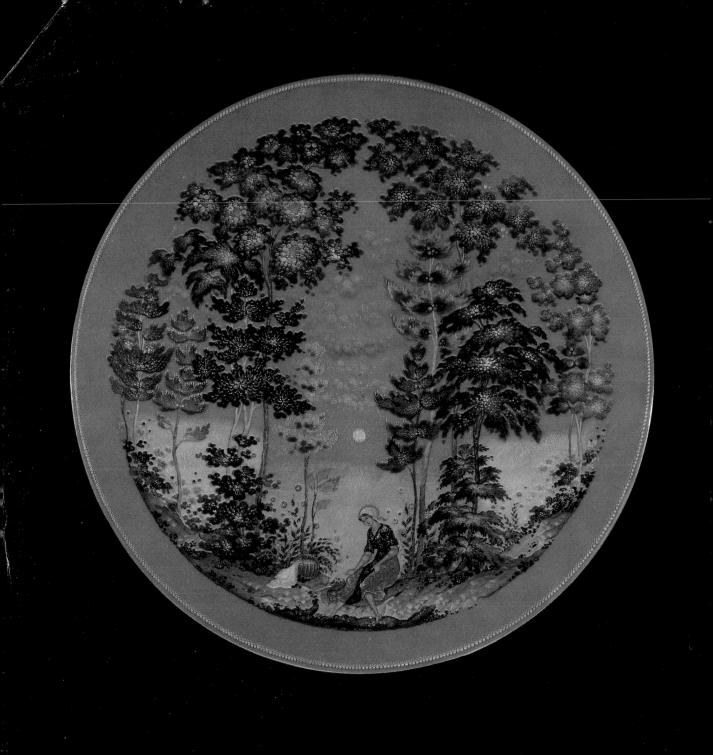

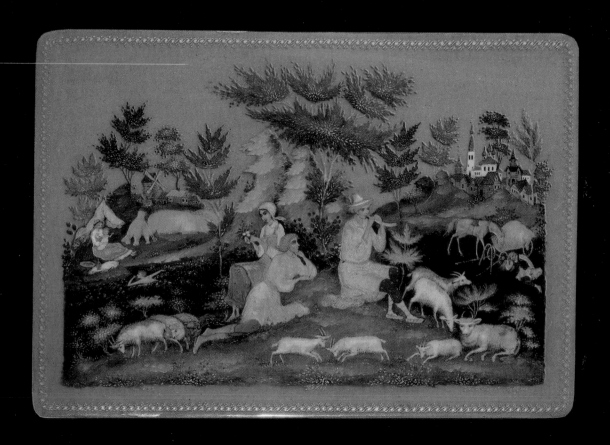

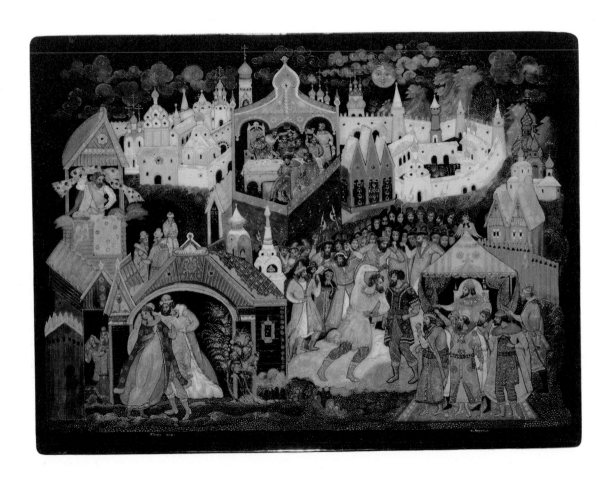

132 Viacheslav Morokin
Casket: *Merchant Kalashnikov.* 1972

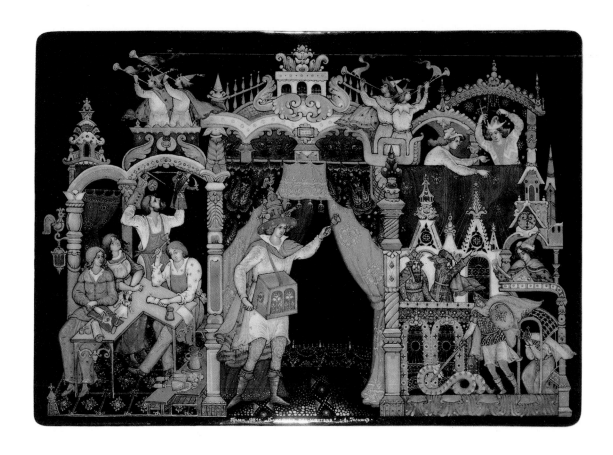

133   Alexander Gelishev
Casket: *Puppet-makers.* 1984

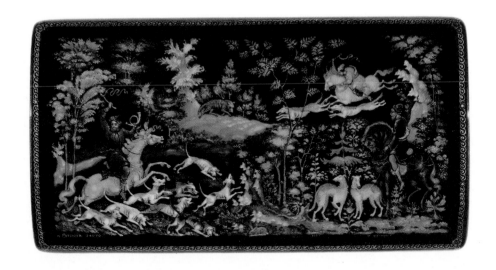

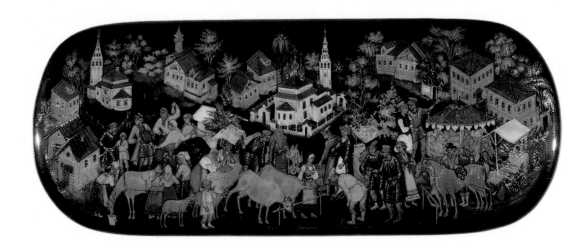

134 Yuri Shchanitsyn
Casket: *The Russian Hunt. Spring. Summer.*
Autumn. Winter. 1984

135 Yekaterina Shchanitsyna
Casket: *The Fair.* 1980

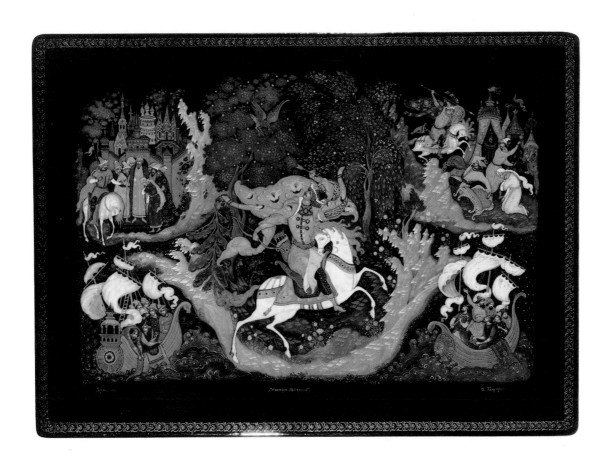

136   Alexei Kochupalov
Casket: *Mikhailo Kazarinov.* 1977

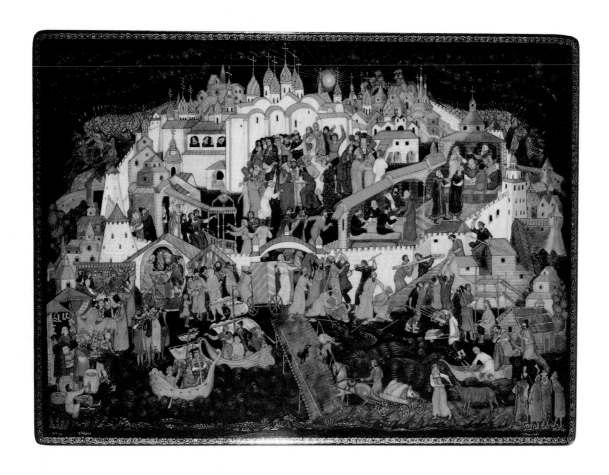

137 Galina Zhiriakova
Casket: *Great Novgorod*. 1978

138 Galina Zhiriakova
Casket: *Great Novgorod*. 1978. Detail

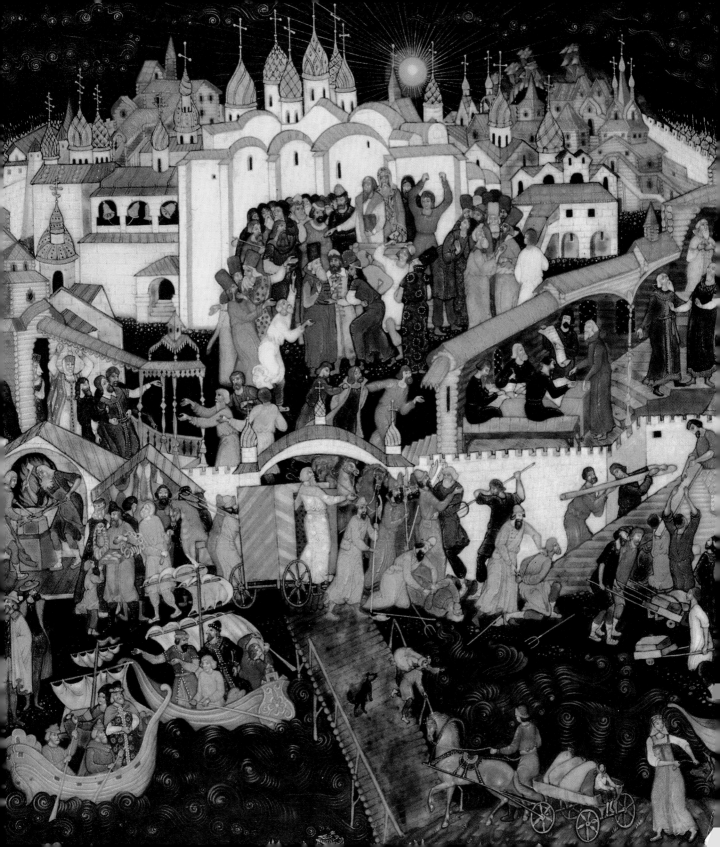

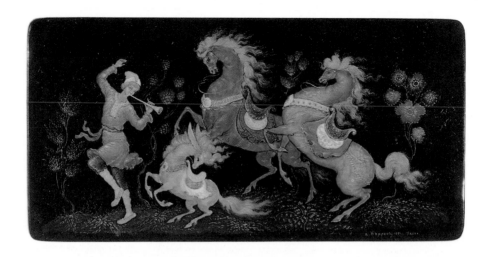

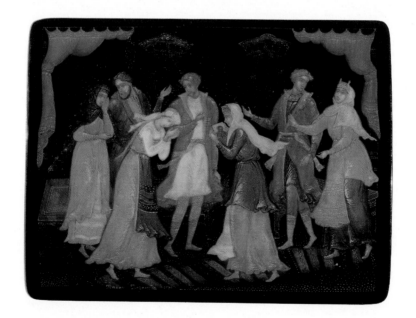

139   Alexander Borunov
Casket: *The Little Hunch-backed Horse.* 1971

140   Nina Bogachova
Casket: *"Oh, mother, why is dust rolling
in the field?"* 1984

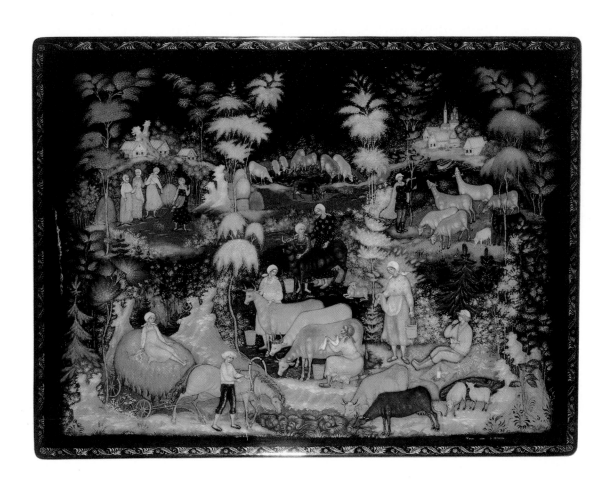

141   Lilia Zverkova
Casket: *Noon*. 1984

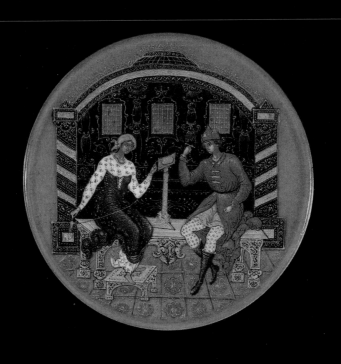

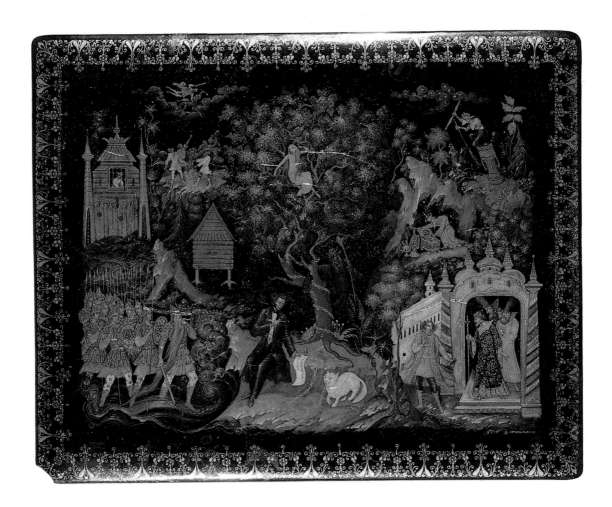

142   Dmitry Butorin
Round box: *The Red Army Man*. 1926

143   Dmitry Butorin
Casket: *Lukomorye*. 1947

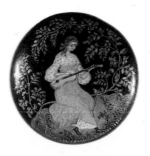

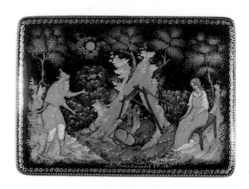

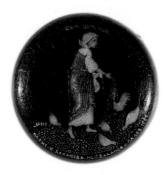

144 Grigory Bakanov
Powder-case: *Guitar-player.* 1926

145 Vladimir Smirnov
Casket: *The Tale of the Fisherman
and the Golden Fish.* 1981

146 Grigory Bakanov
Powder-case: *With the Hens.* 1925

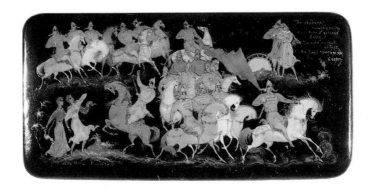

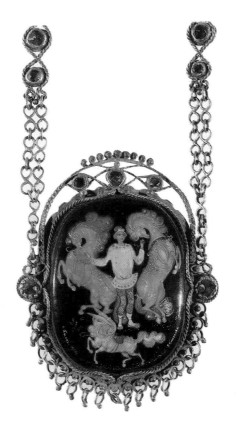

147 Boris Kukuliyev
Casket: *"So long, towns, and huts".* 1969

148 Raisa Smirnova, jeweller Liubov
Kolovangina
Pendant: *The Little Hunch-backed Horse.*
1975

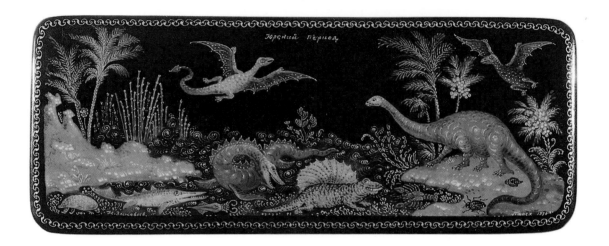

149   Nikolai Zinovyev
Box for stamps: *History of the Earth*. 1930

Mstiora

Mstiora used to be an industrial and merchantile settlement. For a long time its population had engaged in market-gardening and traded in salt and fish. From the seventeenth century icon-painting became their chief occupation. In the late nineteenth century there were 1,300 icon-painters in the settlement. The local icons were made to suit the customers' taste for the ancient austere style. The impeccable copies from ancient icons are indicative of the Mstiora painters' perfect command of all the subtleties of the traditional Russian style. Meanwhile, however, there existed in Mstiora an improvisational style of icon-painting that renounced the traditional austerity and showed a bent for the European manner.

After the revolution the former icon-painters of Mstiora had long been seeking a proper place in the new social context. In October 1918, the Association of Former Icon-painters, Restorers and Related Craftsmen was set up in Mstiora.

In 1923, another cooperative set up by the dedicated artists Alexander Kotiagin, Nikolai Klykov, Yevgeny Yurin, Alexander Briagin, Alexander Merkuryev, Nikolai Briagin and Alexander Kulikov was registered under the title of Ancient Russian Painting Society – the name itself suggesting the aesthetic objective to be pursued by its members. The range of products was not greatly different to the earlier one and basically included the same wooden utensils: sieves, spoons, *matrioshka* dolls, small shelves and decorative mushrooms. Motifs for the paintings were derived from ancient Russian book ornamentation and miniatures. The artists also produced compositions based on historical and daily-life themes, Russian classical and on subjects borrowed from literature and folk songs. At the turn of the '20s and '30s, under the impact of the Palekh experience, Nikolai Klykov, later joined by Ivan Serebriakov and Yevgeny Yurin, began to paint on papier-mâché. Klykov was the first to revert to a more realistic style successfully combining the motifs of the Stroganov icons with the rhythm, composition and characterization peculiar to the popular prints (*lubok*).

In general it took the Mstiora painters an amazingly short time to assimilate the papier-mâché technology and modify the manufacture accordingly. The success of this undertaking was to a great measure ensured by the assistance of the Handicrafts Museum that by this time had been expanded and reorganized into the Institute of Industrial Art. In 1931 the Mstiora painters founded an association for the manufacture of painted papier-mâché articles and gave it the proud, yet typical for the period, name of "The Proletarian Art". The first lacquer wares produced by the association, including the ones mentioned above as well as others, were too iconic in terms of the chosen language of expression. Although the basic guide-lines for the association's policy were correctly selected, the form remained archaic and at variance with the new content.

A notable contribution to the formation of the new style of the Russian miniature was made by Anatoly Bakushinsky, who set great store by the characteristic feature of the Mstiora style of icon-painting. This involved the fringing of the central picture with a series of scenes complementing the main theme of the icon. More often than not these scenes, presenting a sequence of events from the life of the saint, were

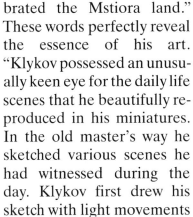

simple in content and less austere in form than the central piece and therefore showed a strong affinity with the imagery structure of the popular prints. Thus the scenes featured such events as banquets, meetings, fights, sea voyages and all kinds of housework. Some Mstiora icons had not been painted to order but for the artist's own pleasure and were therefore more ingenuous, lively and free of the rigidness of the church canons. Bakushinsky suggested that miniaturists should pattern their work on this particular aspect of the traditional Mstiora style. Nikolai Klykov's search for a new vocabulary was carried out along much the same lines.

B. Koromyslov, an expert in the Russian lacquer, writes: "Klykov was credited by his contemporaries with having comprehended and celebrated the Mstiora land." These words perfectly reveal the essence of his art. "Klykov possessed an unusually keen eye for the daily life scenes that he beautifully reproduced in his miniatures. In the old master's way he sketched various scenes he had witnessed during the day. Klykov first drew his sketch with light movements of a sharp pencil, then applied black paint, using a thin brush. Daily sketches gradually made up a whole series of scenes showing haymaking, picking vegetables, harvesting, fishing, hunting and collecting mushrooms. These were fully finished and peculiarly fascinating works".[1]

Landscapes hold the central place in Klykov's miniatures. He infinitely loved his native Central Russian nature and his renderings of it were invariably very precise and poetic, simple but heartfelt.

[1] Б.И. Коромыслов, *Лаковая миниатюра Мстеры*, Л., 1972, с. 27 (B.I. Koromyslov, *The Mstiora Lacquered Miniature*, Leningrad, 1972, p. 27).

A more conventionalized and elevated style was followed by Alexander Kotiagin. His miniatures are utterly expressive, drawn in a rhythm of smooth and light lines.

Alexander Briagin, much like Golikov of Palekh, had a strong taste for romantic subjects. His battle, pursuit and hunting scenes are distinguished by their elaborate composition, the sharp and jerky movements of the characters and the choice of bright, contrasting colours.

The manner of the veteran Mstiora painter Yevgeny Yurin is particularly distinctive. In the mid-30s he created an original style of painting that came to be known as the "Yurin ornament".

Artists in both Mstiora and Kholui had long been fascinated with the art of ornamentation. The splendid garments and buildings in the ancient icons of the Moscow and Stroganov schools were completely embellished with golden ornamentation. Later the miniaturists of Palekh, Mstiora and Kholui widely used the golden ornaments to set off their designs.

Yevgeny Yurin went further. The central component of his paintings is usually a highly conventionalized still-nature: a bouquet of flowers, fruits or berries set against a brown, black, green or blue ground and encircled on all sides of a casket cover with interlaced scrolls, starlets, spots, petals and leaflets. In the corners they are arranged in larger patterns, their shapes harmonious with the central picture. It is amazing how easily, almost playfully, he uses the same simple elements to create unrepetitive, yet stylistically integral ornamental compositions in which the main decorative function is performed by the pattern.

Ivan Fomichov was one of the last Mstiora veterans to assimilate the technique of miniature painting. In fact his first miniature using this technique was painted only in 1937. Fomichov was an artist permanently seeking new themes and language of expression. His miniatures seem to be set on a stage framed by wings. The conventionalized landscape looks like a backdrop against which the action of some fairy-tale is unfolding. The silvery colouring brings to mind that of the ancient Mstiora icons.

Ivan Fomichov had a strong liking for historical themes which he resolved as colourful spectacles. Generally he conceived history as the material for creating a generalized image rather than for elaborating a detailed documentary story in his miniatures.

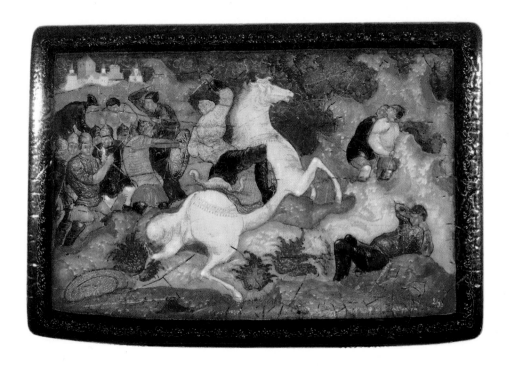

150   Alexander Briagin
Casket: *The Battle*. 1933

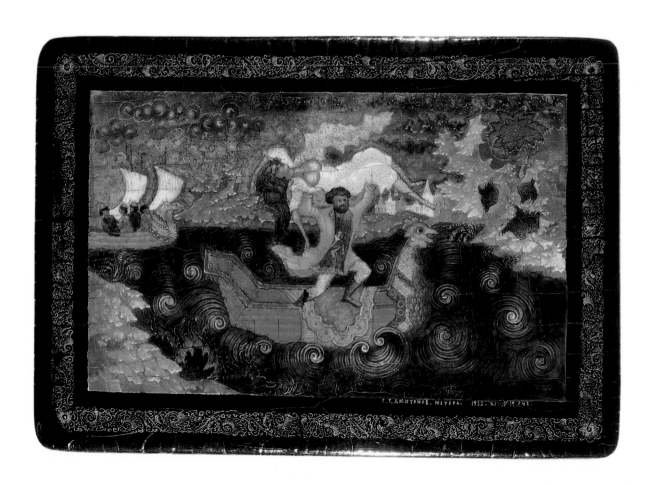

151 Grigory Dmitriyev
Casket: *Stepan Razin*. 1932

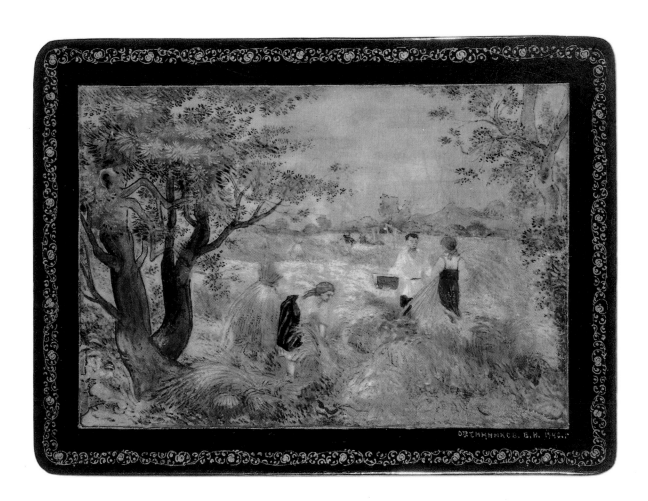

152 Vasily Ovchinnikov
Casket: *Harvesting.* 1936

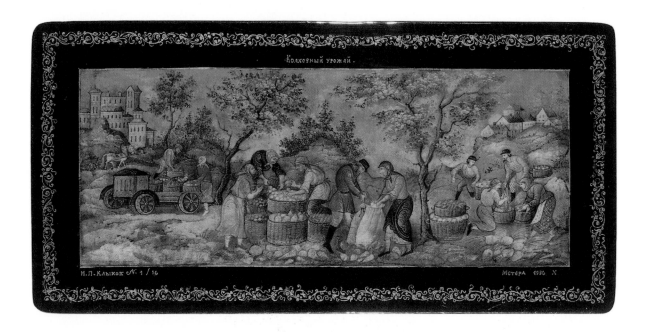

153   Nikolai Klykov
Casket: *Collective Farm's Harvest.* 1936

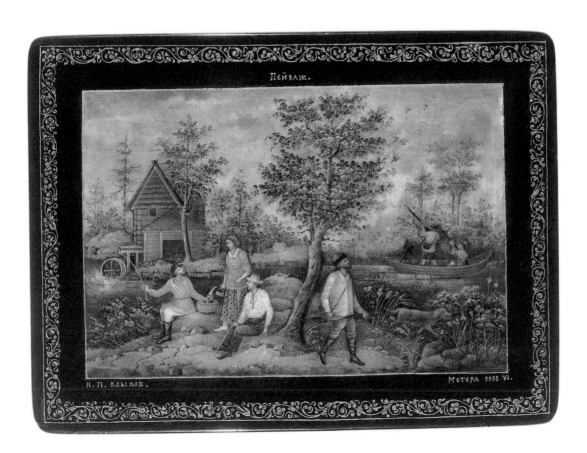

154   Nikolai Klykov
Casket: *Landscape.* 1938

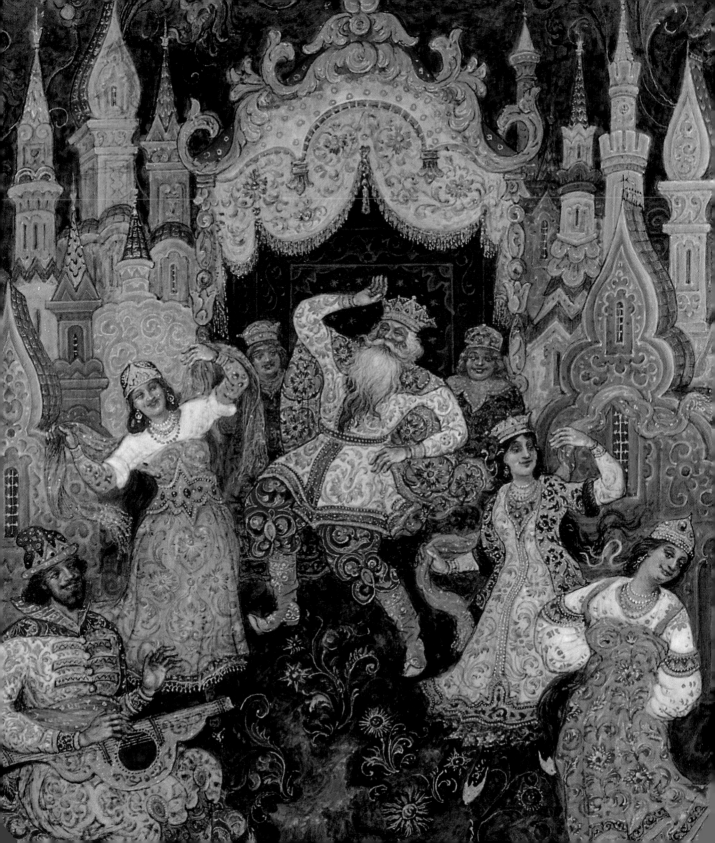

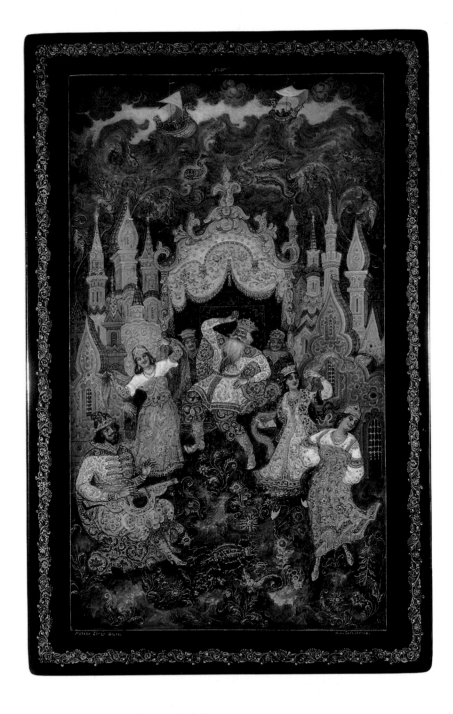

155 Ivan Serebriakov
Casket: *Sadko.* 1948. Detail

156 Ivan Serebriakov
Casket: *Sadko.* 1948

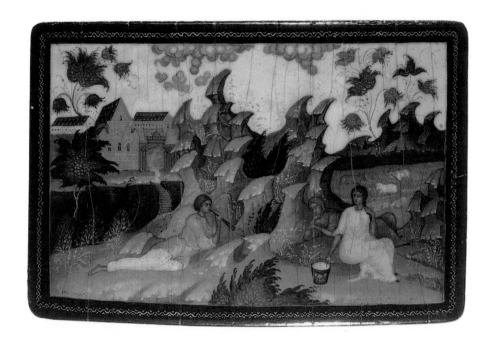

157   Alexander Kotiagin
Casket: *Midday.* 1931

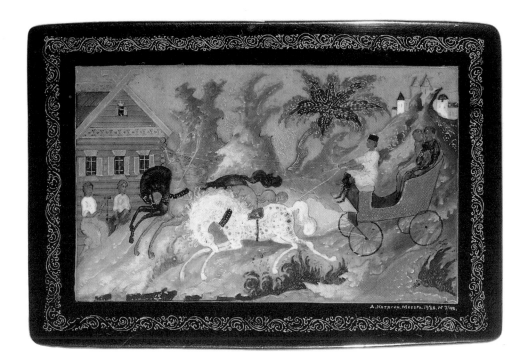

158   Alexander Kotiagin
Casket: *Troika. Evening.* 1932

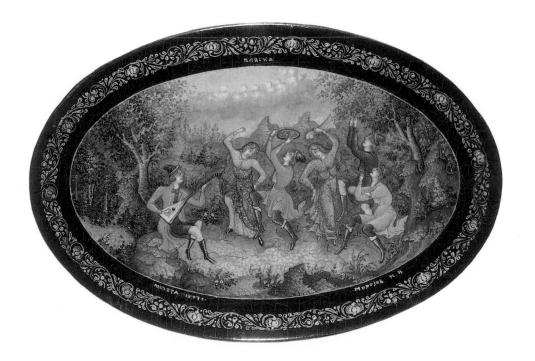

159   Ivan Morozov
Oval casket: *The Dance.* 1947

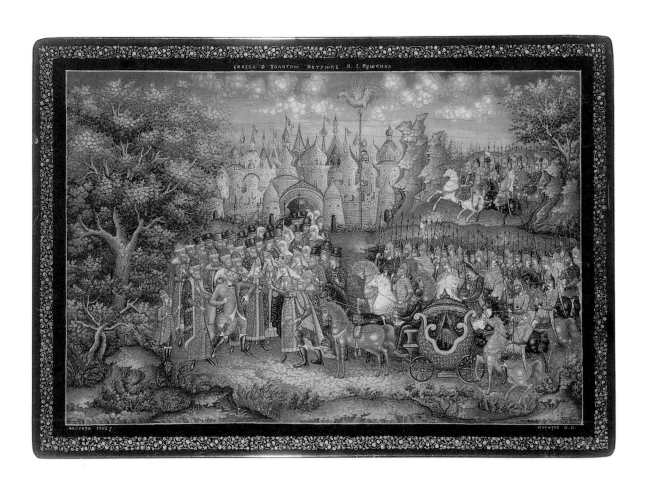

160   Ivan Morozov
Casket: *The Tale of the Golden Cockerel.*
1946

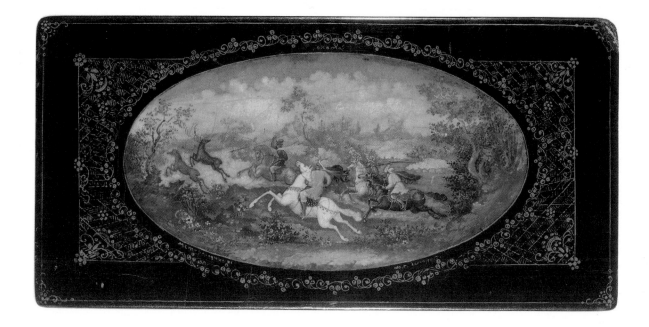

161   Fiodor Shilov
Casket: *The Hunt.* 1946

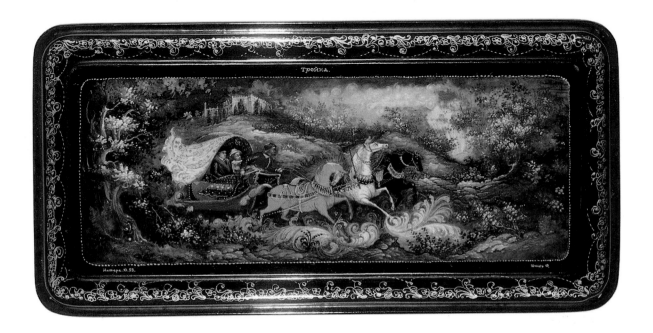

162   Fiodor Shilov
Casket: *Troika.* 1959

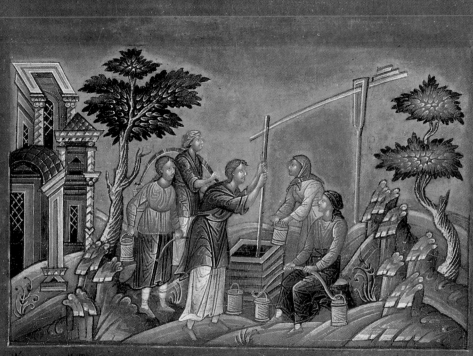

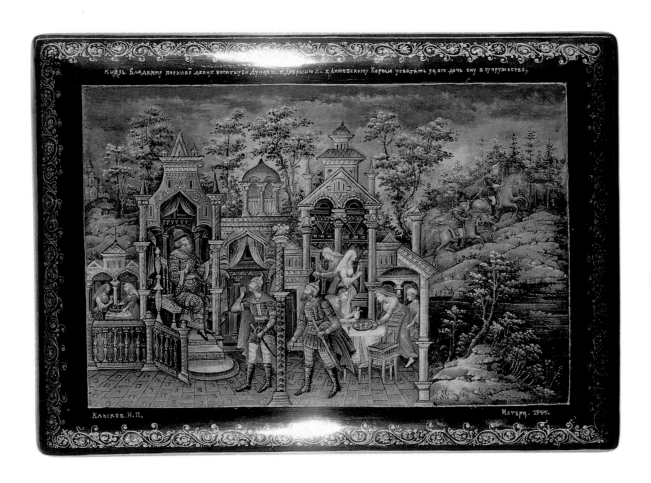

163 Nikolai Klykov
Casket: *At the Well.* 1942

164 Nikolai Klykov
Casket: *Prince Vladimir.* 1942

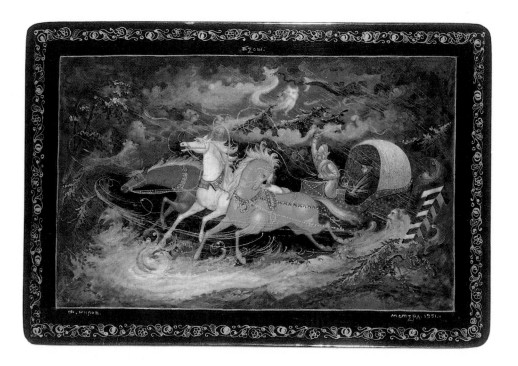

165   Fiodor Shilov
Casket: *The Demons.* 1951

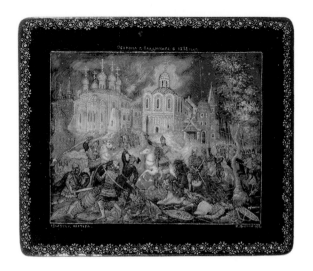

166 Ivan Fomichov
Decorative box: *The Defence of Vladimir
in 1238.* 1946

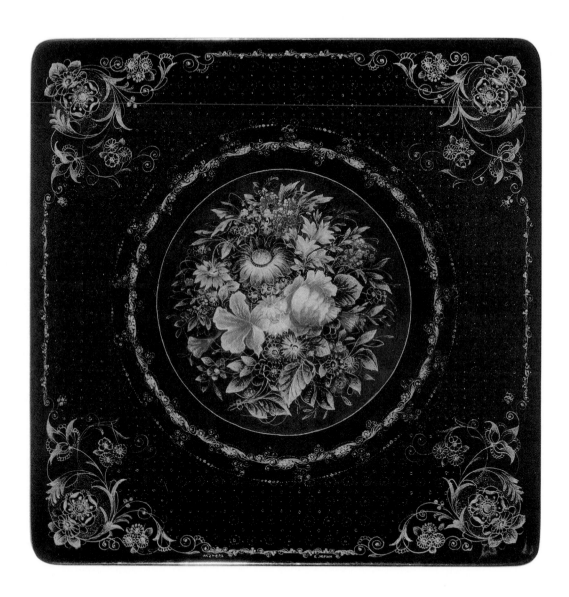

167   Yevgeny Yurin
Casket: *Ornament.* 1954

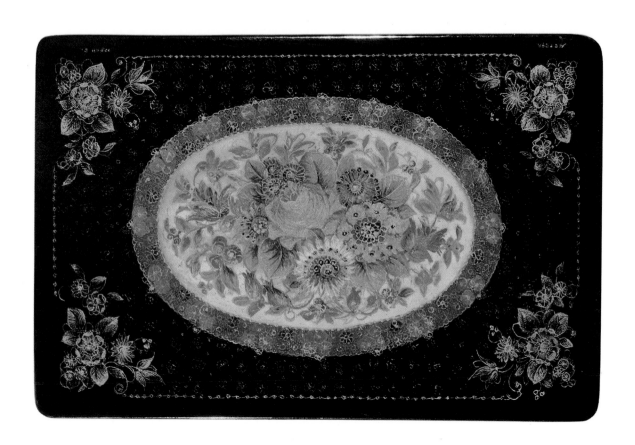

168   Yevgeny Yurin
Casket: *Ornament.* 1970s

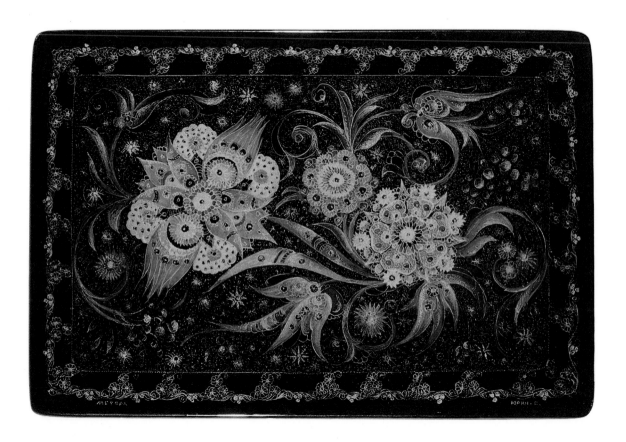

169   Yevgeny Yurin
Casket: *Fairy-tale*. 1970s

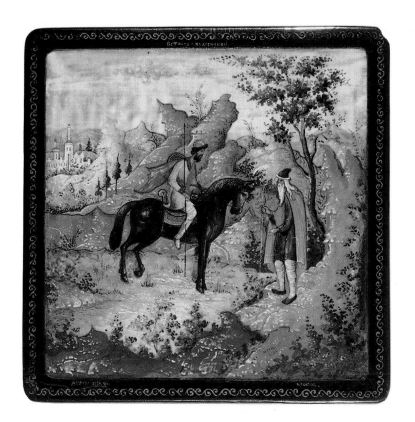

170 Vasily Krotov
Casket: *Meeting with a Sorcerer.* 1950

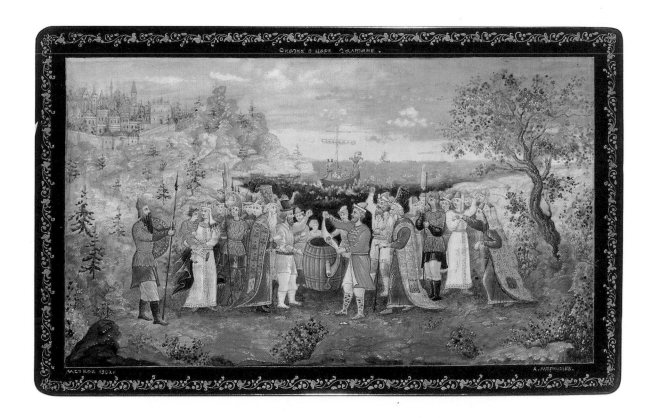

171 Alexander Merkuryev
Casket: *The Tale of Tsar Saltan.* 1953

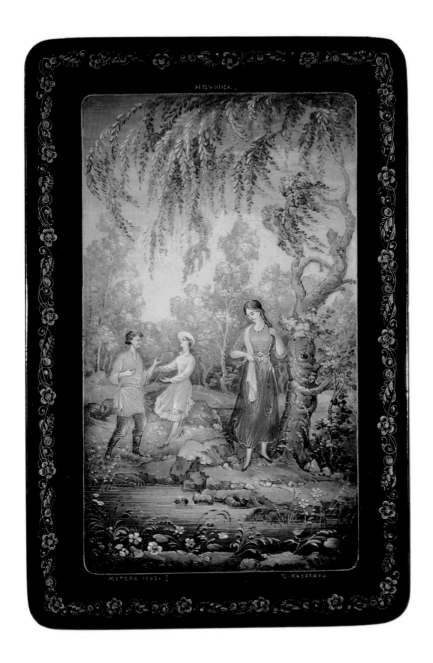

172　Vasily Korsakov
Casket: *The Willow.* 1962

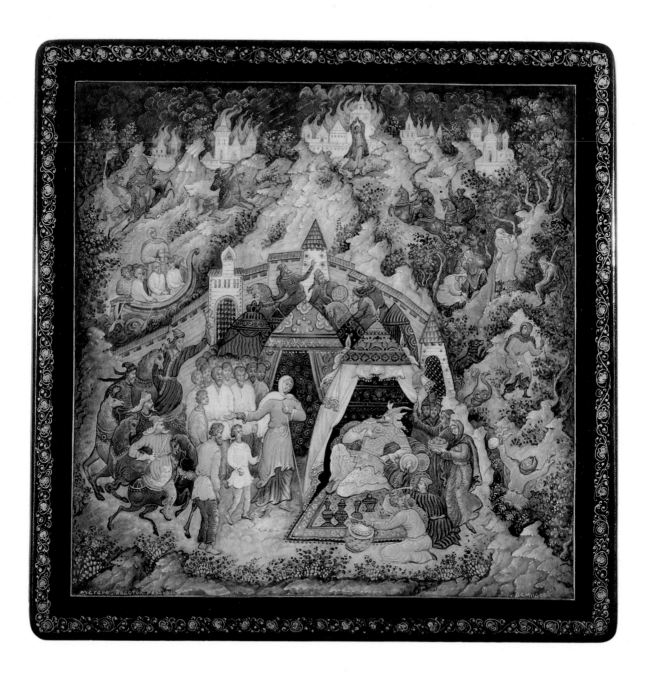

173   Lydia Demidova
Casket: *Avdotya of Riazan*. 1970s

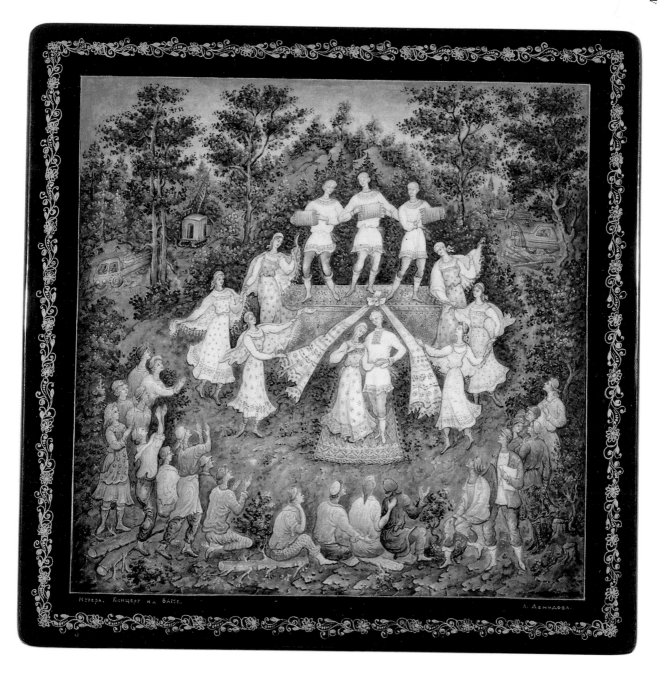

174 Lydia Demidova
Casket: *A Concert on the BAM*. 1970s

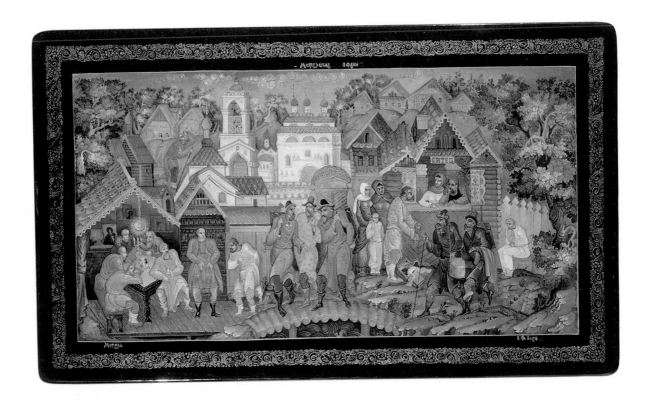

175   Piotr Zayets
Casket: *The Mstiora Peddlers.* 1970s

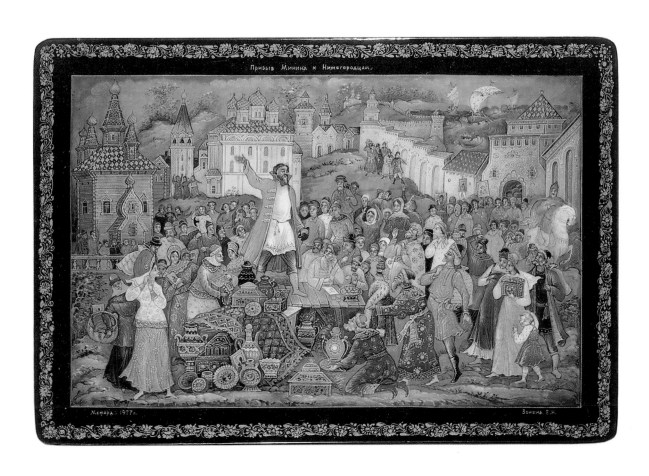

176 Yekaterina Zonina
Casket: *Minin's Appeal to the Residents
of Nizhni Novgorod.* 1977

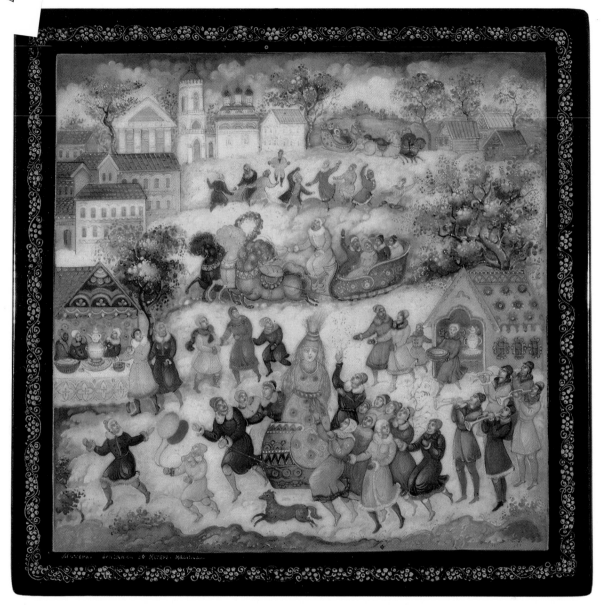

177   Valentina Malakhova
Casket: *Festival in Mstiora*. 1970s

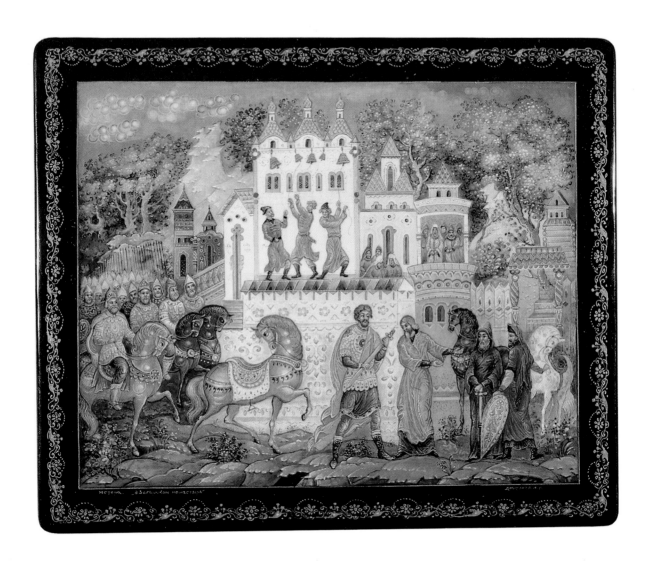

178   Nikolai Dmitriyev
Casket: *At the Trinity–St Sergius
Monastery.* 1980

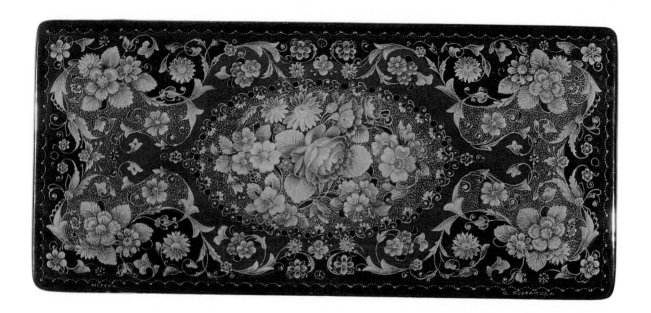

179   Vera Korsakova
Casket: *Floral Ornament.* 1975

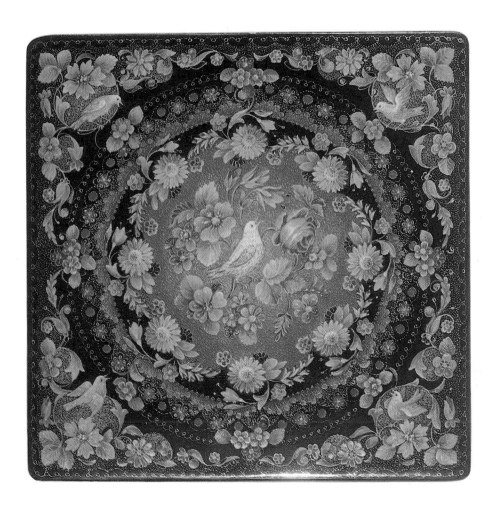

180 Vera Korsakova
Casket: *The Nightingale's Song.* 1980s

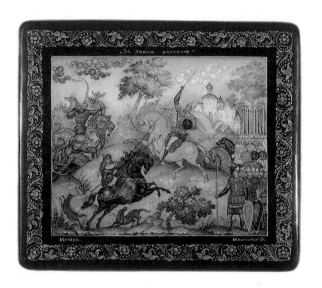

181   Vladimir Moshkovich
Casket: *For the Russian Land*. 1980

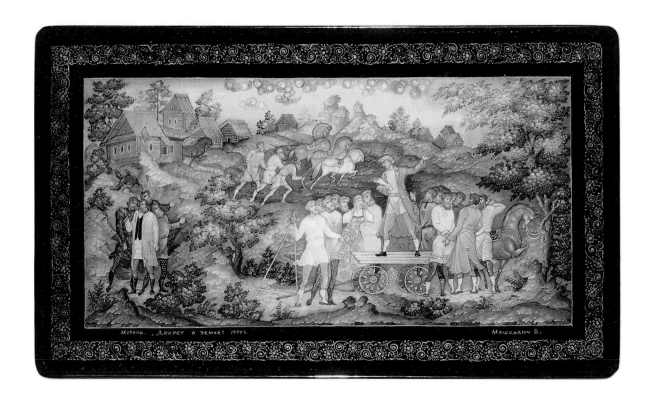

182   Vladimir Moshkovich
Casket: *The Decree on Land*. 1977

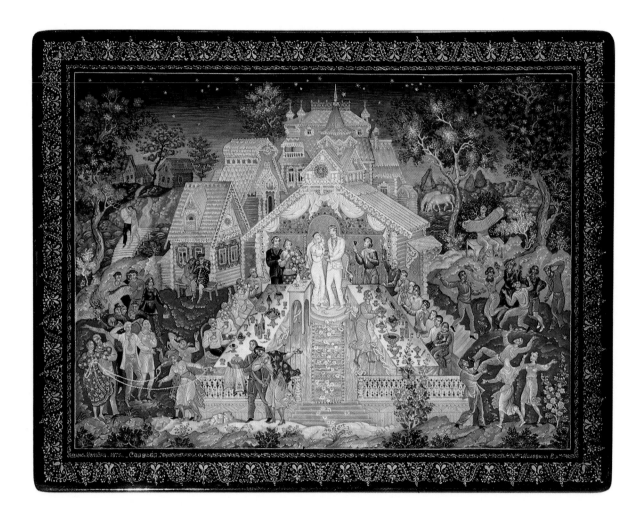

183   Vladimir Molodkin
Casket: *The Wedding.* 1975

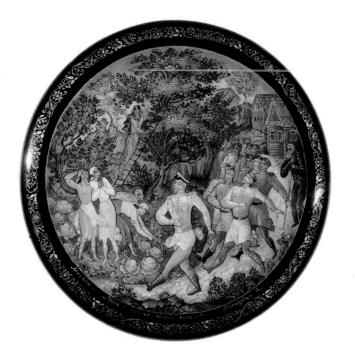

184 Vladimir Molodkin
Portmanteau: *"Company three was returning from the drill".* 1978

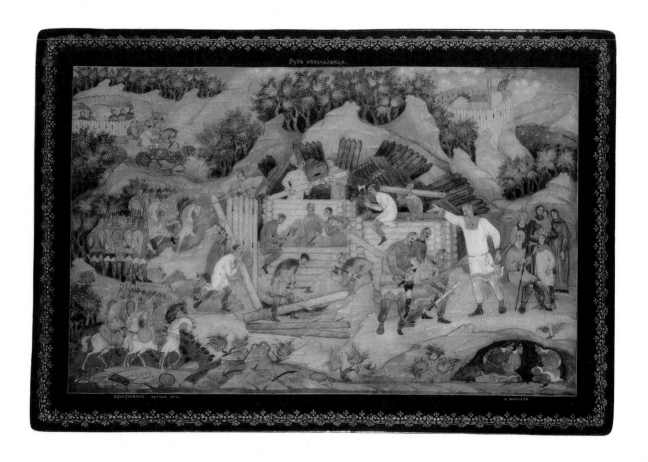

185 Alexander Nikolayev
Casket: *Early Russia*. 1977

186 Alexander Nikolayev
Casket: *Early Russia*. 1977. Detail

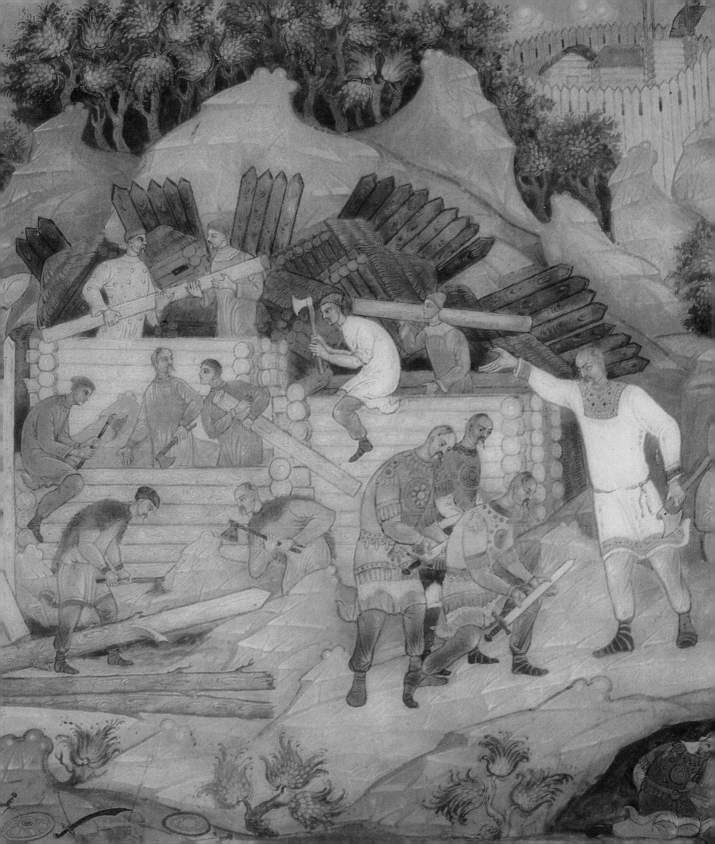

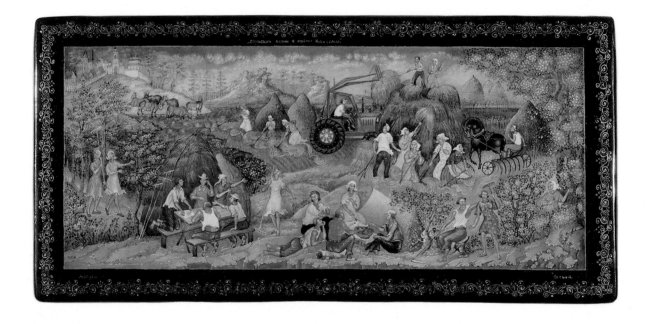

187   Piotr Sosin
Casket: *The Rural Labours.* 1980s

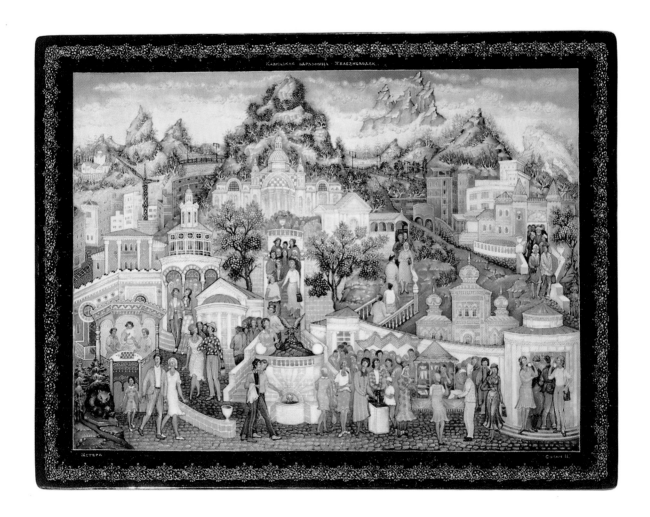

188   Piotr Sosin
Casket: *Zheleznovodsk,*
a Caucasian Health-centre. 1970s

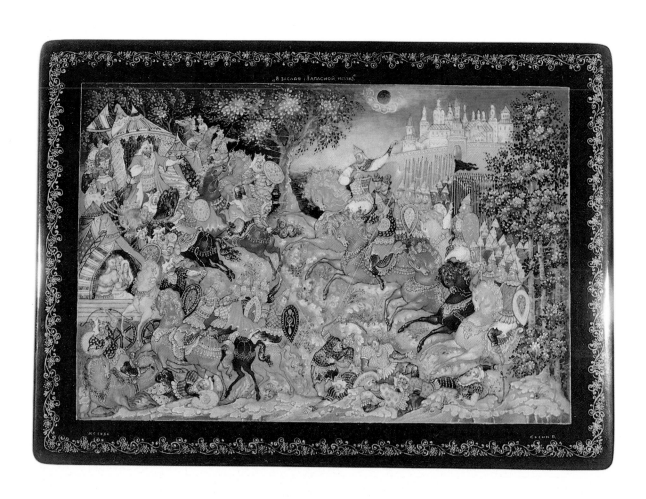

189   Piotr Sosin
Casket: *In Ambush*. 1980

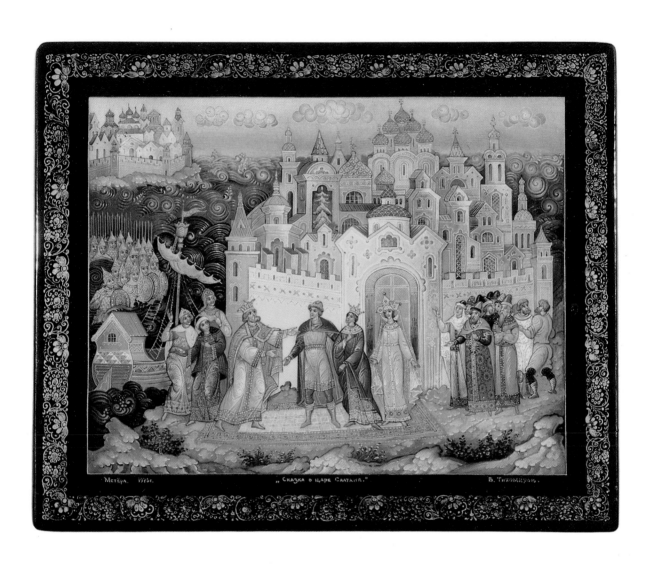

190   Valentin Tikhomirov
Casket: *The Tale of Tsar Saltan*. 1978

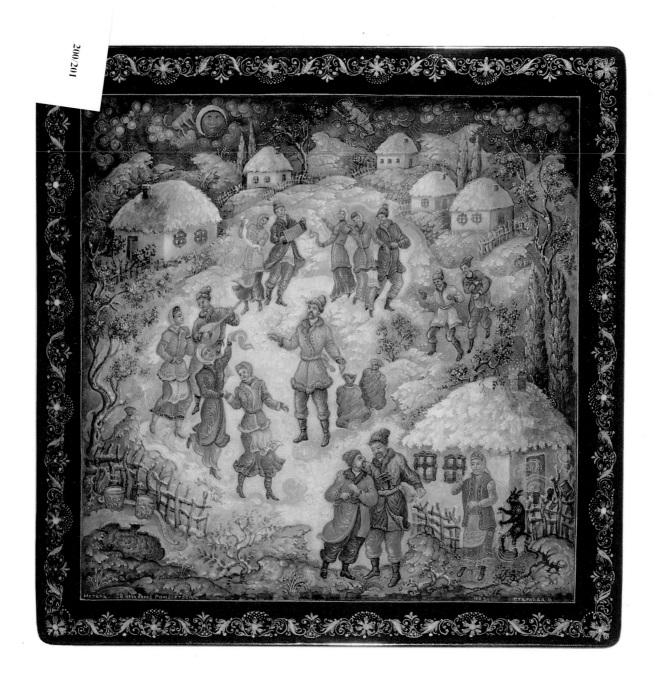

191   Vera Starkova
Casket: *The Night Before Christmas.* 1979

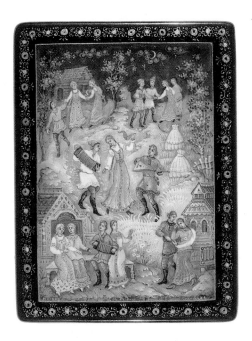

192   Vera Starkova
Casket: *Beyond the Village.* 1970s

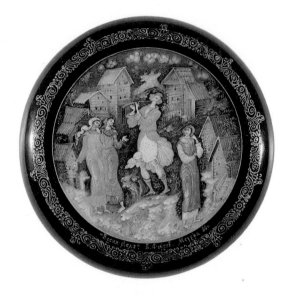

193   Valentin Fokeyev
Powder-case: *Lel's Songs*. 1980

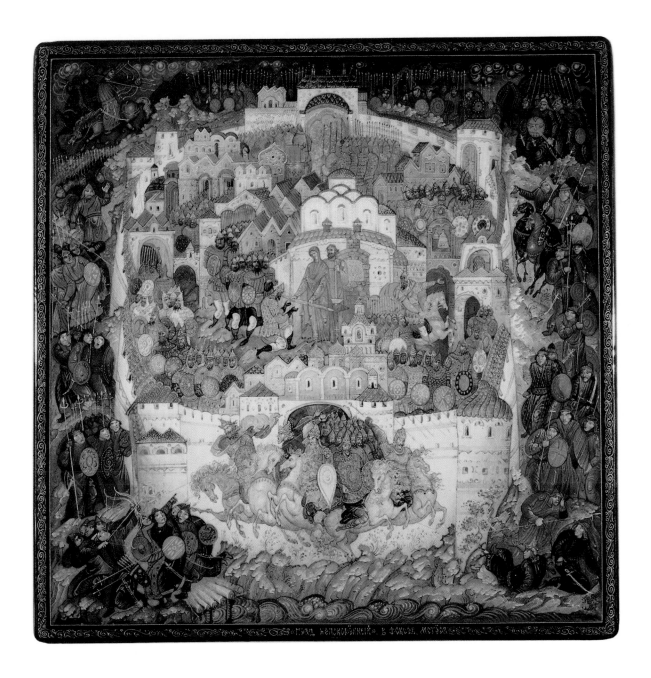

194   Valentin Fokeyev
Casket: *The Unsubdued City.* 1970s

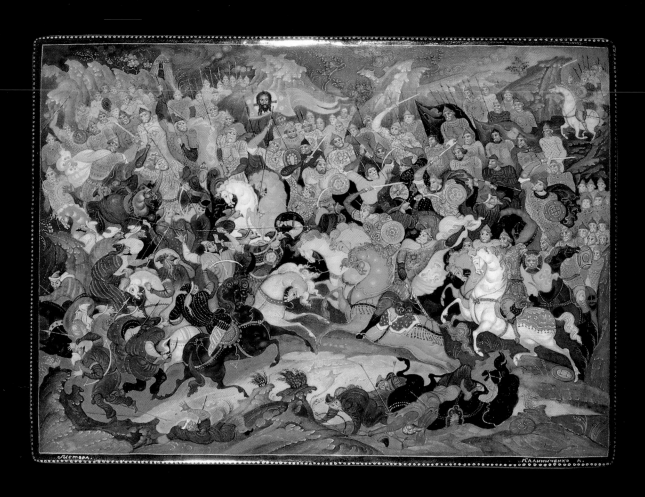

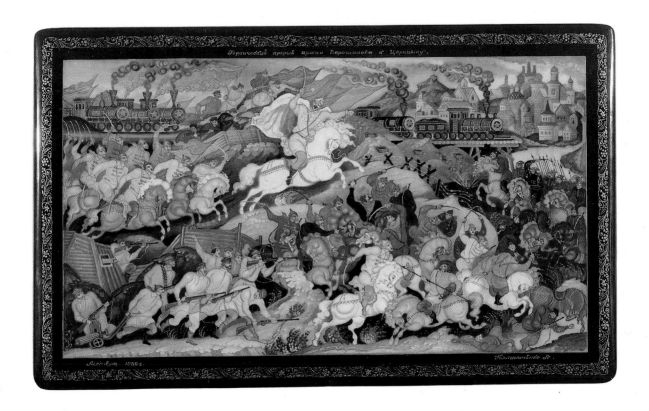

195 Alexander Kalinichenko
Casket: *The Battle*. 1980

196 Alexander Kalinichenko
Casket: *The Voroshilov Army's Heroic
Thrust to Tsaritsyn*. 1980

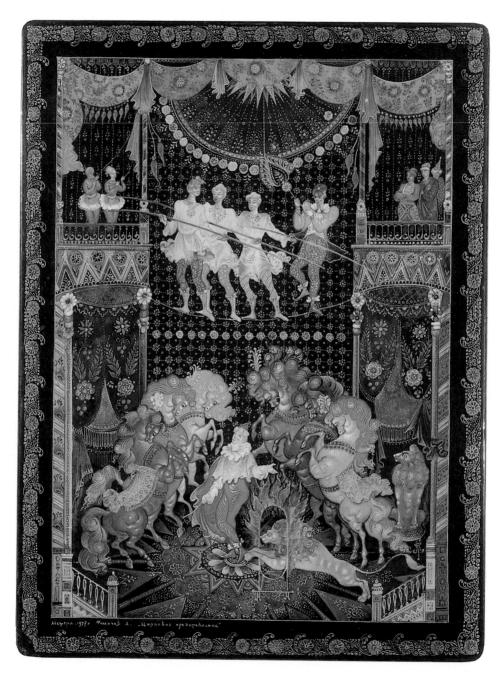

197 Lev Fomichov
Casket: *The Circus Show.* 1977

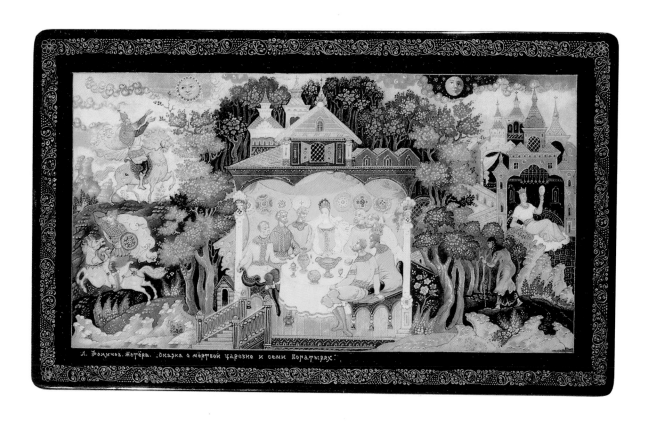

198   Lev Fomichov
Casket: *The Tale of the Dead Princess*. 1970s

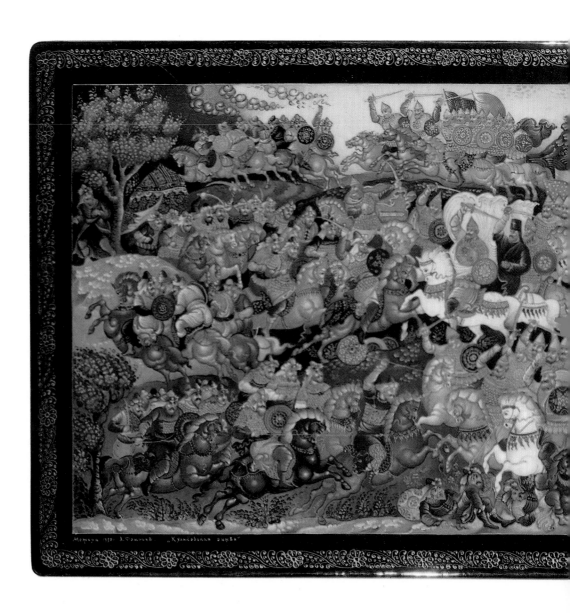

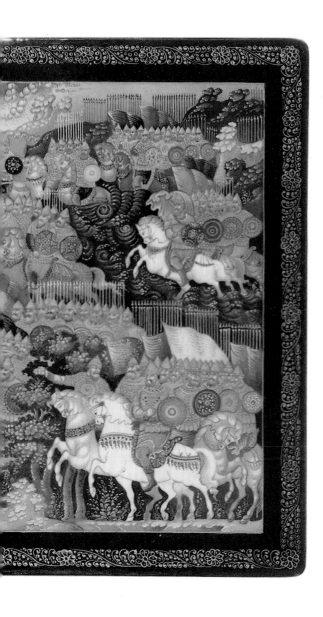

199   Lev Fomichov
Casket: *The Kulikovo Battle*. 1980

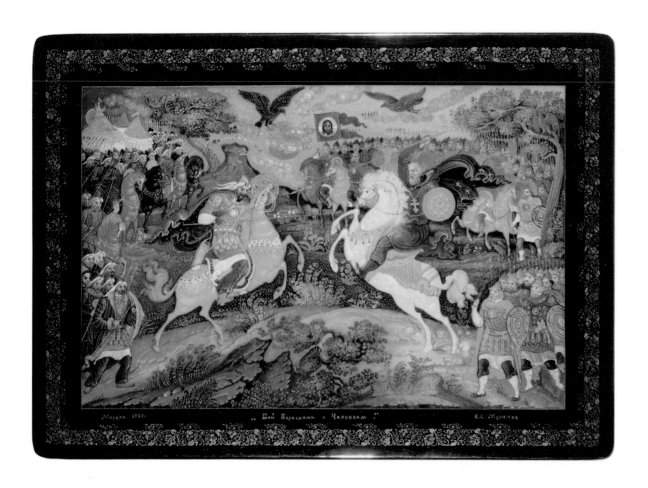

200 Viacheslav Muratov
Casket: *Peresvet Fighting Chelubei*. 1980

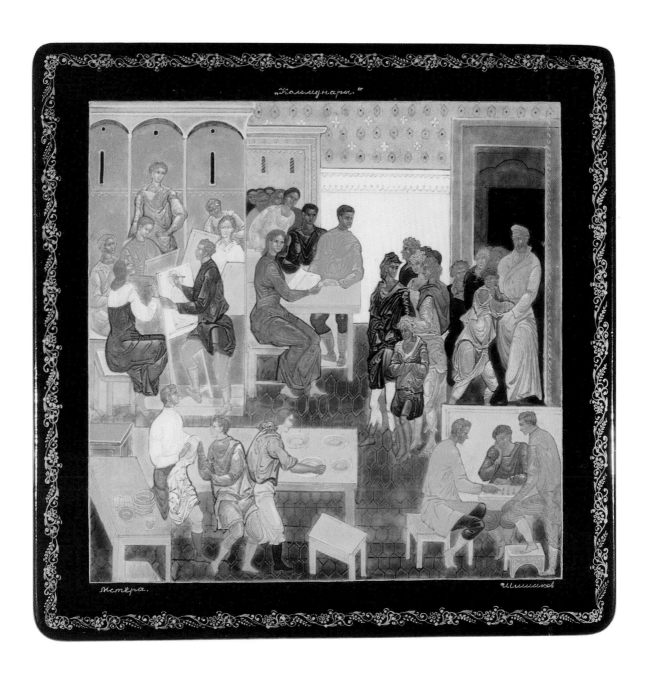

201 Nikolai Shishakov
Casket: *The Communards.* 1969

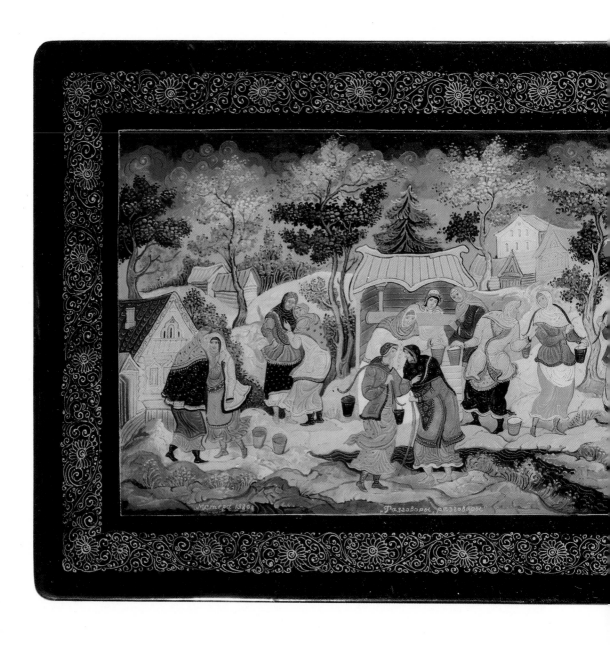

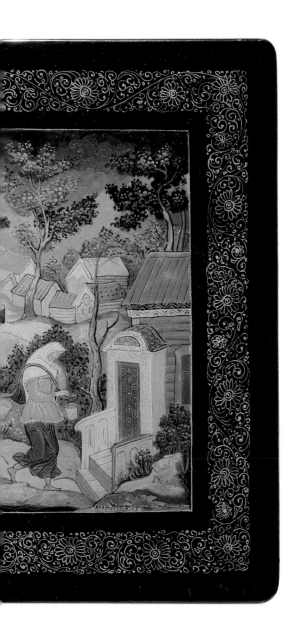

202   Nikolai Shishakov
Casket: *"Tittle-tattle"*. 1980

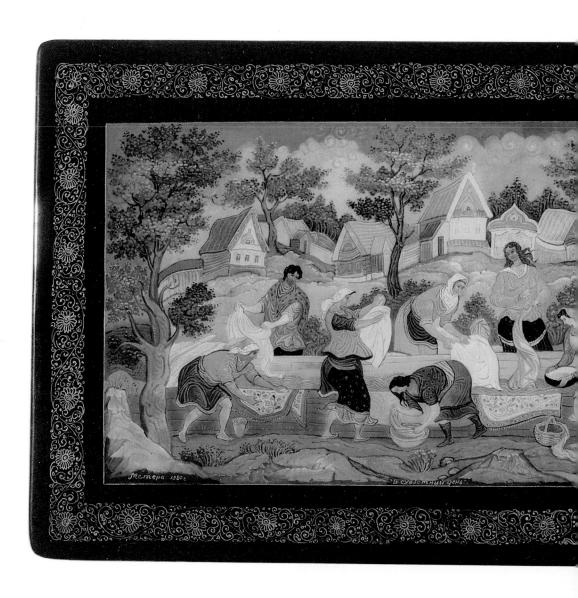

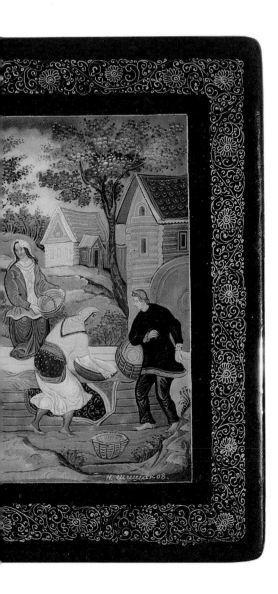

203   Nikolai Shishakov
Casket: *Saturday.* 1980

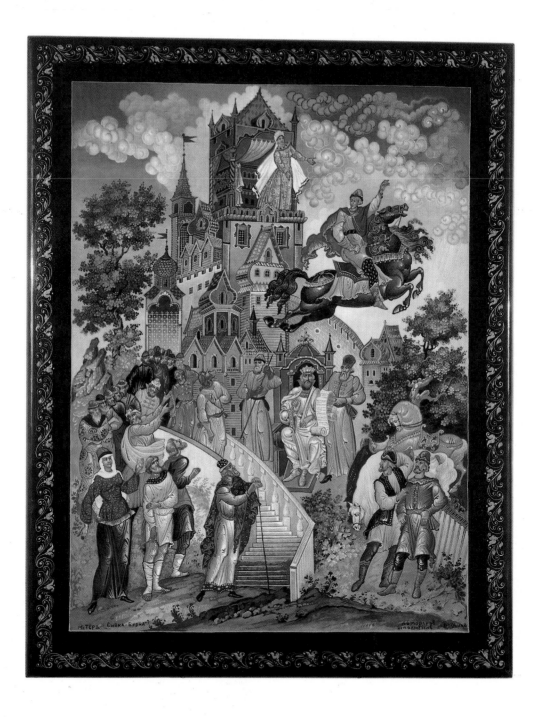

204 Yuri Vavanov
Panel: *Sivka-Burka*. 1981

205 Yuri Vavanov
Panel: *Sivka-Burka*. 1981. Detail

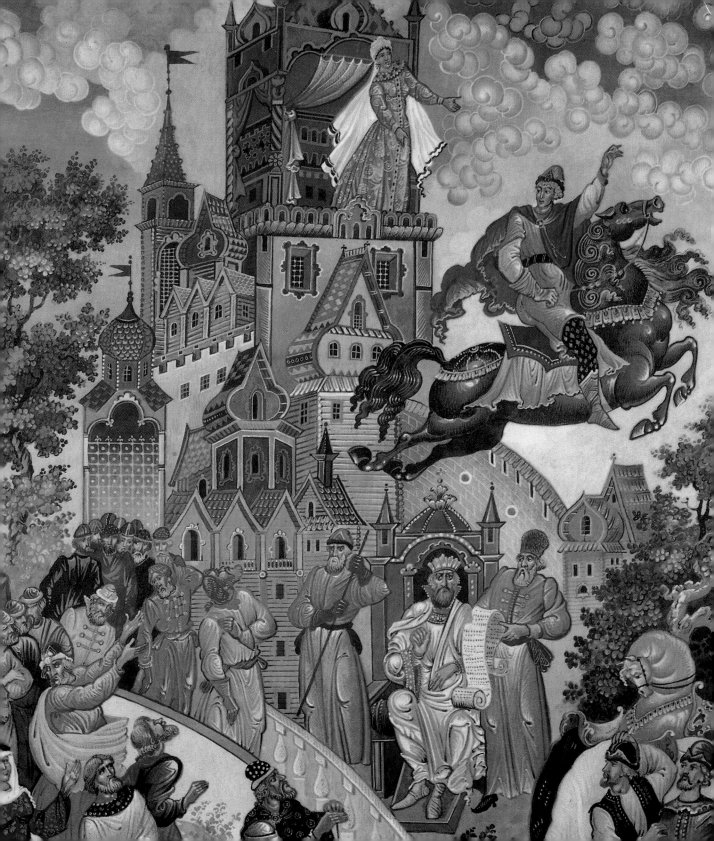

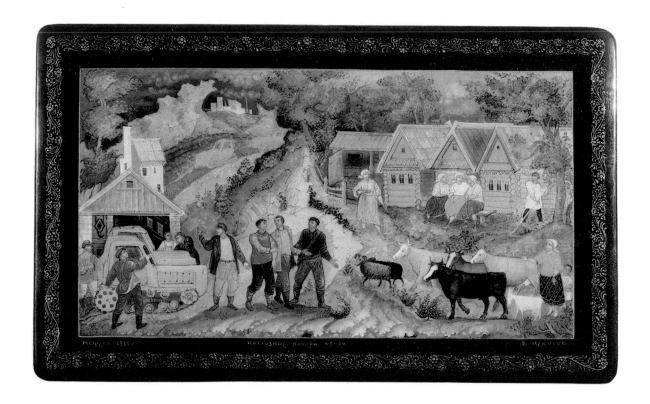

206   Vladislav Nekosov
Casket: *Collective-farm Ploughmen. Evening.*
1980

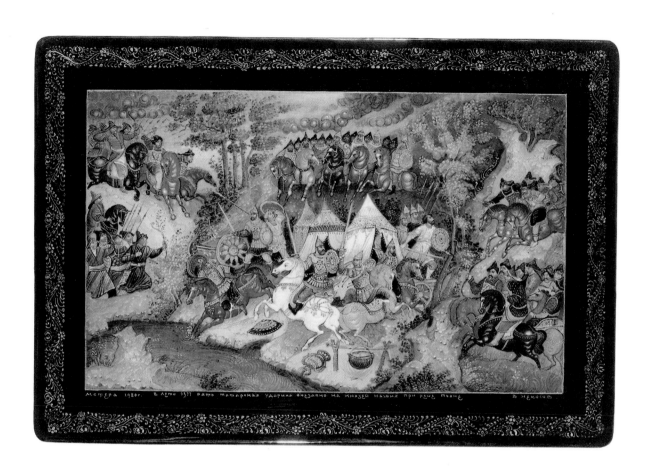

207　Vladislav Nekosov
Casket: *The Battle on the Pyana River.*
1980

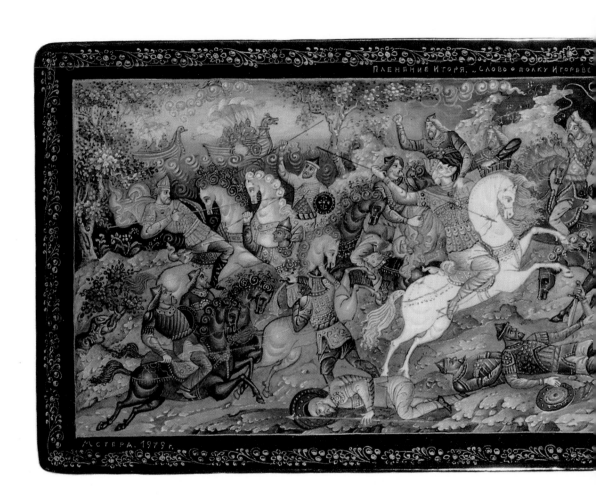

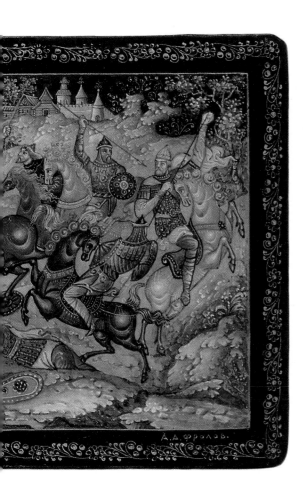

208   Alexander Frolov
Casket: *Igor Taken Prisoner.* 1979

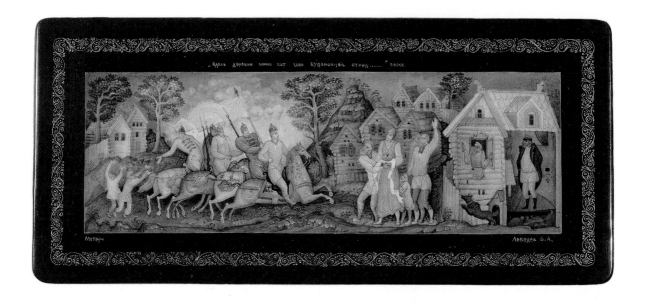

209   Vladimir Lebedev
Casket: *"Through the village,*
past the huts marched a detachment
of Budionny". 1970s

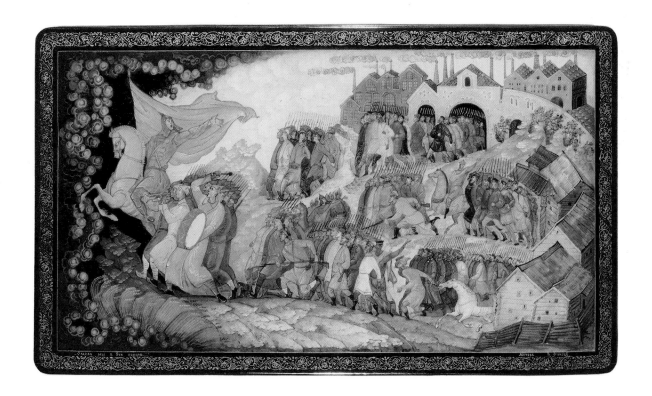

210 Valentin Fokeyev
Casket: *"We won't shirk the battle"*. 1970s

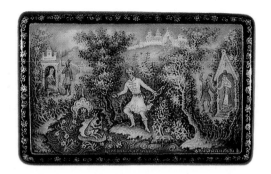

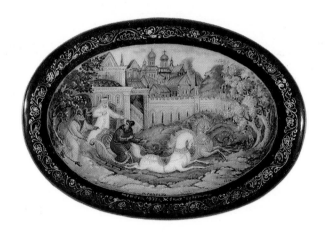

211   Antonina Ovchinnikova
Casket: *The Frog Princess.* 1970s

212   Nikolai Naumov
Portmanteau: *The Groom.* 1977

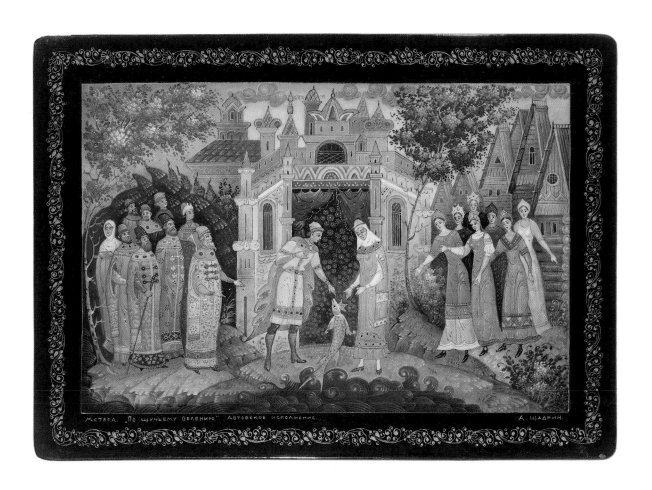

МСТЕРА. "ПО ЩУЧЬЕМУ ВЕЛЕНИЮ." АВТОРСКОЕ ИСПОЛНЕНИЕ.   А. ЩАДРИН.

213   Alexander Shchadrin
Casket: *By a Wave of the Wand.* 1975

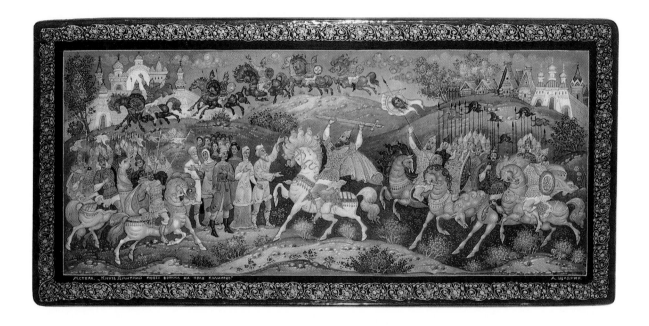

214   Alexander Shchadrin
Casket: *Prince Dmitry Leads His Troops
to the Kulikovo Field.* 1970s

Kholui

Kholui was a merchantile village. Local painters supplied cheap icons that were sold all around Russia. Their manner of execution was noticeably simpler, more naturalistic and unconventional than the traditional style. Thus, quite often such painted icons came into conflict with the canon and the artists incurred the condemnation of, and even penalties from, the church authorities. However, the reprisals had little if any effect on the upsurge of mass manufacture. In the nineteenth century the number of icon-painters in Kholui grew to 700 instead of 300 in the eighteenth century.

After the revolution, in 1919, twenty-five makers of icons, painted metal trays, wooden *matrioshka* dolls, salt-cellars and other utensils set up the Professional Labour Union of Artists, Icon-painters, Designers and Related Craftsmen.

In Kholui the first experiments in painting on papier-mâché go back to 1932 and are associated with the names of Sergei Mokin, Konstantin Kosterin, Dmitry Dobrynin and Vasily Puzanov-Molev. In 1934 they founded the Independent Artists' Cooperative Society.

The lacquer business gained strength rather slowly in Kholui, especially if compared with the spectacular accomplishments of Palekh and the swift progress of Mstiora. Nonetheless the earliest works of the Kholui miniaturists were worthy of the traditions of the local school of painting. Some fascinating designs that were executed by the members of the Kholui cooperative over the first years of its existence are included in this book. The painting on a decorative box cover *At Rest* (pl. 232) is an example of Dmitry Dobrynin's inimitable manner. The simple motif which often recurred in miniatures, was used by the artist to create a profoundly poetic image of peasants. The miniature is reminiscent of the late nineteenth- and early twentieth-century realistic paintings and is utterly expressive of genuine purity and sincerity. Konstantin Kosterin's *The Strength of Defence* (pl. 221) elaborates the theme rather typical of the period of the '30s, when this country was intensively building up its defence potential to be able to repulse any likely agression from outside. The painting provides a characteristic illustration of the lacquer miniature mastering a new range of subjects. Sergei Mokin's innovative execution of *Working the Land* (pl. 219) proves the old truth that new content is expressible only through new form. The application of ancient Russian painting methods to express the dynamic realities of the contemporary world makes sense only if such methods are expertly and thoughtfully modified to conform with modern sensibilities and aesthetic notions.

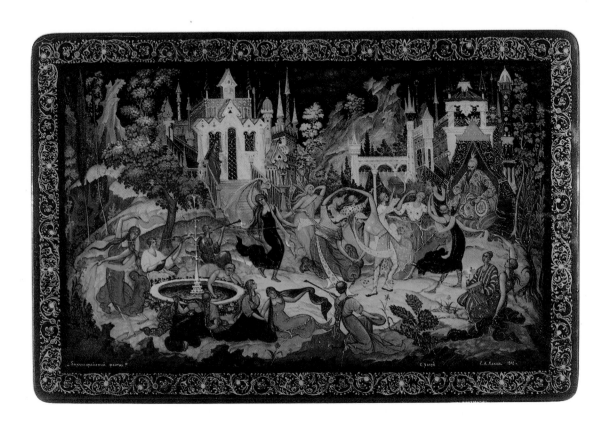

215   Sergei Mokin
Casket: *The Fountain of Bakhchisarai.* 1945

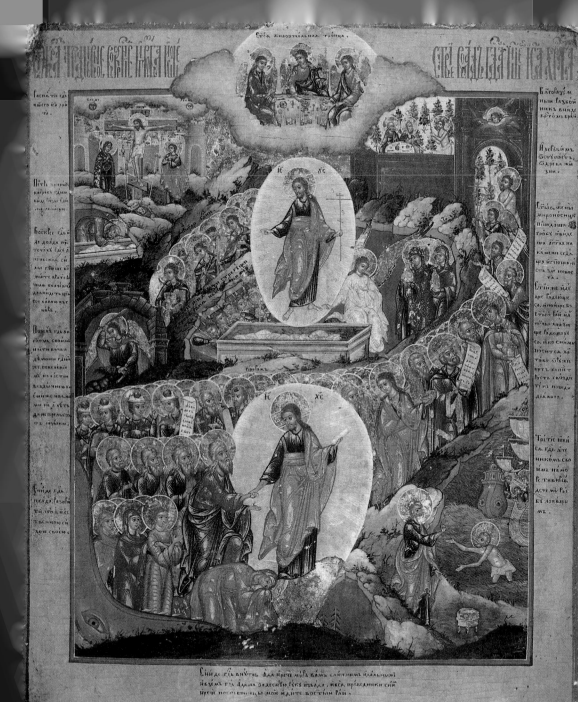

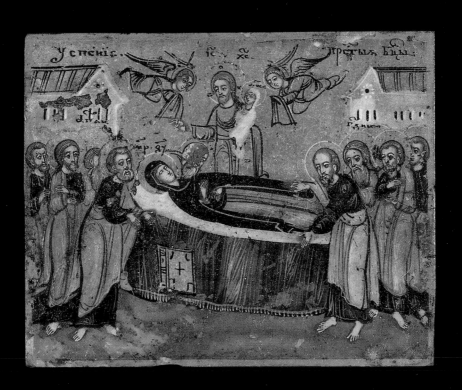

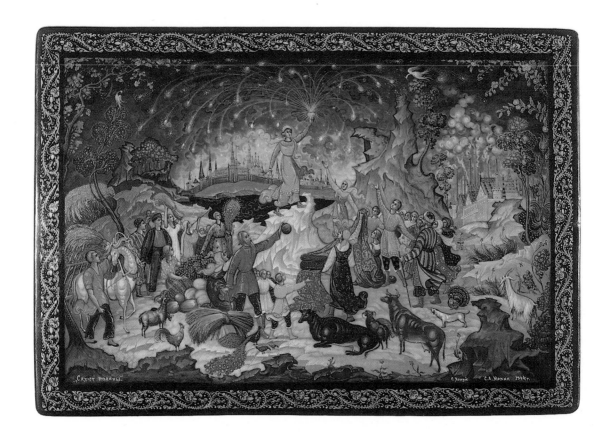

216 Icon: *The Descent into Limbo.*
Early 19th century

217 Icon: *The Assumption.*
Early 19th century

218 Sergei Mokin
Casket: *The Salute.* 1944

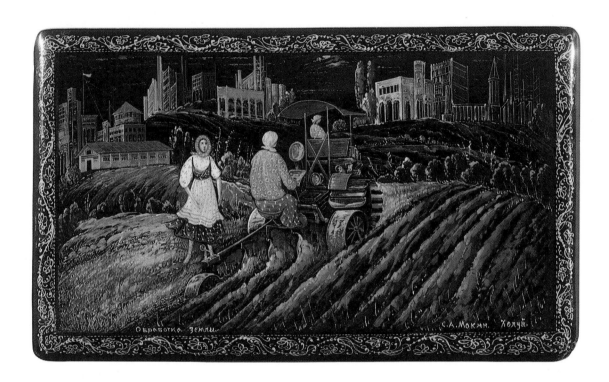

219   Sergei Mokin
Decorative box: *Working the Land.* 1930s

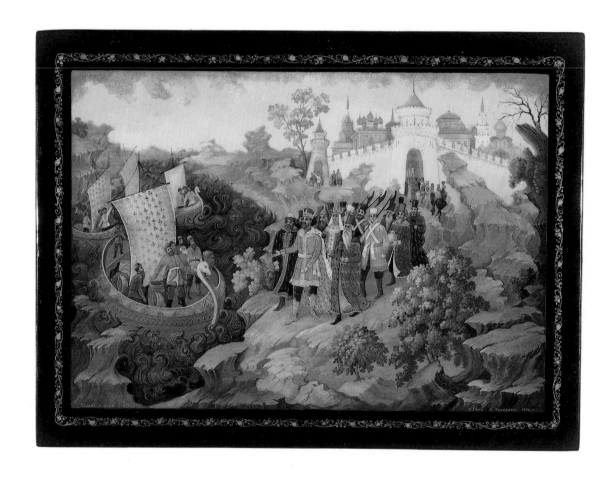

220 Konstantin Kosterin
Panel: *The Tale of Tsar Saltan*. 1943

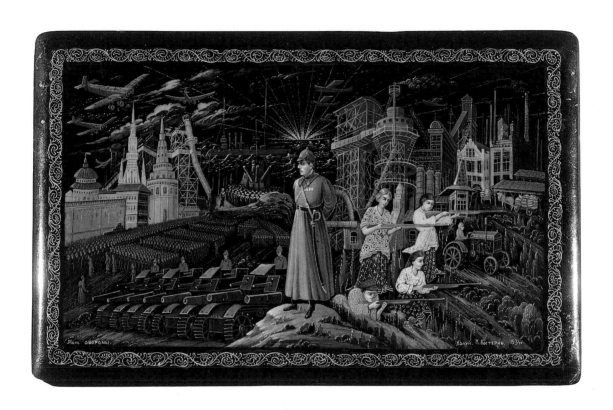

221 Konstantin Kosterin
Casket: *The Strength of Defence*. 1934

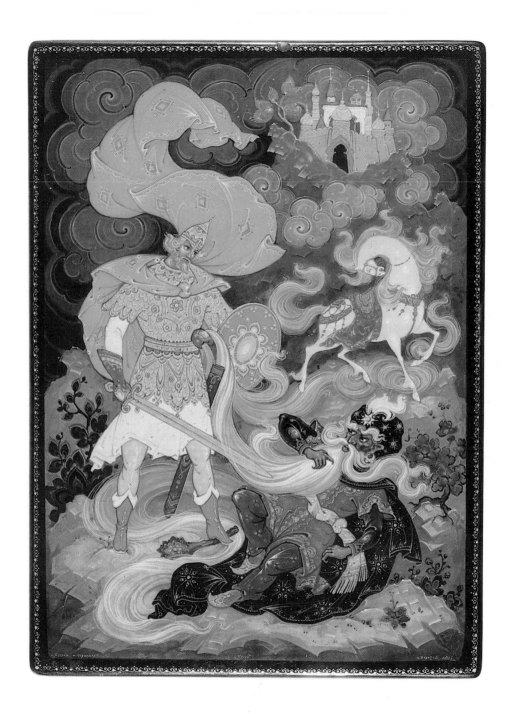

222 Alexander Morozov
Casket: *Ruslan and Chernomor.* 1970

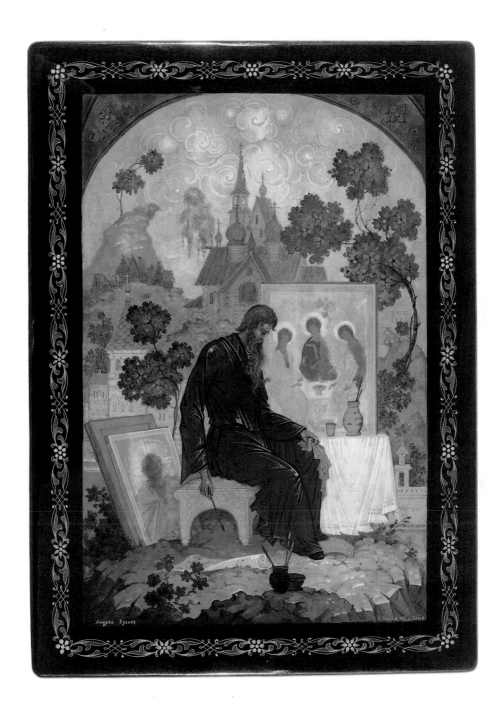

223   Vladimir Belov
Casket: *Andrei Rublev.* 1965

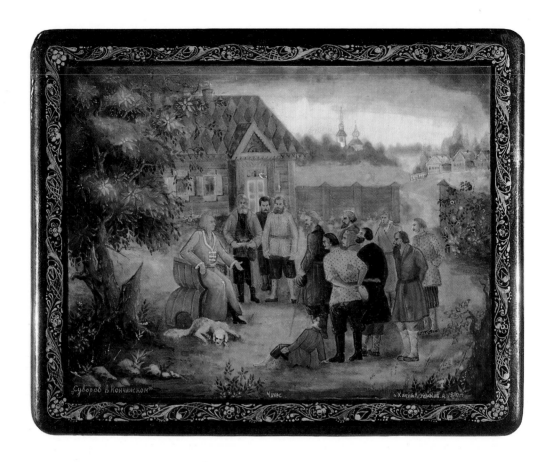

224   Alexei Usikov
Casket: *Suvorov at Konchanskoye.* 1950

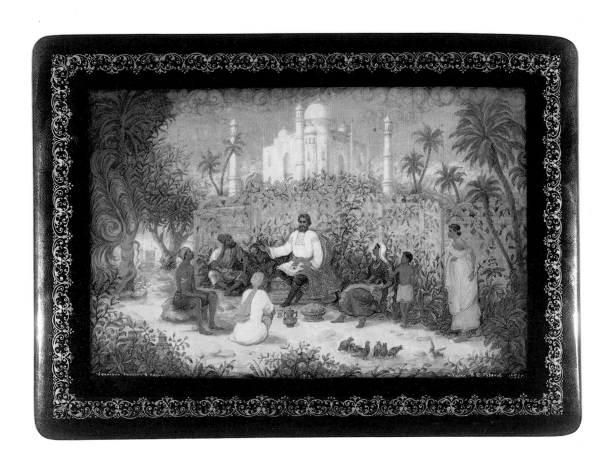

225   Vasily Puzanov-Molev
Casket: *Afanasy Nikitin in India.* 1959

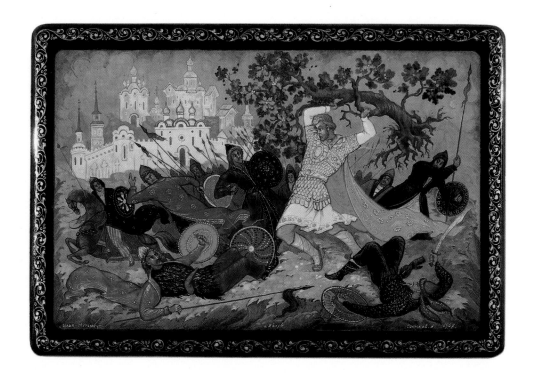

226   Alexander Sotskov
Casket: *Ilya of Murom.* 1967

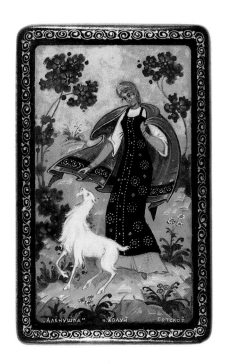

227   Alexander Sotskov
Decorative box: *Alionushka.* 1963

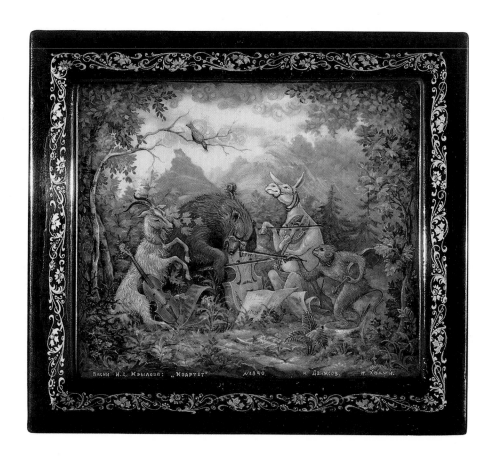

228   Nikolai Denisov
Decorative box: *The Quartette.* 1956

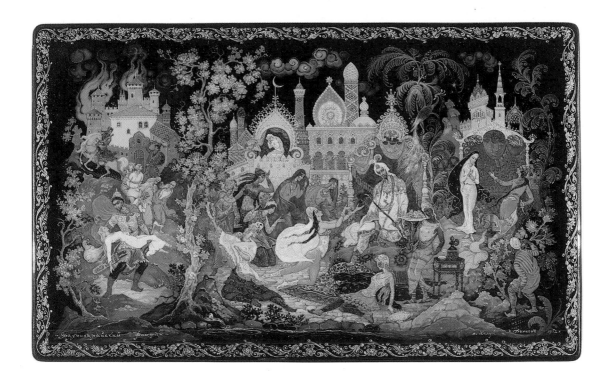

229   Nikolai Denisov
Decorative box: *The Fountain
of Bakhchisarai*. 1972

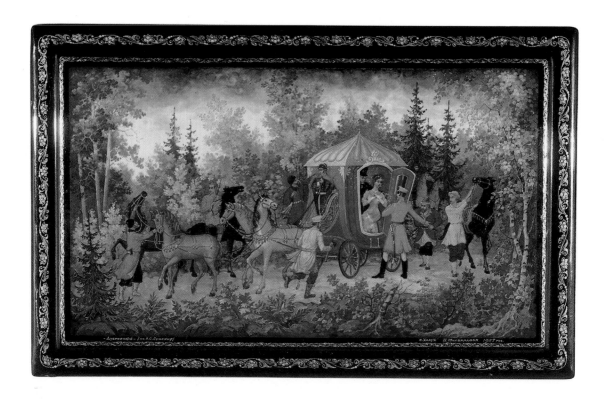

230   Boris Tikhonravov
Casket: *Dubrovsky*. 1957

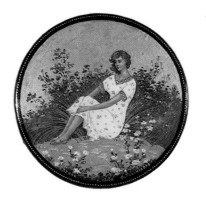

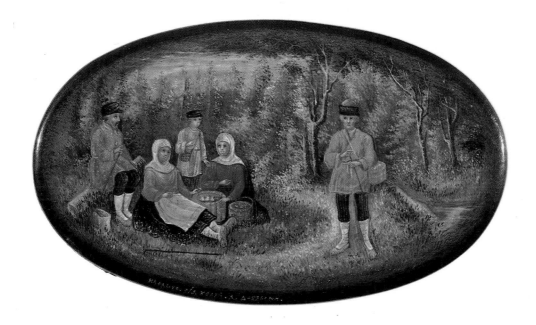

231   Boris Tikhonravov
Brooch: *Alionushka*. 1969

232   Dmitry Dobrynin
Oval box: *At Rest*. 1930s

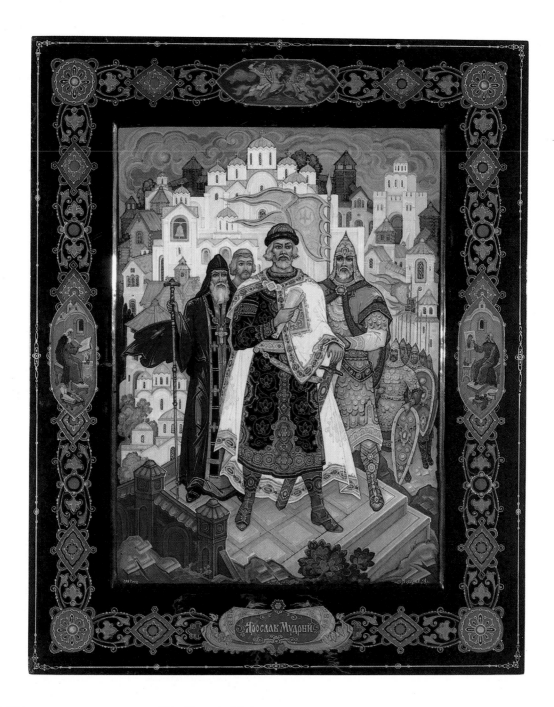

233   Alexander Morozov
Panel: *Yaroslav the Wise*. 1982

234   Alexander Morozov
Panel: *Yaroslav the Wise*. 1982. Detail

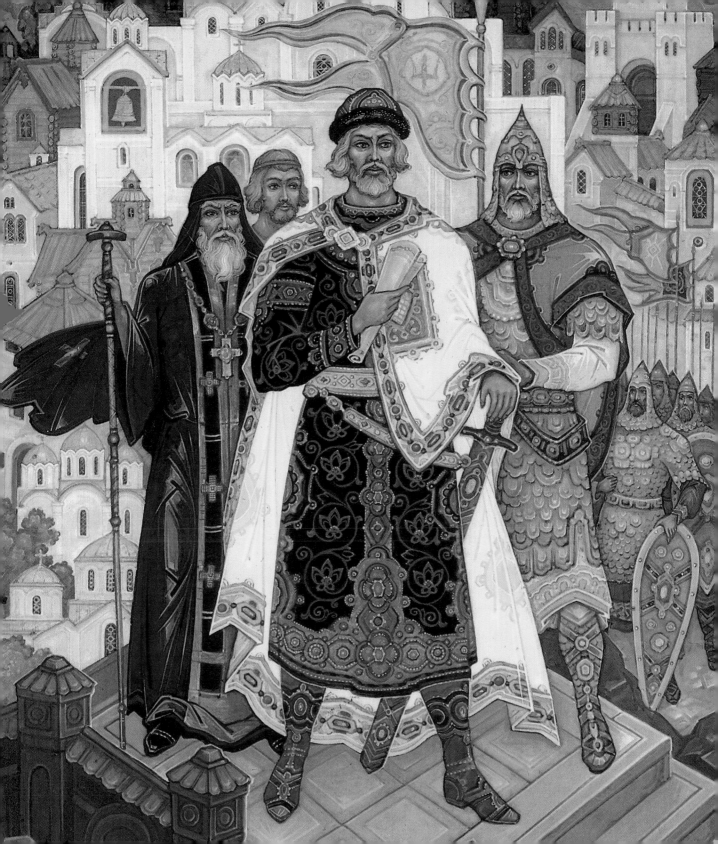

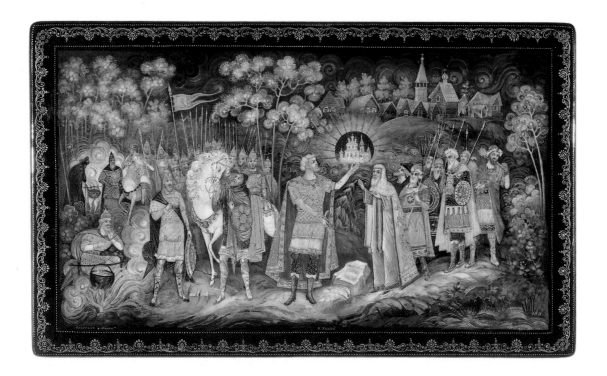

235   Alexei Kosterin
Casket: *The Legend of Borok*. 1984

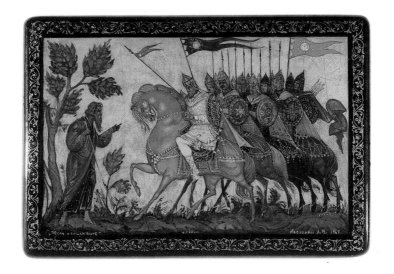

236   Alexei Kosterin
Casket: *The Song of the Wise Oleg.* 1967

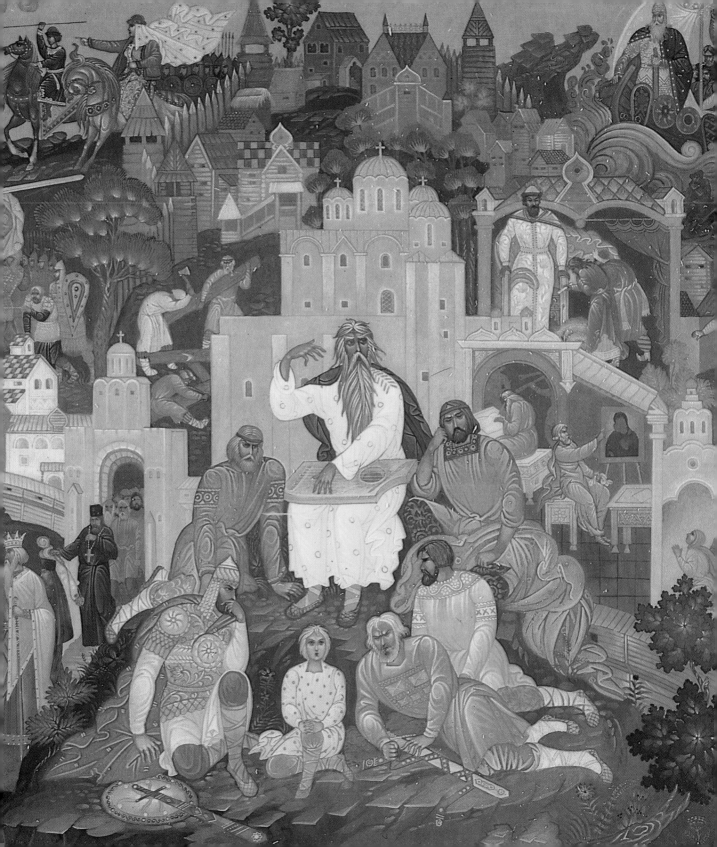

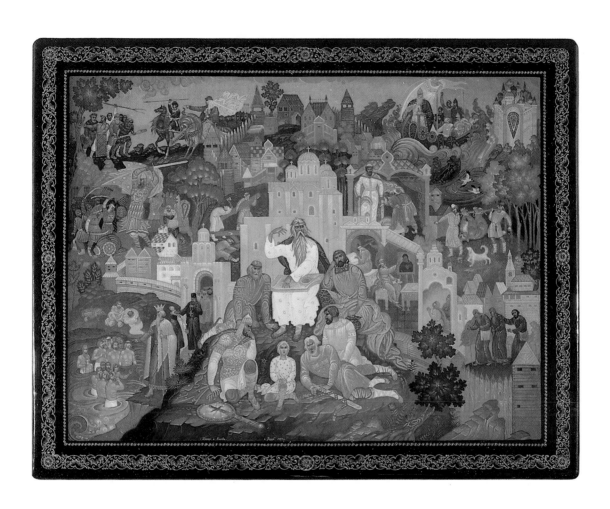

237 Piotr Mitiashin
Casket: *The Song of Kiev.* 1982. Detail

238 Piotr Mitiashin
Casket: *The Song of Kiev.* 1982

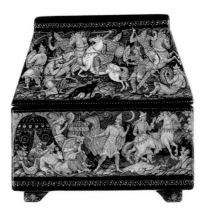

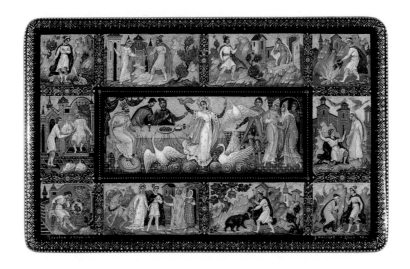

239 Boris Kiseliov
Casket: *The Lay of Igor's Host.* 1979

240 Boris Kiseliov
Decorative box: *The Frog Princess.* 1972

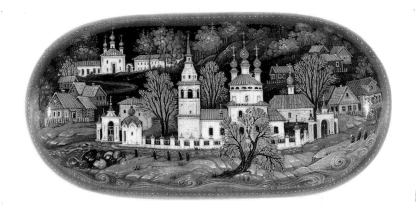

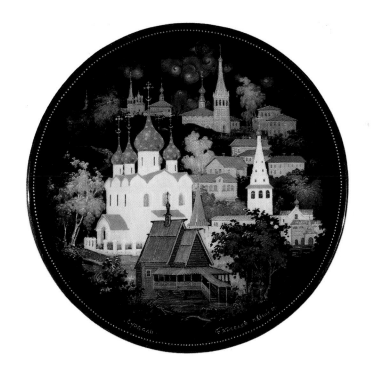

241 Boris Kiseliov
Casket: *Kholui.* 1980

242 Boris Kiseliov
Round box: *Suzdal.* 1964

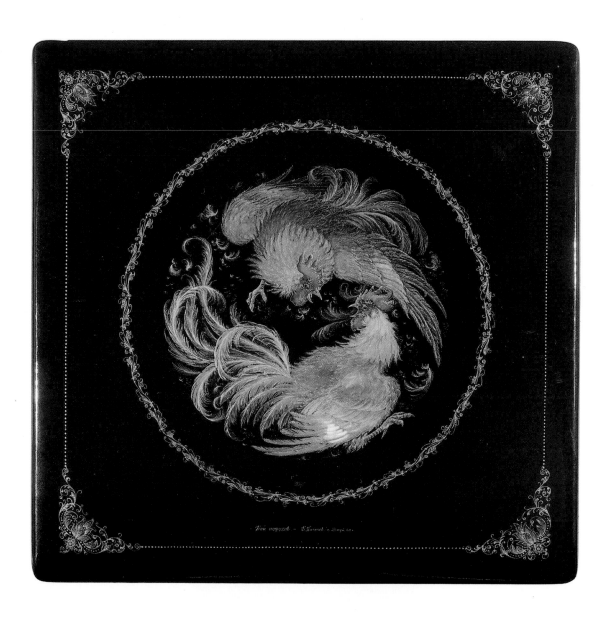

243   Boris Kiseliov
Casket: *Cock-fight*. 1960

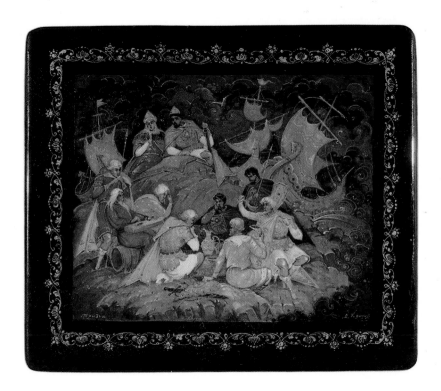

244   Valentin Krotov
Decorative box: *Funeral Feast.* 1960s

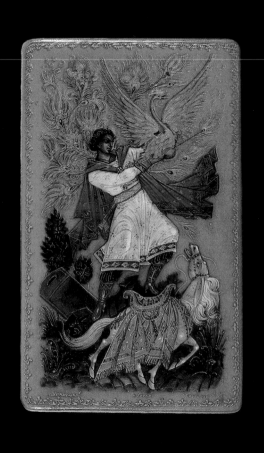

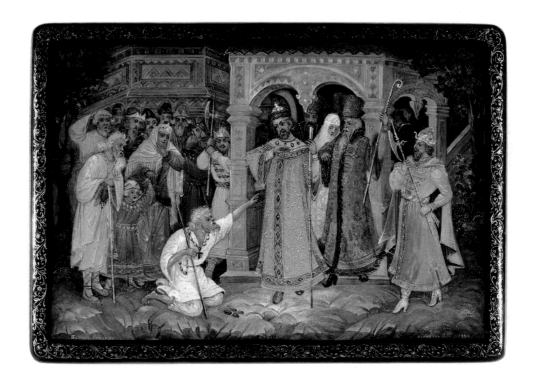

245 Alexei Kosterin
Decorative box: *Ivanushka*. 1967

246 Alexei Kosterin
Decorative box: *Boris Godunov*. 1966

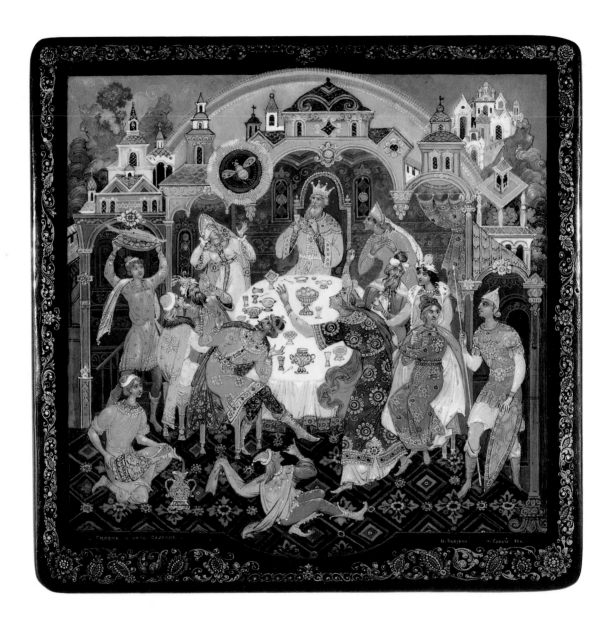

247   Nikolai Baburin
Casket: *The Tale of Tsar Saltan.* 1983

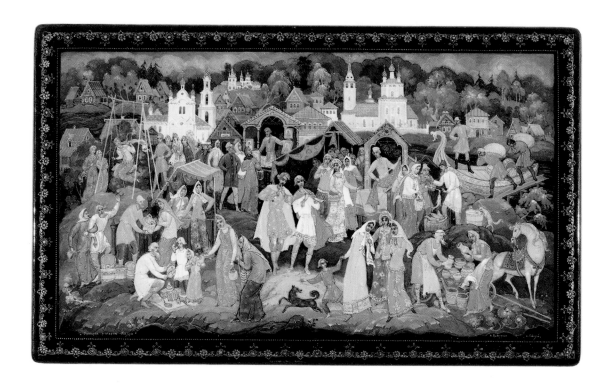

248   Nikolai Baburin
Casket: *Fair in Old Kholui.* 1973

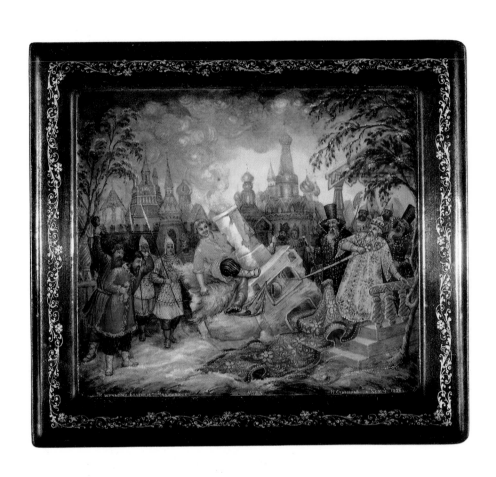

249 Nikolai Starikov
Casket: *By a Wave of the Wand.* 1956

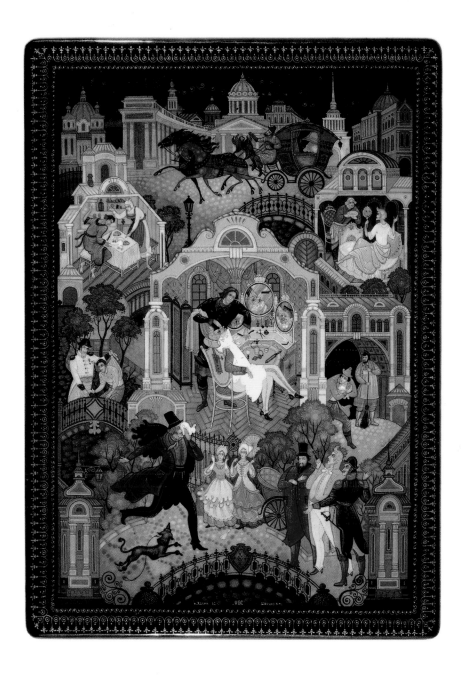

250   Nikolai Shvetsov
Casket: *The Nose.* 1982

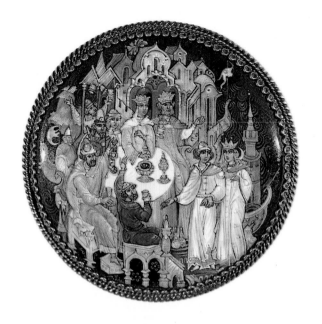

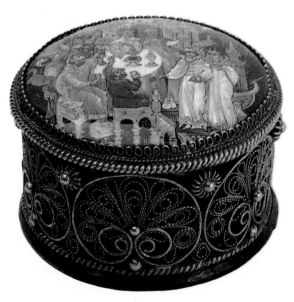

251 Boris Novosiolov
Casket: *Guidon's Guests*. 1978

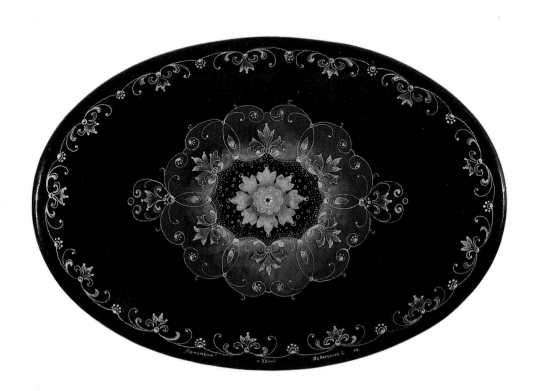

252   Boris Deviatkin
Round box: *Ornament.* 1969

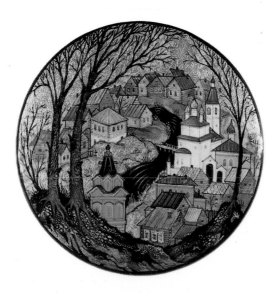

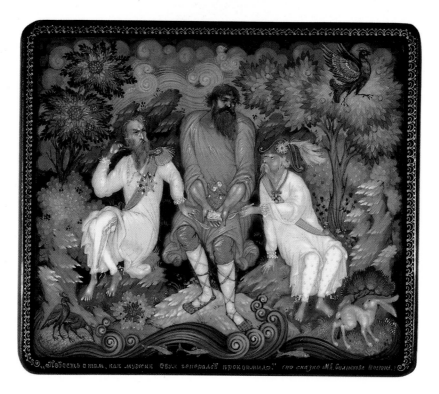

253   Victor Yolkin
Round box: *Autumn*. 1979

254   Victor Yolkin
Decorative box: *The Muzhik
Who Kept Two Generals*. 1982

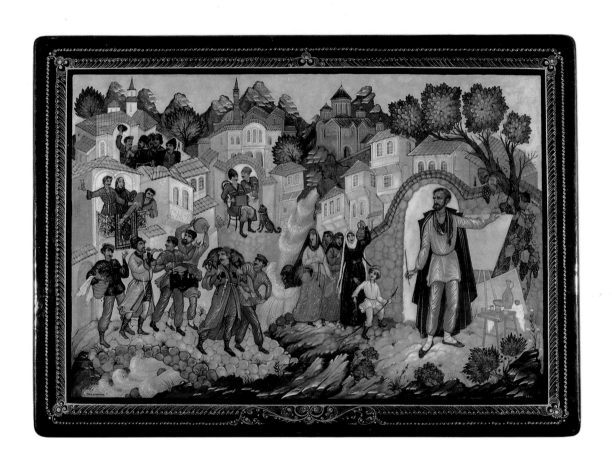

255   Victor Yolkin
Decorative box: *Pirosmani.* 1979

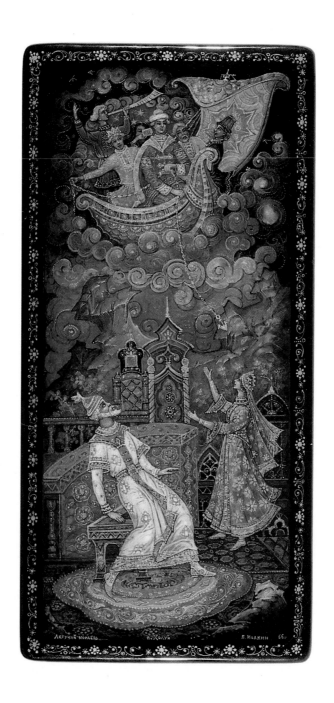

256   Pavel Ivakin
Decorative box: *The Flying Ship*. 1966

The distinctions between the miniatures executed in Palekh, Mstiora and Kholui are visible even to an untrained eye.

The Palekh compositions seem to blossom against the deep black glimmering background. The pattern is graphically expressive, constructed on precise lines and contours and seems to be permeated with the finest gold and silver threads. The treatment of images is explicitly symbolic, figures and gestures are emphatically dynamic, and the colouration is clear and pure.

The background performs quite a notable role in the Palekh miniature. The black colour not only brings out the nuances of the hues but really sets the rhythm of the entire composition. It may signify the sky, the ground or just an abstract space lacking references to time and place. The background is invariably perceived as an independent component of the composition, graphically related to the main picture. Lately Palekh artists have started using bright red, deep blue and ivory-white as well as black for the background. Even so it still functions as an expressive and equal component of the overall colour scheme.

The colouration of the Mstiora miniature is not dominated by contrasting colours. On the contrary, it seeks to achieve a unity of tones — cold blue or warm red, with a predominance of ochre. The picture is set against the coloured background, the latter not being independent but serving to define the concrete space where the action takes place. The Mstiora paintings recall the designs of colourful Persian carpets embroidered in elegant all-over ornaments.

The style of the Kholui miniatures causes one to remember that in the past the local icon-painters used to defy the established rules of painting. Still today the Kholui artists are less bound by canons than their colleagues in Palekh and Mstiora. Keeping within the bounds of pictorial convention, they exercise greater freedom of experimentation and divergence from the rigid rules. While sharing the preference for the black background with the Palekh artists, they are much less restrained by traditions in the treatment of figures. The colouration of their paintings, always bright, rich and sometimes even coarse, imparts a special beauty to the work.

In contrast to those miniaturists who have matured within the modified traditions of ancient Russian painting, the Fedoskino artists employ much less conventionalized means of expression. At the core of the Fedoskino compositions are all the different forms of realistic art.

The modern style of lacquered miniature is by no means static. The contemporary Palekh miniature is appreciably more diversified than in the '20s and '30s, although like the Mstiora paintings it still reluctantly lends itself to major modification. The Fedoskino and Kholui styles are more open to change. Thus many Kholui artists boldly reshape the imagery structure of their miniatures and follow a style originating from the revolutionary paintings and graphic works of the '20s, previously thought to be unsuitable for lacquered miniatures. The design of the Fedoskino lacquer features noticeably more dynamism and expression than earlier.

Contemporary miniaturists do not confine themselves to one particular kind of the decorative arts. In fact they intensively work in such areas as monumental painting and book design, make lacquered insets for the metal components of jewellery, design sets for theatre and cinema, take part in various rehabilitation projects, and at the same time invariably demonstrate good use of the old styles in their work. And to all these various branches of art the miniaturists bring the distinctive properties of their craft.

Despite the differences in style that exist between the four centres of miniature painting, they have some common features. Primarily these involve the choice of themes, which are extensively derived from folklore and literature. The vivid characterization, profound lyricism and acute sense of poetry inherent in Russian folk songs, fairy-tales and ballads are agreeable with the min-

iature artists' quest for elevated harmony. The poetry of Alexander Pushkin, Mikhail Lermontov, Nikolai Nekrasov, the revolutionary prose and poetry, and Maxim Gorky's romantic works offer an infinite source of inspiration for the painters. The range of themes invariably includes patriotic motifs associated with the heroic struggles of the Civil and Second World Wars. From the early '20s the miniaturists have intensively exploited the repertory of contemporary themes, bringing out the poetry inherent in creative labour. They have poeticized the daily life with its simple joys while events of historical significance, like exploration of outer space, have been treated with a good deal of solemnity and raised to the level of allegory and symbol.

While the range of subjects continually grows more diverse, the miniaturists do not change their preference for positive, romantic and lyrical imagery. Humour and mockery are appropriate only when placed in a romantic or fabulous context. The attempts to portray tragically negative characters, expose cruelty, vile emotions and acts have been quite unsuccessful. Such themes lie beyond the bounds of this form of art.

The art of lacquered miniature is deeply rooted in the painting tradition that has been cultivated by more than one generation of well-known and anonymous artists. The fact that one and the same composition could occur countless times in the works of different painters seems to rule out such a category as authorship. Icons were painted according to rules, the Lukutin snuff-boxes were meant for a definite kind of clientele... Yet the merits of the lacquered miniature lie precisely in the artist's ability to express his individual sensibilities and manner while keeping within a limited range of themes and images. That is why miniatures seldom repeat each other and copies are never exact replicas of the original.

To be sure, the degree of artistic independence is varied. There have been mediocre copyists too, but it is not by their works that we judge the art of lacquered miniature. Authorship, as applied to the area of folk arts, is of definite value to us, and if the earliest Palekh designs executed in the Moscow studios bore only the proprietors' names, now the situation has changed: it is absolutely normal for an artist to sign his work.

The art of miniature painting is becoming increasingly individualized. Unlike the pre-revolutionary artists who mainly made copies from easel paintings, the modern miniaturists of Palekh, Mstiora, Kholui and even Fedoskino are totally independent and use no prototypes whatsoever. Individual artistic pursuits have noticeably intensified in each of the four centres where more than one generation of distinctive artists has grown up. It is not within the scope of this review to analyze concrete modern styles. Yet the illustrations have been chosen for this book so as to give a more comprehensive idea of the accomplishments of contemporary miniaturists.

Whatever changes might have been or will be taking place in the art of miniature painting under the impact of changing fashions, styles or individual tastes, it continues to rely largely on tradition and collective work — in the folkloric sense. Essentially this means that here there is a unity of artistic thought. Thus, a contemporary miniaturist works in close association with a group of artists engaged in the same trade. The creative aspirations of individual miniature painters are not opposed to those of the collective.

The modern miniaturist is nothing like the peasant craftsman of the past. He is a highly educated person, fully conscious of his artistic status. Like the leading national artists and sculptors, many contemporary lacquered miniature painters have been awarded honorary titles, orders or medals.

The cooperatives with their primitive organization of labour are no longer to be found in any of the four centres of the lacquered miniature. From the '60s major design works began to exist there. Artists on the staff number 260 in Palekh, 270 in Fedoskino, 300 in Mstiora and 150 in Kholui. These are assisted by skilled joiners, varnishers and polishers. Spacious workshops are perfectly fitted out for lot production of commodity goods and the design of compositions for exhibitions. Special schools provide training in the art of miniature painting while several museums hold the best works of the local masters. Works by Russian miniaturists are represented in the major national collections and their fame has spread far beyond this country's borders.

CATALOGUE

Most of the objects annotated in this catalogue are made
of papier-mâché with the use of the two basic techniques: the Palekh,
Mstiora and Kholui miniature paintings are executed in tempera, gold and
lacquer, while the Fedoskino miniatures are done in oils, gold and lacquer.
Specifications of the medium in the notes on the plates are omitted,
unless the material or techniques used are different.
Measurements of the objects are given in centimeters, followed by inches.

1 P. Korobov Factory
Snuff-box: *Portrait of an Unknown Person.*
Early 19th century
2.2 x 9.4 (⅞" x 3 ¾")
Vocational School Lacquered Miniature
Museum, Fedoskino
In the early 19th century the Korobov factory
supplied snuff-boxes decorated with Russian
prints that were glued on the box cover and
featured historical scenes or portraits. Output of these goods continued for some time
after the Korobov factory was taken over by
Piotr Lukutin.

2 P. Lukutin Factory
Casket: *The Noble Family.* 1820s–1830s
12.2 x 19.8 x 15.3 (4 ¾" x 7 ¾" x 6")
Vocational School Lacquered Miniature
Museum, Fedoskino
In the 1820s–1840s Chinese scenes and ornaments, and the "chinoiserie" style in general,
became fashionable in Russia. The casket
shows in a conventional manner a genre
scene from the life of a rich Chinese family.

3 P. and A. Lukutin Factory
Snuff-box: *Napoleon in Burning Moscow.*
1843–63
3.5 x 9.6 x 5.5 (1 ⅜" x 3 ¾" x 2 ⅛")
Vocational School Lacquered Miniature
Museum, Fedoskino
The miniature shows Napoleon who entered
Moscow on 2 September 1812 to find an
empty city enveloped in flames. The snuffbox is finished in a rich rocaille golden ornament. The ornament is made by glueing a
thin sheet of gold upon a brush-drawn lacquer pattern. After the gold sticks to the
lacquer its surplus parts are removed. The
ornament is set on a background painted in
imitation of iridescent mother-of-pearl.

4 P. and A. Lukutin Factory
Snuff-box: *Sweet-hearts in a Boat.*
1843–63
3.5 x 9.5 x 4.8 (1 ⅜" x 3 ¾" x 1 ⅞")
All-Russia Museum of Decorative and
Folk Arts, Moscow
Presumably the sight of the Bay of Naples
with the smoking Mount Vesuvius in the
background.

5 A. Lukutin Factory
Cigarette-case: *Courting a Woman.* 1863–88
2.9 x 12.7 x 8.1 (1 ⅛" x 5" x 3 ¼")
Miniature Painting Factory Museum,
Fedoskino
In the second half of the nineteenth century
miniaturists used the method of providing a
lustrous lining (as a rule gold leaf or silver
powder) under the painting. The lining
showed through the liquid translucent paint
adding liveliness and brightness to the colours. This technique became traditional for
the Fedoskino miniatures and continues to
be used by contemporary artists.

6 A. Lukutin Factory
Casket: *Fox-hunt.* 1820s–1830s
11.3 x 20.4 x 15.8 (4 ½" x 8" x 6 ¼")
Vocational School Lacquered Miniature
Museum, Fedoskino
The scene is painted on a mother-of-pearl
plate attached to the box cover. The manner
of painting is the same as in the case of
papier-mâché, except that the coats are very
thin and translucent so that the base is visible
through the painting. Mother-of-pearl's
decorative play of colours often suggests a
theme to the artist. This technique is traditional for the Fedoskino miniatures.

7 A. Lukutin Factory
Purse cover: *Demyan's Fish-soup.*

1863–88
0.5 x 8 x 5.1 (¼" x 3 ⅛" x 2")
Vocational School Lacquered Miniature
Museum, Fedoskino
The miniature constitutes an interpretation
of the painting by the Russian artist Andrei
Popov (1832–1896) based on Ivan Krylov's
fable *Demyan's Fish-soup*: the host is so
zealous in treating his guest to fish-soup that
the latter cannot stand it any more and takes
to his heels.

8 P. and A. Lukutin Factory
Cigarette-case: *Peasants in a Pot-house.*
1843–63
2.8 x 8.1 x 13.3 (1 ⅛" x 3 ¼" x 5 ¼")
Vocational School Lacquered Miniature
Museum, Fedoskino
The miniature constitutes a rather free interpretation of the lithograph *Coming Home
from the Fair* by Rudolf Zhukovsky
(1814–1886).

9 P. and A. Lukutin Factory
Snuff-box: *Portrait of a Fisher-woman.*
1843–63
3.4 x 5.2 x 7.8 (1 ⅜" x 2" x 3 ⅛")
Vocational School Lacquered Miniature
Museum, Fedoskino

10 P. and A. Lukutin Factory
Purse cover: *Portrait of Ivan Krylov.*
1843–63
0.3 x 6.2 x 7.5 (⅛" x 2 ½" x 3")
Vocational School Lacquered Miniature
Museum, Fedoskino
Ivan Krylov (1769–1844) was a Russian
fabulist. The miniature is reproduced
from a printed copy of the portrait by the

well-known Russian artist Karl Briullov (1799–1852).

11, 12 A. Lukutin Factory
Photograph album. 1863–88
5 x 33 x 27 (2" x 13" x 10 ⅝")
All-Russia Museum of Decorative and Folk Arts, Moscow
It was typical not just of the Lukutin miniatures but of the late nineteenth-century Russian culture in general to exploit folk, particularly "Ukrainian", themes.

13 P. and A. Lukutin Factory
Snuff-box: *A Peasant Whetting His Scythe.* 1843–63
3.6 x 4.9 x 9.2 (1 ⅜" x 1 ⅞" x 3 ⅝")
Vocational School Lacquered Miniature Museum, Fedoskino
Such scenes from the life of Russian peasants, full of tenderness and tranquillity, were characteristic of the Lukutin miniatures in the second half of the 19th century.

14 P. and A. Lukutin Factory
Cigar-box: *A Game of Piquet.* 1843–63
12 x 22.5 x 16 (4 ¾" x 8 ⅞" x 6 ¼")
All Russia Museum of Decorative and Folk Arts, Moscow

15, 16 A. Lukutin Factory
Pencil-case: *The Village of Fedoskino* and *Troikas.* 1843–88
3.6 x 21.3 x 4.1 (1 ⅜" x 8 ⅜" x 1 ⅝")
Vocational School Lacquered Miniature Museum, Fedoskino
The scenes of festive troika rides were favoured by the miniaturists whose interpretations of this traditional scene always reflected individual sensibilities and artistic temperaments.

17 The Vishniakov Workshop
Round casket: *Peasants on the Way Home from Haymaking.*
Late 19th century
10.3 x 12 (4" x 4 ¾")
All-Russia Museum of Decorative and Folk Arts, Moscow

18 P. and A. Lukutin Factory
Cigarette-case: *Coming on Leave.* 1843–63
2.4 x 14.4 x 8.4 (1" x 5 ⅝" x 3 ¼")
Vocational School Lacquered Miniature Museum, Fedoskino

19 P. and A. Lukutin Factory
Casket: *Red Square.* 1843–63
5.6 x 17 x 12.3 (2 ¼" x 6 ¾" x 4 ⅞")
Vocational School Lacquered Miniature Museum, Fedoskino
The early nineteenth-century sight of the Moscow Kremlin and Red Square.

20 P. and A. Lukutin Factory
Casket: *Morning.* 1843–63
6 x 29.7 x 20 (2 ⅜" x 11 ¾" x 7 ⅞")
Vocational School Lacquered Miniature Museum, Fedoskino

21 N. Lukutin Factory
Menue cover: *A Lady and Two Coachmen.* 1888–1904
0.3 x 14.2 x 10.8 (⅛" x 5 ⅝" x 4 ¼")
Vocational School Lacquered Miniature Museum, Fedoskino
The miniature is copied from the lithograph *Never Mind, I Can Walk* by Rudolf Zhukovsky (1814–1886). The scene is very simple: two coachmen offer a lift to a lady, but she declines.

22 P. and A. Lukutin Factory
Snuff-box: *A Summer Troika.* 1843–63
3.9 x 9.5 x 4.3 (1 ½" x 3 ¾" x 1 ¾")
Vocational School Lacquered Miniature Museum, Fedoskino
(See note on pls. 15, 16). Free interpretation of the prints by Karl Gampeln (late 18th century –1850s) and Alexander Orlovsky (1777–1832).

23 P. and A. Lukutin Factory
Snuff-box: *The Danilkovo Estate.* 1843–63
4 x 9 x 5.2 (1 ⅝" x 3 ½" x 2")
Vocational School Lacquered Miniature Museum, Fedoskino
Danilkovo was the Lukutins' estate in Fedoskino.

24, 25 Dmitry Krylov. 1858–1919
Panel: *Boyaryshnia at the Wattle-fence.*
Late 19th century
0.4 x 24.4 x 30.5 (⅛" x 9 ⅝" x 12")
Vocational School Lacquered Miniature Museum, Fedoskino
This is a miniature interpretation of the painting *Boyaryshnia* by the Russian artist Konstantin Makovsky (1839–1915), whose many works reflected folk motifs.

26 Nikolai Tsybin. 1887–1939
Casket: *A Winter Troika.* 1932
4.6 x 8.5 x 7.2 (1 ¾" x 3 ⅜" x 2 ⅞")
Miniature Painting Factory Museum, Fedoskino
See note on pls. 15, 16.

27 Alexei Leznov. 1886–1946
Pencil-case: *Flowers.* 1944
2 x 20 x 5.3 (¾" x 7 ⅞" x 2 ⅛")
Miniature Painting Factory Museum, Fedoskino

28 Mikhail Popenov. 1889–1952
Casket: *Haymaking Season.* 1947
8.7 x 9.2 x 7.5 (3 ⅜" x 3 ⅝" x 3")
Miniature Painting Factory Museum, Fedoskino

29 Afanasy Kulikov. 1884–1949
Casket: *Radio in the Village.* 1920s
4.7 x 12.2 x 12.2 (1 ⅞" x 4 ¾" x 4 ¾")
Folk Art Museum at the Institute of Industrial Art, Moscow
Afanasy Kulikov was a professional artist who supplied models for the Fedoskino miniaturists in the 1920s.

30 Vasily Lavrov. 1894–1951
Casket: *Drinking Tea.* 1935
4.8 x 16.5 x 11.6 (1 ⅞" x 6 ½" x 4 ⅝")
Vocational School Lacquered Miniature Museum, Fedoskino
This scene is traditional for the Fedoskino miniatures: peasants or artisans are engaged in a leisurely conversation over tea poured from a big *samovar.* This particular painting is based on a nineteenth-century miniature that in turn was a copy from a photograph.

31 Alexei Kruglikov. 1884–1960
Casket: *Summer Troikas*. 1943
9.2 x 26.6 x 19.6 (3 ⅝" x 10 ½" x 7 ¾")
Miniature Painting Factory Museum,
Fedoskino
See note on pls. 15, 16.

32 Alexei Kruglikov. 1884–1960
Casket: *St. Basil's Cathedral*. 1943
10.3 x 17.5 x 19.1 (4" x 6 ⅞" x 7 ½")
Miniature Painting Factory Museum,
Fedoskino
St. Basil's Cathedral or the Cathedral of the
Intercession of the Virgin is the monument of
ancient Russian architecture in the southern
end of Red Square overlooking the Moscow
Kremlin. The cathedral was built in 1555–60
by the architects Barma and Postnik to mark
the victory over the Kazan Khanate.

33 Mikhail Chizhov. Born 1923.
Merited Artist of the RSFSR, Winner of
the Repin State Prize of the RSFSR
Round casket. "Tortoise-shell" technique.
1960s
7.8 x 5.8 (3 ⅛" x 2 ¼")
Miniature Painting Factory Museum,
Fedoskino
One of the oldest Fedoskino decorative
techniques is an imitation of tortoise-shell.

34 Vasily Korsakov. 1917–1983
Decorative box. *Zierovka* technique. 1964
2.5 x 7 x 3 (1" x 2 ¾" x 1 ⅛")
All-Russia Museum of Decorative and
Folk Arts, Moscow
Zierovka is an ornament scratched on a
lacquered silver or tin sheet. The wavy radiat-
ing lines are preliminarily outlined on a
template.
This ornamentation technique is also typical
of the Fedoskino miniatures.

35 N. Lukutin Factory
Round box: *Portrait of an Old Man*.
1888–1904
3.4 x 5.8 (1 ⅜" x 2 ¼")
Miniature Painting Factory Museum,
Fedoskino
The Fedoskino miniaturists took portrait
orders from their clientele. Owing to the

great expressivity of individual characteris-
tics this portrait can be rated as the best work
of this particular genre.

36 P. and A. Lukutin Factory
Snuff-box decorated with "filigree"
ornament. 1843–63
3.25 x 9.8 x 4.8 (1 ¼" x 3 ⅞" x 1 ⅞")
All-Russia Museum of Decorative and
Folk Arts, Moscow
The box is decorated with the traditional
"filigree" ornament — diversely shaped,
inlaid chased metal plaques.

37 The Vishniakovs Workshop
Tea-caddy: *Lunching Children*. Late 19th
century
12 x 18 x 11.5 (4 ¾" x 7 ⅛" x 4 ½")
All-Russia Museum of Decorative and
Folk Arts, Moscow

38 Mikhail Chizhov. Born 1923. Merited
Artist of the RSFSR, Winner of the Repin
State Prize of the RSFSR
Round casket: *Russian Winter Festival
in Fedoskino*. 1968
6.1 x 19.6 (2 ⅜" x 7 ¾")
Miniature Painting Factory Museum, Fedos-
kino

39 Mikhail Chizhov. Born 1923.
Merited Artist of the RSFSR, Winner of
the Repin State Prize of the RSFSR
Decorative box. 1960s
2.5 x 7.3 x 3 (1" x 2 ⅞" x 1 ⅛")
Miniature Painting Factory Museum,
Fedoskino
See note on pl. 3.

40 Mikhail Chizhov. Born 1923.
Merited Artist of the RSFSR, Winner of
the Repin State Prize of the RSFSR
Casket: *Evening in the Country*. 1972
5 x 15.3 x 12 (2" x 6" x 4 ¾")
All-Russia Museum of Decorative and
Folk Arts, Moscow

41 Victor Antonov. Born 1936
Round casket: *The Family*. 1977
4.7 x 6 (1 ⅞" x 2 ⅜")

All-Russia Museum of Decorative and
Folk Arts, Moscow

42 Mikhail Korniyenko. Born 1926
Casket: *Moscow Suburb*. 1978
2.8 x 10.5 x 5.2 (1 ⅛" x 4 ½" x 2")
All-Russia Museum of Decorative and
Folk Arts, Moscow

43 Alexander Kozlov. Born 1932
Decorative box: *March*. 1979
3 x 8 x 5.5 (1 ⅛" x 3 ⅛" x 2 ⅛")
All-Russia Museum of Decorative and
Folk Arts, Moscow
The landscape is painted on a mother-
of-pearl plate attached to the box cover.
See note on pl. 6.

44 Yuri Karapayev. Born 1936.
Merited Artist of the RSFSR
Casket: *The Northern Song*. 1970
2.5 x 6 x 8 (1" x 2 ⅜" x 3 ⅛")
All-Russia Museum of Decorative and
Folk Arts, Moscow
A scene repeatedly occurring in Fedoskino
miniatures is the round dance — an old
peasant ritual performed to the accompani-
ment of drawling songs.

45, 46 Victor Lipitsky. Born 1921.
Merited Artist of the RSFSR
Casket: *The Scarlet Flower*. 1979
8.5 x 19.8 x 26.5 (3 ⅜" x 7 ¾" x 10 ⅜")
Miniature Painting Factory Museum,
Fedoskino
The Scarlet Flower is a Russian fairy-tale re-
corded by the Russian writer Sergei Aksakov
(1791–1859). The magic flower led a Russian
girl to a far-away island where she met a mon-
ster who was in fact a bewitched prince. The
girl showed no fear of her host's dreadful ap-
pearance. She loved him for his kindness and
her love broke the spell. The miniature shows
the girl arriving on the strange island.

47 Sergei P. Rogatov. Born 1920
Oval casket: *Birch-tree*. 1960s
4.2 x 11.5 x 7.9 (1 ⅝" x 4 ½" x 3 ⅛")
Miniature Painting Factory Museum,
Fedoskino

48 Gennady Larishev. Born 1929.
People's Artist of the RSFSR
Casket: *A Seredniak (Peasant of Average Means).* 1968
3.5 x 7.3 x 7.3 (1 ⅜" x 2 ⅞" x 2 ⅞")
All-Russia Museum of Decorative and Folk Arts, Moscow
A scene from the period of collectivization — amalgamation of private peasant plots into collective farms in the 1930s. The miniature shows a peasant of average means who contemplates joining the collective farm.

49 A. Lukutin Factory
Match-box: *A Peasant Dance.* 1863–88
8.1 x 9.5 x 9.5 (3 ¼" x 3 ¾" x 3 ¾")
Vocational School Lacquered Miniature Museum, Fedoskino
A copy of the work by the French porcelain and glass artist Paul Marie Roussel (1804–1877) who drew several sketches of peasant life during his trip to Russia in the second half of the nineteenth century.

50 Gennady Larishev. Born 1929.
People's Artist of the RSFSR
Casket: *Snow-maiden.* 1977
7.2 x 21.2 x 14 (2 ⅞" x 8 ⅜" x 5 ½")
Snow-maiden is a Russian fairy-tale about a childless old couple who dreamed of a daughter. So they sculptured a girl out of snow, but then suddenly she came to life. The miniature shows peasants startled by this miraculous transformation.

51 Sergei Monashov. Born 1923
Decorative box: *Maids' Room.* 1970s
4 x 4.9 x 3.5 (1 ⅝" x 1 ⅞" x 1 ⅜")
All-Russia Museum of Decorative and Folk Arts, Moscow
See note on pl. 36.

52 Oleg Kurzov. Born 1938
Set of pendants: *Seasons.* 1970s
1 x 3.5 x 4.2 (⅜" x 1 ⅜" x 1 ⅝")
All-Russia Museum of Decorative and Folk Arts, Moscow

53 Gennady Skripunov. Born 1923
Casket: *Kakhovka.* 1977
5 x 12 x 10 (2" x 4 ¾" x 3 ⅞")
All-Russia Museum of Decorative and Folk Arts, Moscow
Kakhovka is a city on the left bank of the Dnieper river. Here, in 1920, the Red Army dealt the crucial blow against the White Guards in the course of its offensive on the southern front of the Civil War. The popular song *Kakhovka* is dedicated to this event.

54 Lydia Stroganova. Born 1938
Decorative box. "Tortoise-shell" technique. 1980
3.5 x 6.5 x 3.5 (1 ⅜" x 2 ½" x 1 ⅜")
All-Russia Museum of Decorative and Folk Arts, Moscow
See note on pl. 33.

55 Viacheslav Sviatchenkov. Born 1954
Decorative box: *In the Boat.* 1981
3.5 x 3 x 2 (1 ⅜" x 1 ⅛" x ¾")
All-Russia Museum of Decorative and Folk Arts, Moscow

56 Alexander Tolstov. Born 1929. Merited Artist of the RSFSR
Casket: *Winter in the Country.* 1974
3.7 x 10.5 x 9 (1 ½" x 4 ⅛" x 3 ½")
All-Russia Museum of Decorative and Folk Arts, Moscow

57 Nikolai Petrov. 1863–1936
Casket: *Round-dance.* 1925
6 x 16 x 11 (2 ⅜" x 6 ¼" x 4 ⅜")
Miniature Painting Factory Museum, Fedoskino
See note on pl. 44.

58 Vasily Kruglikov. 1881–1947
Casket: *Scared by Snake.* 1930s
4 x 12 x 8.5 (1 ⅝" x 4 ¾" x 3 ⅜")
All-Russia Museum of Decorative and Folk Arts, Moscow
Miniature interpretation of the painting *Scared by Snake* by the Russian artist Konstantin Trutovsky (1826–1893), who extensively derived themes from Russian and Ukrainian peasant life-styles. His works were used as models by the Fedoskino miniaturists more than once.

59, 60 Ivan Strakhov. 1918–1979.
Merited Artist of the RSFSR, Winner of the Repin State Prize of the RSFSR
Casket: *The Tourist Routes.* 1972
9.3 x 26.5 x 19.6 (3 ⅝" x 10 ⅜" x 7 ¾")
Miniature Painting Factory Museum, Fedoskino

61 Ivan Strakhov. 1918–1979.
Merited Artist of the RSFSR, Winner of the Repin State Prize of the RSFSR
Casket: *Winter in Fedoskino.* 1977
4.3 x 13.5 x 8.8 (1 ¾" x 5 ⅜" x 3 ½")
Miniature Painting Factory Museum, Fedoskino

62 Sergei Kozlov. Born 1955
Casket: *The New Marches.* 1981
4 x 25 x 15 (1 ⅝" x 9 ⅞" x 5 ⅞")
All-Russia Museum of Decorative and Folk Arts, Moscow
A symbolic presentation of the revolutionary transformations, the downfall of the old regime and the birth of the new life.

63 Yelena Khomutinnikova. Born 1957.
Winner of the Leninist Komsomol Prize
Decorative box: *Katiusha.* 1979
2.8 x 5.2 x 10.3 (1 ⅛" x 2" x 4")
Miniature Painting Factory Museum, Fedoskino

64 Sergei Chistov. Born 1946
Decorative box: *Construction Workers.* 1978
3.8 x 7.5 x 6 (1 ½" x 3" x 2 ⅜")
All-Russia Museum of Decorative and Folk Arts, Moscow

65 Yuri Gusev. Born 1933
Casket: *Russian Ornament.* 1980
4 x 16.1 x 8.5 (1 ⅝" x 6 ⅜" x 3 ⅜")
Ministry of Culture of the RSFSR, Moscow
Intricate golden ornament is a traditional decoration of the Fedoskino articles. See note on pl. 3.

66 Ivan Platonov. 1887–1967
Tea-caddy. 1945
6.1 x 12 x 8.7 (2 ⅜" x 4 ¾" x 3 ⅜")
Miniature Painting Factory Museum, Fedoskino

67 Ivan Semionov. 1883–1950
Casket: *The Salute.* 1944
7.5 x 8.5 x 7.2 (3" x 3 ⅜" x 2 ⅞")
Miniature Painting Factory Museum, Fedoskino
The salute in Moscow marking the complete liberation of the Soviet territory from the Nazi invaders in 1944.

68 Nikolai Soloninkin. Born 1945.
Winner of the Leninist Komsomol Prize
Panel: *Portrait of Mikhail Chizhov.* 1984
1.8 x 10.8 x 14.5 (¾" x 4 ¼" x 5 ¾")
Vocational School Lacquered Miniature Museum, Fedoskino
The miniature portrays the Fedoskino artist Mikhail Chizhov.

69 Victor Lipitsky. Born 1921.
Merited Artist of the RSFSR
Casket: *Leo Tolstoy.* 1985
4.2 x 14.7 x 14.7 (1 ⅝" x 5 ¾" x 5 ¾")
The artist's property
Leo Tolstoy (1828–1910) — a great Russian writer, author of the novels *War and Peace*, *Anna Karenina* and *Resurrection.*

70 Mikhail Pashinin. Born 1921.
Merited Artist of the RSFSR
Decorative box: *Alexander Pushkin.* 1971
2.3 x 5.5 x 8.2 (⅞" x 2 ⅛" x 3 ¼")
Miniature Painting Factory Museum, Fedoskino
Alexander Pushkin (1799–1837) – a great Russian poet. He is shown in St. Petersburg, on the embankment of the Neva river.

71 Anatoly Kuznetsov. Born 1954
Decorative box: *A Story of Lenin.* 1980s
3 x 4.5 x 5.5 (1 ⅛" x 1 ¾" x 2 ⅛")
All-Russia Museum of Decorative and Folk Arts, Moscow
Vladimir I. Lenin (Ulyanov, 1870–1924), founder of the Soviet Communist Party and the Soviet State.

72 Sergei Rogatov. Born 1955
Round casket: *The Fair.* 1979
1.5 x 9.2 (⅝" x 3 ⅝")
All-Russia Museum of Decorative and Folk Arts, Moscow

73 Piotr Puchkov. Born 1932
Round casket: *The Kremlin Ornaments.* 1978
6.0 x 8.0 (2 ⅜" x 3 ⅛")
All-Russia Museum of Decorative and Folk Arts, Moscow
The panoramic view of the Moscow Kremlin.

74 Nikolai Vakurov. 1879–1952
Panel: *Yemelyan Pugachov.* 1936
17 x 12 (6 ¾" x 4 ¾")
Museum of Palekh Art, Palekh
Yemelyan Pugachov (1740–1775), a Cossack from the Don, leader of the 1773–75 peasant war, executed after his army was crushed.

75 Icon: *The Fiery Ascent of the Prophet Elijah.* Early 18th century
106 x 85.6 (41 ¾" x 33 ¾")
Museum of Palekh Art, Palekh

76 Icon: *The Archangel Michael the Voivode.* The Volga Region.
First half of the 17th century. Detail
Tempera on wood. 33 x 27 (13" x 10 ⅝")
Pavel Korin Collection Museum, Moscow

77 Ivan Golikov. 1886–1937.
Merited Artist of the RSFSR
Casket: *The Beasts.* 1925
4.4 x 13.7 x 9 (1 ¾" x 5 ⅜" x 3 ½")
Museum of Palekh Art, Palekh
The motif is borrowed from the 18th-century Palekh icon *St. John the Baptist.*

78 Ivan Golikov. 1886–1937.
Merited Artist of the RSFSR
Casket: *The Dance.* 1925
4 x 13.7 x 9 (1 ⅝" x 5 ⅜" x 3 ½")
Museum of Palekh Art, Palekh

79, 80 Ivan Golikov. 1886–1937.
Merited Artist of the RSFSR
Tray: *Troika.* 1926
Tempera on lacquered metal.
2 x 40.5 x 29.5 (¾" x 16" x 11 ⅝")
Museum of Palekh Art, Palekh
See note on pls. 15, 16.

81 Ivan Golikov. 1886–1937.
Merited Artist of the RSFSR
Casket: *The Tale of the Fisherman and the Golden Fish.* 1927
8.7 x 28 x 9.5 (3 ⅜" x 11" x 3 ¾")
Museum of Palekh Art, Palekh
Based on the fairy-tale of the same name by Alexander Pushkin (1799–1837). A poor old fisherman caught a magic golden fish who fulfilled every wish of his capricious wife. At last the old woman said she wished to be a "sea mistress" and lost everything she had gained.

82 Ivan Golikov. 1886–1937.
Merited Artist of the RSFSR
Panel: *The Battle.* 1927
12 x 20 (4 ¾" x 7 ⅞")
Tretyakov Gallery, Moscow

83 Pavel Bazhenov. 1904–1941
Decorative plate: *The Corvée.* 1932
Diam. 27.8 (11")
Museum of Palekh Art, Palekh
The corvée is the work of the serfs for the landlord.

84 Pavel Bazhenov. 1904–1941
Casket: *Churila Plenkovich.* 1934
4.7 x 19.3 x 26.7 (1 ⅞" x 7 ⅝" x 10 ½")
Museum of Palekh Art, Palekh
Churila Plenkovich is a hero of the Russian folk ballads, a prankish dandy and lady-killer.

85 Pavel Bazhenov. 1904–1941
Casket: *The Crane and the Heron.* 1941
4.5 x 17 x 9.2 (1 ¾" x 6 ¾" x 3 ⅝")
Museum of Palekh Art, Palekh
Based on the Russian fairy-tale about endless match-making. The crane and the heron are making proposals to each other but every time one of them happens to be out of spirits.

86 Ivan Zubkov. 1883–1938
Oval box: *Herdsman's Pastime.* 1926
3.2 x 8.8 x 5.5 (1 ¼" x 3 ½" x 2 ⅛")
Tretyakov Gallery, Moscow
Based on a Russian folk song.

87 Ivan Zubkov. 1883–1938
Cigarette-case: *The Ploughman.* 1926
2 x 13.2 x 8.5 (¾" x 5 ¼" x 3 ⅜")
Museum of Palekh Art, Palekh

88 Tamara Zubkova. 1917–1973.
Merited Artist of the RSFSR, Winner of the Repin State Prize of the RSFSR
Casket: *"What's on his mind?"* 1946
6 x 22 x 15 (2 ⅜" x 8 ⅝" x 5 ⅞")
Museum of Palekh Art, Palekh
Based on a contemporary Russian lyrical song about a young fellow who goes in circles around a girl's house, winking at her time and again. "What's on his mind?" wonders the girl.

89 Ivan Zubkov. 1883–1938
Oval casket: *Harvesting.* 1929
3.6 x 19.3 x 9.5 (1 ⅜" x 7 ⅝" x 3 ¾")
Museum of Palekh Art, Palekh

90 Ivan Markichev. 1883–1955.
People's Artist of the RSFSR
Casket: *Haymaking.* 1926
4.8 x 10 x 8.8 (1 ⅞" x 3 ⅞" x 3 ½")
Russian Museum, Leningrad

91 Ivan Markichev. 1883–1955.
People's Artist of the RSFSR
Casket: *Harvesting.* 1925
4.3 x 13.5 x 8.5 (1 ¾" x 5 ⅜" x 3 ⅜")
Museum of Palekh Art, Palekh

92, 93 Ivan Golikov. 1886–1937.
Merited Artist of the RSFSR
Panel: *Yaroslavna Weeping.* 1933
Tempera on wood. 36 x 24 (14 ⅛" x 9 ½")
Tretyakov Gallery, Moscow
An episode from the 12th-century Russian epic *The Lay of Igor's Host.* Yaroslavna, the wife of Prince Igor who was captured by the Polovtsians, bemoans the bitter lot of her husband and his army.

94 Vladimir Kotukhin. 1897–1957
Brooch: *Troika.* 1929
3 x 6 (1 ⅛" x 2 ⅜")
Museum of Palekh Art, Palekh
See note on pls. 15, 16.

95 Alexander Kotukhin. 1886–1961.
People's Artist of the RSFSR
Casket: *Pushkin's Fairy-tales.* 1939
9.5 x 26.5 x 19.5 (3 ¾" x 10 ⅜" x 7 ⅝")
Tretyakov Gallery, Moscow
Based on the fairy-tales by Alexander Pushkin (1799–1837): *The Tale of Tsar Saltan* (see note on pls. 171, 190), *The Tale of the Dead Princess and Seven Knights* (see note on pl. 129), *The Tale of the Fisherman and the Golden Fish* (see note on pl. 81).

96 Stanislav Butorin. Born 1940
Decorative box: *"Hey, crony, why don't you come in?"* 1974
3 x 5.7 x 5.7 (1 ⅛" x 2 ¼" x 2 ¼")
Russian Museum, Leningrad
Based on a comic folk song.

97 Stanislav Butorin. Born 1940
Round casket: *The Sun Pantry.* 1978
6.5 x 5.0 (2 ½" x 2")
All-Russia Museum of Decorative and Folk Arts, Moscow
Based on the story of the same name by Mikhail Prishvin (1873–1954) about an orphaned brother and sister who lived by themselves during the war and had some wonderful adventures in the woods.

98 Sergei Solonin. 1892–1952
Casket: *The Lower Depths.* 1932
3.5 x 9.4 x 13.8 (1 ⅜" x 3 ¾" x 5 ⅜")
Museum of Palekh Art, Palekh
Based on the play of the same name by the outstanding proletarian writer Maxim Gorky (Alexei Peshkov, 1868–1936). The play shows the people who have found themselves at the very bottom of society and live in doss-houses.

99 Dmitry Turin. 1899–1945
Casket: *Count Nulin.* 1934
7.8 x 27.2 x 9.3 (3 ⅛" x 10 ¾" x 3 ⅝")
Museum of Palekh Art, Palekh
Based on the poem of the same name by Alexander Pushkin (1799–1837). The miniature shows one of the characters getting ready to leave for a hunt.
Museum of Palekh Art, Palekh

100 Vasily Salabanov. 1902–1941
Casket: *The Nose.* 1935
4.8 x 15.8 x 22.2 (1 ⅞" x 6 ¼" x 8 ¾")
Museum of Palekh Art, Palekh
Based on the story of the same name by the great Russian writer Nikolai Gogol (1809–1852) about the misadventures of a person who has lost his nose.

101 Aristarkh Dydykin. 1874–1954
Decorative plate: *Demyan's Fish-soup.* 1931
20 x 2.7 (7 ⅞" x 1 ⅛")
Museum of Palekh Art, Palekh
See note on pl. 7.

102 Aristarkh Dydykin. 1874–1954
Casket: *The Reapers.* 1933
4.3 x 17 x 8.8 (1 ¾" x 6 ¾" x 3 ½")
Museum of Palekh Art, Palekh

103 Ivan Bakanov. 1870–1936.
Merited Artist of the RSFSR
Panel: *Morning in the Country.* 1929
0.6 x 16 x 11 (¼" x 6 ¼" x 4 ⅜")
Russian Museum, Leningrad
Based on the Russian folk song "Don't wake me so early in the morning".

104 Ivan Bakanov. 1870–1936.
Merited Artist of the RSFSR
Casket: *Palekh.* 1934
4.3 x 26.8 x 19.5 (1 ¾" x 10 ½" x 7 ⅝")
Museum of Palekh Art, Palekh

105 Ivan Bakanov. 1870–1936.
Merited Artist of the RSFSR
Casket: *By the Roadway.* 1934
8.4 x 26.9 x 19.6 (3 ¼" x 10 ⅝" x 7 ¾")
Museum of Palekh Art, Palekh
Based on the Russian folk song about a young girl who walks along the roadway to a well and is stopped by a young lad.

106 Ivan Dorofeyev. 1902–1969
Powder-case: *Leisure-time.* 1936

Tempera and lacquer on wood.
5.2 x 1.3 (2" x ½")
Museum of Palekh Art, Palekh

107 Alexei Vatagin. 1881–1947
Powder-case: *The Reaper.* 1932
7.2 x 2.4 (2 ⅞" x 1")
Museum of Palekh Art, Palekh

108 Ivan Vakurov. 1885–1968.
People's Artist of the RSFSR
Casket: *The Forest Tale.* 1932
10 x 27.1 x 21 (3 ⅞" x 10 ⅝" x 8 ¼")
Museum of Palekh Art, Palekh
Based on the fairy-play of the same name by
the Ukrainian writer Lesia Ukrainka (Larisa
P. Kosach-Kvitka, 1871–1913).

109 Ivan Vakurov. 1885–1968.
People's Artist of the RSFSR
Casket: *The Wood Goblin.* 1928
5.2 x 17 x 8.5 (2" x 6 ¾" x 3 ⅜")
All-Russia Museum of Decorative and
Folk Arts, Moscow
The wood goblin is an ancient folklore
character going back to the times of
paganism.

110 Boris Yermolayev. Born 1934.
People's Artist of the RSFSR
Casket: *The Arabian Tales.* 1968
8 x 20 x 12 (3 ⅛" x 7 ⅞" x 4 ¾")
Museum of Palekh Art, Palekh

111 Alexander Doshlygin. Born 1953
Casket: *The Tale of the Fisherman and
the Golden Fish.* 1980
4.5 x 17.7 x 12.5 (1 ¾" x 7" x 4 ⅞")
Museum of Palekh Art, Palekh
See note on pl. 81.

112, 113 Anna Kotukhina. Born 1915.
People's Artist of the USSR, Winner of
the Repin State Prize of the RSFSR
Panel: *Birch-tree.* 1956
0.7 x 20 x 40 (¼" x 7 ⅞" x 15 ¾")
Museum of Palekh Art, Palekh
The miniature is dedicated to the "Birch-
tree" Russian Folk Dance Company.

114 Pavel Chalunin. 1918–1980.
Merited Artist of the RSFSR
Casket: *Peresvet Fighting Chelubei.* 1945
7 x 18 x 22.5 (2 ¾" x 7 ⅛" x 8 ⅞")
Museum of Palekh Art, Palekh
Peresvet was the Russian monk and warrior,
while Chelubei the Mongolian fighting man.
Their duel preceded the Kulikovo Battle of
1380 in which the Russian army led by Prince
Dmitry of the Don crushed the horde of
Khan Mamai.

115 Grigory Bureyev. 1900–1972.
Merited Artist of the RSFSR
Casket: *The Gypsies.* 1946
5 x 12 x 20 (2" x 4 ¾" x 7 ⅞")
All-Russia Museum of Decorative and
Folk Arts, Moscow
Based on the poem *The Gypsies* by Alexander Pushkin (1799–1837). Aleko, a nobleman,
abandoned his society and joined the gypsies.
However, he was unable to accept their free
ways. Out of jealousy he killed his beloved
Zemphira and the gypsies sent him away
from the camp saying: "Your love of freedom
— how you flaunt it! / Yet for yourself alone
you want it!"

116 Nikolai Zinovyev. 1888–1979.
Hero of Socialist Labour, People's Artist
of the USSR, Winner of the Repin State
Prize of the RSFSR
Casket: *The Little Hunch-backed Horse.* 1967
4 x 19 x 27 (1 ⅝" x 7 ½" x 10 ⅝")
Museum of Palekh Art, Palekh
Based on the tale of the same name by Piotr
Yershov (1815–1869). A peasant's son Ivan
commits numerous exploits helped by his
friend — the little hunch-backed horse.

117 Kaleria Kukuliyeva. Born 1937
Round casket: *The Garland of the Danube.*
1967
3.8 x 21 (1 ½" x 8 ¼")
Museum of Fine Arts, Ivanovo

118, 119 Oleg An. Born 1952
Casket: *Seven Muzhiks.* 1979
5 x 27.2 x 20.5 (2" x 10 ¾" x 8 ⅛")
All-Russia Museum of Decorative and
Folk Arts, Moscow

Based on the poem *Who Is Well-off in Russia*
by the famous Russian poet Nikolai Nekrasov
(1821–1877). Seven muzhiks from seven
villages have decided to find out "who's
living a free and jolly life in Russia".

120 Vadim Zotov. Born 1936
Casket: *Autumn.* 1984
3 x 20 x 12 (1 ⅛" x 7 ⅞" x 4 ¾")
Art Foundation of the RSFSR, Moscow

121 Vadim Zotov. Born 1936
Casket: *Morning.* 1984
3 x 20 x 14 (1 ⅛" x 7 ⅞" x 5 ½")
Art Foundation of the RSFSR, Moscow

122 Alexander Klipov. Born 1942
Casket: *Alexander Pushkin Meets
Ivan Pushchin.* 1984
5 x 12 x 12 (2" x 4 ¾" x 4 ¾")
Museum of Palekh Art, Palekh
Ivan Pushchin (1798–1859) was a friend of
the great Russian poet (see note on pl. 70).
For participation in the anti-tsar uprising on
14 December 1825 Pushchin was sentenced to
life penal servitude of which he served twenty
years. Author of *The Notes about Pushkin.*
Ivan Pushchin visited the disfavoured
poet during his exile in the village of
Mikhailovskoye. The miniature shows the
meeting of the friends.

123 Tatyana Andriyashkina. Born 1952
Powder-case: *In the Wood.* 1984
6.5 x 2 (2 ½" x ¾")
Museum of Palekh Art, Palekh

124 Irina Livanova. Born 1937
Portmanteau: *Picking Berries.* 1984
2.5 x 5 x 6 (1" x 2" x 2 ⅜")
Museum of Palekh Art, Palekh

125, 126 Grigori Melnikov. Born 1916.
People's Artist of the RSFSR
Panel: *Ivan Golikov.* 1967
40.2 x 60 (15 ⅞" x 23 ⅝")
Museum of Palekh Art, Palekh
Ivan Golikov (1886–1937) was one of the
founders of the Ancient Painting Coopera-

tive Society and the most brilliant and gifted representative of the new Palekh art.

127 Nikolai Gribov. Born 1948
Casket: *The Hunt.* 1981
34.5 x 4.7 x 3.5 (13 5/8" x 1 7/8" x 1 3/8")
Museum of Palekh Art, Palekh

128 Olga Subbotina. Born 1954
Casket: *The Trumpet Blared.* 1984
3 x 10 x 5 (1 1/8" x 3 7/8" x 2")
Ministry of Culture of the RSFSR, Moscow
Based on the Russian folk song. By custom the young bride had to conceal her braid under the head-dress. The miniature shows the scene of dressing the bride: "The trumpet blared early in the morning, and the young maid shed a few tears over her beautiful braid," the song goes.

129 Nikolai Lopatin. Born 1947
Casket: *The Tale of the Dead Princess.* 1979
6 x 9.7 x 14.3 (2 3/8" x 3 7/8" x 5 5/8")
Museum of Palekh Art, Palekh
Based on the fairy-tale of the same name by Alexander Pushkin (1799–1837). The evil Queen ordered her step-daughter to be left alone in the thick wood, but the Princess found refuge in the tower of seven knight-brothers. Then the Queen sent her a poisoned apple, the Princess fell into deadly coma but was awakened by her groom Prince Yelisei.

130 Valentin Khodov. Born 1942.
Merited Artist of the RSFSR
Decorative plate: *Summer.* 1980
Diam. 26 (10 1/4")
All-Russia Museum of Decorative and Folk Arts, Moscow

131 Gennady Kochetov. Born 1941
Casket: *Noon.* 1984
4.3 x 10 x 15 (1 3/4" x 3 7/8" x 5 7/8")
The artist's property

132 Viacheslav Morokin. Born 1945
Casket: *Merchant Kalashnikov.* 1972
5.7 x 26.4 x 19.5 (2 1/4" x 10 3/8" x 7 5/8")
Museum of Palekh Art, Palekh
Based on the poem of the same name by the great Russian poet Mikhail Lermontov (1814–1841). Merchant Kalashnikov challenges Ivan the Terrible's retainer Kiribeyevich, who has been making passes at his wife, to a fight. The merchant kills his rival and the angry tsar orders him to be put to death.

133 Alexander Gelishev. Born 1954
Casket: *Puppet-makers.* 1984
4 x 20 x 14 (1 5/8" x 7 7/8" x 5 1/2")
Museum of Palekh Art, Palekh

134 Yuri Shchanitsyn. Born 1947
Casket: *The Russian Hunt. Spring. Summer. Autumn. Winter.* 1984
7 x 12 x 6 (2 3/4" x 4 3/4" x 2 3/8")
Ministry of Culture of the RSFSR

135 Yekaterina Shchanitsyna. Born 1947
Casket: *The Fair.* 1980
6 x 14.5 x 3.5 (2 3/8" x 5 3/4" x 1 3/8")
All-Russia Museum of Decorative and Folk Arts, Moscow

136 Alexei Kochupalov. Born 1940.
People's Artist of the RSFSR
Casket: *Mikhailo Kazarinov.* 1977
5 x 24 x 17 (2" x 9 1/2" x 6 3/4")
Museum of Palekh Art, Palekh
Mikhailo Kazarinov, a Russian epic hero, rescues his sister from captivity.

137, 138 Galina Zhiriakova. Born 1948
Casket: *Great Novgorod.* 1978
6 x 27.5 x 20.5 (2 3/8" x 10 7/8" x 8 1/8")
All-Russia Museum of Decorative and Folk Arts, Moscow
A scene from the history of the Russian free city of Novgorod. Known from the year 859 it was the capital of the Novgorod Republic between 1131 and 1478. The city maintained trade relations with many states of the East and West and was renowned for its versatile crafts and unique architecture. In 1478 Novgorod was forcibly united with the centralized Russian state by Ivan III.

139 Alexander Borunov. Born 1920.
Merited Artist of the RSFSR
Casket: *The Little Hunch-backed Horse.* 1971
2 x 12 x 6 (3/4" x 4 3/4" x 2 3/8")
Museum of Palekh Art, Palekh
See note on pl. 116.

140 Nina Bogachova. Born 1941
Casket: *"Oh, mother, why is dust rolling in the field?"*. 1984
9 x 8 x 10 (3 1/2" x 3 1/8" x 3 7/8")
Art Foundation of the RSFSR, Moscow
A melancholy Russian folk song sung by a girl in foreboding of her departure from her parental home: the match-makers are on their way.

141 Lilia Zverkova. Born 1941
Casket: *Noon.* 1984
4.2 x 20 x 26.6 (1 5/8" x 7 7/8" x 10 1/2")
Art Foundation of the RSFSR, Moscow

142 Dmitry Butorin. 1891–1960.
Merited Artist of the RSFSR
Round box: *The Red Army Man.* 1926
2.7 x 7.8 (1 1/8" x 3 1/8")
Tretyakov Gallery, Moscow

143 Dmitry Butorin. 1891–1960.
Merited Artist of the RSFSR
Casket: *Lukomorye.* 1947
4 x 23.5 x 18.6 (1 5/8" x 9 1/4" x 7 3/8")
Museum of Palekh Art, Palekh
Based on the poem *Ruslan and Liudmila* by Alexander Pushkin (1799–1837). In the foreword the poet mentions some characters of the Russian fairy-tales: the mermaid, the witch and the wood goblin. The action is set in the fairy-tale land of Lukomorye.

144 Grigory Bakanov. 1881–1927
Powder-case: *Guitar-player.* 1926
1.5 x 3.5 (5/8" x 1 3/8")
Museum of Palekh Art, Palekh

145 Vladimir Smirnov. Born 1951
Casket: *The Tale of the Fisherman and the Golden Fish.* 1981
4.2 x 6 x 4.4 (1 5/8" x 2 3/8" x 1 3/4")
Museum of Palekh Art, Palekh
See note on pl. 81.

146 Grigory Bakanov. 1881–1927
Powder-case: *With the Hens.* 1925
2.5 x 4 (1" x 1 ⅝")
Museum of Palekh Art, Palekh

147 Boris Kukuliyev. Born 1936.
People's Artist of the RSFSR
Casket: *"So long, towns and huts".* 1969
3 x 3 x 9 (1 ⅛" x 1 ⅛" x 3 ½")
Museum of Fine Arts, Ivanovo
Based on a Soviet song.

148 Raisa Smirnova (born 1935), jeweller **Liubov Kolovangina** (born 1947)
Pendant: *The Little Hunch-backed Horse.* 1975
0.7 x 6.5 x 5.5 (¼" x 2 ½" x 2 ⅛")
All-Russia Museum of Decorative and Folk Arts, Moscow
See note on pl. 116.

149 Nikolai Zinovyev. 1888–1979.
Hero of Socialist Labour, People's Artist of the USSR, Winner of the Repin State Prize of the RSFSR
Box for stamps: *History of the Earth.* 1930
3.4 x 14.3 x 3.4 (1 ⅜" x 5 ⅝" x 1 ⅜")
Tretyakov Gallery, Moscow

150 Alexander Briagin. 1888–1948
Casket: *The Battle.* 1933
5 x 12.5 x 8.5 (2" x 4 ⅞" x 3 ⅜")
Art Museum, Mstiora (branch of the Vladimir-Suzdal Museum Centre of Art and Architecture)
An abstract battle scene touched with romantic colouring characteristic of Briagin's miniatures.

151 Grigory Dmitriyev. 1888–1939
Casket: *Stepan Razin.* 1932
5.5 x 18 x 14 (2 ⅛" x 7 ⅛" x 5 ½")
Art Museum, Mstiora
Based on the popular Russian folk song about Stepan Razin. Stepan Razin (1630–1671), a Cossack from the Don, leader of the 1670–71 peasant war, was executed and became the hero of many folk songs. The song relates how Razin's Cossacks sailed up the Volga river after a foray. Their booty included a Persian princess. The miniature shows the moment of the song when Razin, unwilling to quarrel with his comrades over the woman, throws her into the river.

152 Vasily Ovchinnikov. 1885–1952
Casket: *Harvesting.* 1936
5.3 x 18.5 x 9.5 (2 ⅛" x 7 ¼" x 3 ¾")
Art Museum, Mstiora

153 Nikolai Klykov. 1861–1944
Casket: *Collective Farm's Harvest.* 1936
6 x 18 x 9 (2 ⅜" x 7 ⅛" x 3 ½")
Art Museum, Mstiora

154 Nikolai Klykov. 1861–1944
Casket: *Landscape.* 1938
5 x 14.5 x 10 (2" x 5 ¾" x 3 ⅞")
Art Museum, Mstiora

155, 156 Ivan Serebriakov. 1888–1967
Casket: *Sadko.* 1948
7 x 19 x 28.3 (2 ¾" x 7 ½" x 11 ⅛")
Art Museum, Mstiora
Based on the epic of the same name about Sadko, a merchant and psaltery-player from Novgorod. The miniature shows the last episode: the Sea King was so pleased with Sadko's psaltery playing that he let him go back to the land.

157 Alexander Kotiagin. 1882–1943
Casket: *Midday.* 1931
10 x 12 x 10 (3 ⅞" x 4 ¾" x 3 ⅞")
Art Museum, Mstiora

158 Alexander Kotiagin. 1882–1943
Casket: *Troika. Evening.* 1932
4.5 x 13 x 8.5 (1 ¾" x 5 ⅛" x 3 ⅜")
Art Museum, Mstiora
See note on pls. 15, 16.

159 Ivan Morozov. 1884–1962.
Merited Artist of the RSFSR
Oval casket: *The Dance.* 1947
4 x 13 x 6 (1 ⅝" x 5 ⅛" x 2 ⅜")
Art Museum, Mstiora

160 Ivan Morozov. 1884–1962.
Merited Artist of the RSFSR
Casket: *The Tale of the Golden Cockerel.* 1946
6.6 x 23.5 x 16.5 (2 ⅝" x 9 ¼" x 6 ½")
Art Museum, Mstiora
Based on the fairy-tale of the same name by Alexander Pushkin (1799–1837). An old star-gazer presented Tsar Dodon with a golden cockerel. From then on the cockerel crowed every time Dodon's state was threatened with a foreign invasion. Dodon became invincible. Once returning from a campaign and bringing with him an overseas Queen, the Tsar met the star-gazer at the city gates. The old man claimed the Queen as the recompense promised by the Tsar. In his anger Dodon knocked the star-gazer dead with his sceptre. In the same instant the golden cockerel pecked the Tsar on the top of his head and he fell down dead.

161 Fiodor Shilov. 1915–1967
Casket: *The Hunt.* 1946
5 x 18 x 9 (2" x 7 ⅛" x 3 ½")
Art Museum, Mstiora

162 Fiodor Shilov. 1915–1967
Casket: *Troika.* 1959
7.5 x 19.5 x 9.5 (3" x 7 ⅝" x 3 ¾")
Art Museum, Mstiora
See note on pls. 15, 16.

163 Nikolai Klykov. 1861–1944
Casket: *At the Well.* 1942
6 x 22 x 15.5 (2 ⅜" x 8 ⅝" x 6 ⅛")
Art Museum, Mstiora
The solemn, refined and highly conventionalized language of icon-painting imparts grandeur and inner significance to the ordinary scene.

164 Nikolai Klykov. 1861–1944
Casket: *Prince Vladimir.* 1942
13 x 23 x 16 (5 ⅛" x 9" x 6 ¼")
Art Museum, Mstiora
The miniature shows the opening episode of the ancient Kiev epic: Prince Vladimir of Kiev sends his two knights, Dunai and Dobrynia, as match-makers to the Lithuanian Princess Apraksa.

165 Fiodor Shilov. 1915–1967
Casket: *The Demons.* 1951

4.4 x 12.8 x 8.8 (1 ¾" x 5" x 3 ½")
Art Museum, Mstiora
Based on the poem of the same name by Alexander Pushkin (1799–1837), which describes the fears of a traveller caught by a snowstorm in the steppe at night:

"Spinning storm-clouds, rushing storm-clouds,
Hazy skies, a hazy night
And the furtive moon that slyly
Sends the flying snow alight.
On we drive, the waste is boundless,
Nameless plains skim past, and hills.
Gripped by fear, I sit unmoving
Tink-tink-tinkle go the bells".

166 Ivan Fomichov. 1890–1972.
People's Artist of the RSFSR, Winner of the Repin State Prize of the RSFSR
Decorative box: *The Defence of Vladimir in 1238.* 1946
4 x 7.5 x 6.5 (1 ⅝" x 3" x 2 ½")
Art Museum, Mstiora
The miniature shows the siege of Vladimir by Khan Batu during the invasion of 1208–55.

167 Yevgeny Yurin. 1898–1983.
People's Artist of the RSFSR
Casket: *Ornament.* 1954
4 x 14 x 14 (1 ⅝" x 5 ½" x 5 ½")
Art Museum, Mstiora
The decorative ornament developed into a distinctive style of the Mstiora lacquered miniature and largely stemmed from the traditional iconic ornamentation.

168 Yevgeny Yurin. 1898–1983.
People's Artist of the RSFSR
Casket: *Ornament.* 1970s
4.4 x 15.7 x 10.5 (1 ¾" x 6 ⅛" x 4 ⅛")
All-Russia Museum of Decorative and Folk Arts, Moscow

169 Yevgeny Yurin. 1898–1983.
People's Artist of the RSFSR
Casket: *Fairy-tale.* 1970s
4.5 x 15.5 x 10.6 (1 ¾" x 6 ⅛" x 4 ⅛")
All-Russia Museum of Decorative and Folk Arts, Moscow

170 Vasily Krotov. 1884–1967
Casket: *Meeting with a Sorcerer.* 1950
5 x 10 x 10 (2" x 3 ⅞" x 3 ⅞")
Art Museum, Mstiora
Based on *The Song of the Wise Oleg* by Alexander Pushkin (1799–1837). Oleg was the first historically verified Russian prince (?–912), renowned for his triumphant campaigns against Constantinople. The legend holds that once a soothsayer prophesied that the prince would receive death from his favourite horse. Oleg parted with the horse but having later learned that the horse had died, he wished to see it and was fatally bitten by the snake that crept out from the horse's skull.

171 Alexander Merkuryev. 1892–1977
Casket: *The Tale of Tsar Saltan.* 1953
5.5 x 19.5 x 12 (2 ⅛" x 7 ⅝" x 4 ¾")
Art Museum, Mstiora
Based on the fairy-tale of the same name by Alexander Pushkin (1799–1837). The miniature shows the episode when the courtiers, deceived by counterfeit order of Tsar Saltan decide to put the queen and the prince in a barrel and throw it into the sea.

172 Vasily Korsakov. Born 1921
Casket: *The Willow.* 1962
4.2 x 10.5 x 15.8 (1 ⅝" x 4 ⅛" x 6 ¼")
All-Russia Museum of Decorative and Folk Arts, Moscow
The motif is borrowed from a contemporary Russian song about the sufferings of a girl who was betrayed by her beloved:

"Oh you green willow-tree
Don't keep it back from me,
Say, where my love is?"

173 Lydia Demidova. Born 1927
Casket: *Avdotya of Riazan.* 1970s
3.5 x 16.3 x 16.3 (1 ⅜" x 6 ⅜" x 6 ⅜")
All-Russia Museum of Decorative and Folk Arts, Moscow
Based on the Russian historical song (presumably of the 13th century) about a woman named Avdotya whose native town of Riazan had been ravaged by the enemy. Avdotya went to the Golden Horde and having overcome many obstacles moved Khan Bakhmet to let the Russian captives return with her to their homeland.

174 Lydia Demidova. Born 1927
Casket: *A Concert on the BAM.* 1970s
3.5 x 19 x 18.7 (1 ⅜" x 7 ½" x 7 ⅜")
All-Russia Museum of Decorative and Folk Arts, Moscow
The BAM (Baikal-Amur Main Line) is the railroad spanning East Siberia and the Far East. Many theatre and dance companies mounted field peformances for the BAM construction workers.

175 Piotr Zayets. Born 1951
Casket: *The Mstiora Peddlers.* 1970s
4.5 x 25 x 14.5 (1 ¾" x 9 ⅞" x 5 ¾")
All-Russia Museum of Decorative and Folk Arts, Moscow
Petty peddlers in Mstiora (called *ofenias*) bought up icons from local workshops and sold them throughout Russia. In the meantime they took orders for icons that they passed over to the Mstiora painters.

176 Yekaterina Zonina. Born 1919
Casket: *Minin's Appeal to the Residents of Nizhni Novgorod.* 1977
6 x 20.3 x 14 (2 ⅜" x 8" x 5 ½")
All-Russia Museum of Decorative and Folk Arts, Moscow
The miniature recreates the historical event of the early 17th century when Russia was nearly broken down under the onset of invaders. In the autumn of 1611 the elder of a suburbian community in Nizhni Novgorod, Kozma Minin (?–1616), called on the residents of the city to offer means for freeing their land.

177 Valentina Malakhova. Born 1933
Casket: *Festival in Mstiora.* 1970s
3.5 x 18.5 x 18.5 (1 ⅜" x 7 ¼" x 7 ¼")
All-Russia Museum of Decorative and Folk Arts, Moscow
Scenes from the festival to welcome spring in contemporary Mstiora.

178 Nikolai Dmitriyev. Born 1916
Casket: *At the Trinity–St. Sergius Monastery.* 1980
3.8 x 17.5 x 14.3 (1 ½" x 6 ⅞" x 5 ⅝")
All-Russia Museum of Decorative and Folk Arts, Moscow

The legend goes that before the Kulikovo Battle (1380) the Moscow prince Dmitry of the Don (1350–1389) went to the Trinity–St. Sergius Monastery to solicit benediction from Superior Sergius of Radonezh (1321–1391) who sent two monk warriors, Peresvet and Osliabia, with the prince.

179 Vera Korsakova. Born 1918
Casket: *Floral Ornament.* 1975
3.8 x 18 x 8.3 (1 ½" x 7 ⅛" x 3 ¼")
All-Russia Museum of Decorative and Folk Arts, Moscow

180 Vera Korsakova. Born 1918
Casket: *The Nightingale's Song.* 1980s
4.5 x 12.3 x 12.3 (1 ¾" x 4 ⅞" x 4 ⅞")
All-Russia Museum of Decorative and Folk Arts, Moscow

181 Vladimir Moshkovich. Born 1946
Casket: *For the Russian Land.* 1980
3 x 7.7 x 6.7 (1 ⅛" x 3" x 2 ⅝")
All-Russia Museum of Decorative and Folk Arts, Moscow
See note on pl. 114.

182 Vladimir Moshkovich. Born 1946
Casket: *The Decree on Land.* 1977
3.8 x 17.3 x 10.2 (1 ½" x 6 ¾" x 4")
All-Russia Museum of Decorative and Folk Arts, Moscow
The miniature recreates the events that unfolded in the village after the October Revolution. Under Lenin's Decree on Land passed on 27 October 1917 all the manor, church and monastery lands were nationalized and divided between peasants.

183 Vladimir Molodkin. Born 1945
Casket: *The Wedding.* 1975
4.5 x 24.5 x 19 (1 ¾" x 9 ⅝" x 7 ½")
All-Russia Museum of Decorative and Folk Arts, Moscow

184 Vladimir Molodkin. Born 1945
Portmanteau: *"Company three was returning from the drill".* 1978
4.5 x 8.5 (1 ¾" x 3 ⅜")
All-Russia Museum of Decorative and Folk Arts, Moscow
Based on a Soviet song.

185, 186 Alexander Nikolayev. Born 1938
Casket: *Early Russia.* 1977
15.7 x 30.5 x 20.7 (6 ⅛" x 12" x 8 ⅛")
All-Russia Museum of Decorative and Folk Arts, Moscow
Based on the novel of the same name by the Soviet writer Valentin Ivanov (1902–1975). The novel is about that period of Russia's ancient history when the Slavic tribes began to unite against Byzantine as well as bellicose nomadic tribes (6th–9th centuries A.D.).

187 Piotr Sosin. Born 1936
Casket: *The Rural Labours.* 1980s
7 x 24 x 11.5 (2 ¾" x 9 ½" x 4 ½")
All-Russia Museum of Decorative and Folk Arts, Moscow

188 Piotr Sosin. Born 1936
Casket: *Zheleznovodsk, a Caucasian Health-centre.* 1970s
4.5 x 24 x 18.5 (1 ¾" x 9 ½" x 7 ¼")
All-Russia Museum of Decorative and Folk Arts, Moscow
Zheleznovodsk is a major health resort famous for its medicinal mineral waters in the Stavropol Territory of the Northern Caucasus.

189 Piotr Sosin. Born 1936
Casket: *In Ambush.* 1980
4.8 x 22 x 15.7 (1 ⅞" x 8 ⅝" x 6 ⅛")
All-Russia Museum of Decorative and Folk Arts, Moscow
The miniature recreates the 1380 Kulikovo Battle that played a crucial role in the Russian state's struggle for independence. The outcome of the Kulikovo Battle was largely determined by a surprise attack launched by the Russian ambush regiment that put the enemy to flight.

190 Valentin Tikhomirov. Born 1947
Casket: *The Tale of Tsar Saltan.* 1978
4 x 17.5 x 14.5 (1 ⅝" x 6 ⅞" x 5 ¾")
All-Russia Museum of Decorative and Folk Arts, Moscow
See note on pl. 171. The miniature shows one of the last episodes of the tale: Tsar Saltan arrives on Buyan Island where he meets his wife, his son, Prince Guidon, and the Prince's young wife — the Swan-Princess.

191 Vera Starkova. Born 1926
Casket: *The Night Before Christmas.* 1979
3.5 x 16.3 x 16.3 (1 ⅜" x 6 ⅜" x 6 ⅜")
All-Russia Museum of Decorative and Folk Arts, Moscow
Based on the fantastic tale of the same name by Nikolai Gogol (1809–1852). During the outdoor fête in a Ukrainian village the capricious beauty Oksana promises Vakula the blacksmith that she will marry him if he brings her the Tsarina's golden slippers. On that magic night Vakula flies to St. Petersburg on the back of the devil and brings the slippers to his beloved.

192 Vera Starkova. Born 1926
Casket: *Beyond the Village.* 1970s
3.3 x 6 x 8 (1 ¼" x 2 ⅜" x 3 ⅛")
All-Russia Museum of Decorative and Folk Arts, Moscow

193 Valentin Fokeyev. Born 1940
Powder-case: *Lel's Songs.* 1980
4.7 x 7 (1 ⅞" x 2 ¾")
All-Russia Museum of Decorative and Folk Arts, Moscow
Based on the fantasy-play *The Snow-maiden* by the outstanding Russian dramatist Alexander Ostrovsky (1823–1886). The Snow-maiden, daughter of the Spring and the Frost, decided to live among the people of the Kingdom of Berendei. One day she heard the sweet songs of young Lel and fell in love with him.

194 Valentin Fokeyev. Born 1940
Casket: *The Unsubdued City.* 1970s
3.7 x 18.7 x 18.7 (1 ½" x 7 ⅜" x 7 ⅜")
All-Russia Museum of Decorative and Folk Arts, Moscow
The theme for the miniature is suggested by 13th-century Russian history. However, the events are treated symbolically rather than literally. The city is the generalized image of all Russian cities while the woman handing the golden sword to the warrior is Russia herself sending her sons forth to defend their

mother-country. The miniature mirrors the eternal struggle of the forces of Good and Evil.

195 Alexander Kalinichenko. Born 1946
Casket: *The Battle.* 1980
10 x 17 x 12 (3 ⅞" x 6 ¾" x 4 ¾")
All-Russia Museum of Decorative and Folk Arts, Moscow
See note on pls. 178, 189.

196 Alexander Kalinichenko. Born 1946
Casket: *The Voroshilov Army's Heroic Thrust to Tsaritsyn.* 1980
4.4 x 20.2 x 12.3 (1 ¾" x 8" x 4 ⅞")
All-Russia Museum of Decorative and Folk Arts, Moscow
Klim Voroshilov (1881–1969) commanded the Red Army that drove the White Guards out of the city of Tsaritsyn (now Volgograd) during the Civil War (1918–20).

197 Lev Fomichov. Born 1932.
Merited Artist of the RSFSR, Winner of the Repin State Prize of the RSFSR
Casket: *The Circus Show.* 1977
4.2 x 18.5 x 24 (1 ⅝" x 7 ¼" x 9 ½")
All-Russia Museum of Decorative and Folk Arts, Moscow
Boldly experimenting with contemporary themes, Lev Fomichov transforms the circus show into festive milieu of the living fairy-tale.

198 Lev Fomichov. Born 1932.
Merited Artist of the RSFSR, Winner of the Repin State Prize of the RSFSR
Casket: *The Tale of the Dead Princess.* 1970s
2.5 x 24 x 14.5 (1" x 9 ½" x 5 ¾")
All-Russia Museum of Decorative and Folk Arts, Moscow
See note on pl. 129.

199 Lev Fomichov. Born 1932.
Merited Artist of the RSFSR, Winner of the Repin State Prize of the RSFSR
Casket: *The Kulikovo Battle.* 1980
12.8 x 24.5 x 14.5 (5" x 9 ⅝" x 5 ¾")
All-Russia Museum of Decorative and Folk Arts, Moscow
See note on pl. 189.

200 Viacheslav Muratov. Born 1948.
Winner of the Leninist Komsomol Prize
Casket: *Peresvet Fighting Chelubei.* 1980
4.6 x 20.5 x 14.4 (1 ¾" x 8 ⅛" x 5 ⅝")
All-Russia Museum of Decorative and Folk Arts, Moscow
See note on pl. 114.

201 Nikolai Shishakov. Born 1925.
People's Artist of the RSFSR, Winner of the Repin State Prize of the RSFSR
Casket: *The Communards.* 1969
5.5 x 18 x 18 (2 ⅛" x 7 ⅛" x 7 ⅛")
Art Museum, Mstiora
The miniature mirrors the various activities of the communists to support and educate homeless children in the first years of Soviet power.

202 Nikolai Shishakov. Born 1925.
People's Artist of the RSFSR, Winner of the Repin State Prize of the RSFSR
Casket: *"Tittle-tattle".* 1980
All-Russia Museum of Decorative and Folk Arts, Moscow
Based on the Soviet lyrical song about a village girl whose love affair is not approved by the villagers:
"The narrow track meanders
Through snow-drifts, along the fence,
And as I pass by the well I hear
Women tittle-tattle about me.
Tittle-tattle, tittle-tattle.
One word leads to another.
The tittle-tattle will soon subside
While the love will stay . . ."

203 Nikolai Shishakov. Born 1925.
People's Artist of the RSFSR, Winner of the Repin State Prize of the RSFSR
Casket: *Saturday.* 1980
4.4 x 24 x 14.3 (1 ¾" x 9 ½" x 5 ⅝")
All-Russia Museum of Decorative and Folk Arts, Moscow

204, 205 Yuri Vavanov. Born 1937
Panel: *Sivka-Burka.* 1981
39 x 48.5 (15 ⅜" x 19 ⅛")
All-Russia Museum of Decorative and Folk Arts, Moscow
Based on the Russian folk tale about a peasant's son who married the Tsar's

daughter. The magic horse named Sivka-Burka took him to the window of a high tower where the Princess was sitting and he tore the ring off her finger.

206 Vladislav Nekosov. Born 1940
Casket: *Collective-farm Ploughmen. Evening.* 1980
4.3 x 20.5 x 12.5 (1 ¾" x 8 ⅛" x 4 ⅞")
All-Russia Museum of Decorative and Folk Arts, Moscow
The contemporary Mstiora miniaturists are coming up with innovative representations of the farming scenes that vividly communicate the rhythms of the eternal cycles of nature that set the pace of rural life even in our impetuous times.

207 Vladislav Nekosov. Born 1940
Casket: *The Battle on the Pyana River.* 1980
6 x 20.2 x 13.6 (2 ⅜" x 8" x 5 ⅜")
All-Russia Museum of Decorative and Folk Arts, Moscow
The miniature recreates an episode from Russian history: in 1377 the enemy launched a surprise attack on the Russian camp on the Pyana river.

208 Alexander Frolov. Born 1935
Casket: *Igor Taken Prisoner.* 1979
4.3 x 24.3 x 11.3 (1 ¾" x 9 ⅝" x 4 ½")
All-Russia Museum of Decorative and Folk Arts, Moscow
An illustration to the opera *Prince Igor* by Alexander Borodin (1833–1898). The libretto of the opera is based on the late 12th-century Russian epic *The Lay of Igor's Host.* In 1185 the Russian army led by Prince Igor was crushed by the Polovtsian troops. Igor was taken prisoner but managed to escape.

209 Vladimir Lebedev. Born 1953
Casket: *"Through the village, past the huts marched a detachment of Budionny".* 1970s
3.3 x 18.2 x 8.2 (1 ¼" x 7 ⅛" x 3 ¼")
All-Russia Museum of Decorative and Folk Arts, Moscow

Based on the song from the times of the Civil War (1918–20). Semion Budionny (1883–1973), a war hero, was commander of the First Cavalry Army.

210 Valentin Fokeyev. Born 1940
Casket: *"We won't shirk the battle".* 1970s
3.5 x 24.7 x 14.5 (1 ⅜" x 9 ¾" x 5 ¾")
All-Russia Museum of Decorative and Folk Arts, Moscow
Based on the song going back to the period of the revolution and Civil War (1917–20). The song celebrates the determination of workers and peasants not to spare their lives upholding the cause of the revolution and Soviet power.

211 Antonina Ovchinnikova. Born 1926
Casket: *The Frog Princess.* 1970s
3.5 x 6.5 x 4 (1 ⅜" x 2 ½" x 1 ⅝")
All-Russia Museum of Decorative and Folk Arts, Moscow
Based on a Russian fairy-tale. The Tsar's three sons shot arrows in three different directions and each took a bride for himself where his arrow fell. The youngest son Ivan had to marry the Frog Princess who happened to be a beautiful girl spell-bound by the evil sorcerer. Ivan killed the sorcerer and broke the spell.

212 Nikolai Naumov. Born 1916
Portmanteau: *The Groom.* 1977
2.7 x 7.8 x 5.5 (1 ⅛" x 3 ⅛" x 2 ⅛")
All-Russia Museum of Decorative and Folk Arts, Moscow
Based on the tale of the same name by Alexander Pushkin (1799–1837) about a young bride who during the wedding party exposed the groom as a brigand. The miniature shows the opening episode of the tale.

213 Alexander Shchadrin. Born 1925
Casket: *By a Wave of the Wand.* 1975
5.5 x 17.5 x 12.3 (2 ⅛" x 6 ⅞" x 4 ⅞")
All-Russia Museum of Decorative and Folk Arts, Moscow
Based on the Russian fairy-tale about a magic pike who helped Yemelia, the peasant's son, find wealth, happiness and marry the daughter of the Tsar.

214 Alexander Shchadrin. Born 1925
Casket: *Prince Dmitry Leads His Troops to the Kulikovo Field.* 1970s
6 x 2.4 x 10.5 (2 ⅜" x 1" x 4 ⅛")
All-Russia Museum of Decorative and Folk Arts, Moscow
See note on pls. 178, 189.

215 Sergei Mokin. 1891–1945.
Merited Artist of the RSFSR
Casket: *The Fountain of Bakhchisarai.* 1945
7.7 x 29.5 x 19.5 (3" x 11 ⅝" x 7 ⅝")
Lacquered Miniature Museum, Kholui
See note on pl. 229. The Crimean Khan Girei is shown in his harem.

216 Icon: *The Descent into Limbo.* Early 19th century
Tempera and gold on wood.
27 x 33 (10 ⅝" x 13")
Lacquered Miniature Museum, Kholui

217 Icon: *The Assumption.* Early 19th century
Tempera and gold on wood.
11 x 8.5 (4 ⅜" x 3 ⅜")
Lacquered Miniature Museum, Kholui

218 Sergei Mokin. 1891–1945.
Merited Artist of the RSFSR
Casket: *The Salute.* 1944
6.5 x 23 x 13 (2 ½" x 9" x 5 ⅛")
Folk Art Museum at the Institute of Industrial Art, Moscow
The miniature, dedicated to the Soviet Army's victories in the Second World War, expresses the joy of returning to a life of peace.

219 Sergei Mokin. 1891–1945.
Merited Artist of the RSFSR
Decorative box: *Working the Land.* 1930s
4.5 x 15 x 9 (1 ¾" x 5 ⅞" x 3 ½")
Folk Art Museum at the Institute of Industrial Art, Moscow

220 Konstantin Kosterin. 1899–1984
Panel: *The Tale of Tsar Saltan.* 1943
24.3 x 18 (9 ⅝" x 7 ⅛")
Lacquered Miniature Museum, Kholui
See notes on pls. 171, 190. Prince Guidon receives travelling merchants.

221 Konstantin Kosterin. 1899–1984
Casket: *The Strength of Defence.* 1934
4.5 x 18 x 11.5 (1 ¾" x 7 ⅛" x 4 ½")
Folk Art Museum at the Institute of Industrial Art, Moscow

222 Alexander Morozov. Born 1942
Casket: *Ruslan and Chernomor.* 1970
4 x 17.5 x 24 (1 ⅝" x 6 ⅞" x 9 ½")
Art Foundation of the RSFSR, Moscow
Based on the poem *Ruslan and Liudmila* by Alexander Pushkin (1799–1837). Ruslan, the hero of the poem, is fighting Chernomor, the abductor of his wife.

223 Vladimir Belov. Born 1923.
Merited Artist of the RSFSR
Casket: *Andrei Rublev.* 1965
2.5 x 17 x 23.5 (1" x 6 ¾" x 9 ¼")
Folk Art Museum at the Institute of Industrial Art, Moscow
Andrei Rublev (about 1360/70–about 1430) — the great Russian icon-painter. In the miniature he is shown working on his famous icon *Old Testament Trinity* permeated with the idea of concord and harmony.

224 Alexei Usikov. Born 1924
Casket: *Suvorov at Konchanskoye.* 1950
4 x 13.5 x 10.5 (1 ⅝" x 5 ⅜" x 4 ⅛")
Lacquered Miniature Museum, Kholui
Alexander Suvorov (1730–1800) — the generalissimo of the Russian army who never sustained a defeat. Konchanskoye was his ancestral estate where he spent the last years of his life in the company of veteran soldiers.

225 Vasily Puzanov-Molev. 1892–1961.
Merited Artist of the RSFSR
Casket: *Afanasy Nikitin in India.* 1959
4.7 x 18 x 13 (1 ⅞" x 7 ⅛" x 5 ⅛")
Folk Art Museum at the Institute of Industrial Art, Moscow
Afanasy Nikitin (?–1472), a merchant from the city of Tver, author of the book *The Voyage Across the Three Seas*, travelled to

Persia, India, Arabia, Turkey and Somalia in 1466–72.

226 Alexander Sotskov. Born 1937
Casket: *Ilya of Murom.* 1967
3.7 x 13 x 8.7 (1 ½" x 5 ⅛" x 3 ⅜")
Lacquered Miniature Museum, Kholui
Ilya of Murom is the hero of the 13th–16th century Russian epic, personifying the folk ideals of the valiant warrior.

227 Alexander Sotskov. Born 1937
Decorative box: *Alionushka.* 1963
2.8 x 3.3 x 8.5 (1 ⅛" x 1 ¼" x 3 ⅜")
Folk Art Museum at the Institute of Industrial Art, Moscow
Alionushka is the personage of Russian fairy-tales.

228 Nikolai Denisov. Born 1929.
Merited Artist of the RSFSR
Decorative box: *The Quartette.* 1956
8 x 12 x 10.5 (3 ⅛" x 4 ¾" x 4 ⅛")
Lacquered Miniature Museum, Kholui
Based on the fable of the same name by Ivan Krylov (1769–1844) about four untalented musicians who tried to play in tune by changing places until the nightingale told them that it was the skill rather than the right position that they lacked.

229 Nikolai Denisov. Born 1929.
Merited Artist of the RSFSR
Decorative box: *The Fountain of Bakhchisarai.* 1972
4 x 25.5 x 15.5 (1 ⅝" x 10" x 6 ⅛")
Folk Art Museum at the Institute of Industrial Art, Moscow
See note on pl. 215. The Crimean Khan Girei, deeply enamoured of his new captive, Polish princess Maria, forgets his previous love Zarema. Zarema, devoured by jealousy, kills her rival. By Girei's order Zarema is executed and a fountain of tears is built to express the Khan's undying grief.

230 Boris Tikhonravov. 1929–1977
Casket: *Dubrovsky.* 1957
11.5 x 22 x 13.5 (4 ½" x 8 ⅝" x 5 ⅜")
Folk Art Museum at the Institute of Industrial Art, Moscow
Dubrovsky, the hero of the story of the same name by Alexander Pushkin (1799–1837), was the chieftain of rebellious peasants. He fell in love with the daughter of the offender of his family Troyekurov, but she was given in marriage to someone else. The miniature shows the episode when Dubrovsky holds up the wedding carriage in the wood.

231 Boris Tikhonravov. 1929–1977
Brooch: *Alionushka.* 1969
Art Foundation of the RSFSR, Moscow
Diam. 5 (2")
See note on pl. 227.

232 Dmitry Dobrynin. 1884–1936
Oval box: *At Rest.* 1930s
3.5 x 13 x 7.5 (1 ⅜" x 5 ⅛" x 3")
Folk Art Museum at the Institute of Industrial Art, Moscow

233, 234 Alexander Morozov. Born 1942
Panel: *Yaroslav the Wise.* 1982
39.5 x 49 (15 ½" x 19 ¼")
Art Foundation of the RSFSR, Moscow
Prince Yaroslav the Wise (about 978–1054) reigned in Kievan Russia from 1019. His reign was a flourishing period in the history of the state. Town construction developed extensively, the St. Sofia Cathedral was built and the foundations of the Kiev-Pechorsky Monastery were laid. Yaroslav personally headed the drawing up of the ancient Russian code of laws known as *The Russian Truth*, and established dynastic relations with many countries of Europe.

235 Alexei Kosterin. Born 1929
Casket: *The Legend of Borok.* 1984
4 x 26 x 15.5 (1 ⅝" x 10 ¼" x 6 ⅛")
Lacquered Miniature Museum, Kholui
Borok is a waste land near Kholui where Prince Dmitry Pozharsky joined the troops of Kozma Minin in the Russian liberation war of 1610–18.

236 Alexei Kosterin. Born 1929
Casket: *The Song of the Wise Oleg.* 1967
3.2 x 9.5 x 6.7 (1 ¼" x 3 ¾" x 2 ⅝")
Folk Art Museum at the Institute of Industrial Art, Moscow
See note on pl. 170.

237, 238 Piotr Mitiashin. Born 1948
Casket: *The Song of Kiev.* 1982
3 x 28 x 22 (1 ⅛" x 11" x 8 ⅝")
Lacquered Miniature Museum, Kholui
The miniature shows an episode from the history of Kievan Russia — the earliest state of the Eastern Slavs in the 9th–early 12th centuries, its hey-day being associated with the name of Prince Yaroslav the Wise (see note on pls. 233, 234).

239 Boris Kiseliov. Born 1928.
People's Artist of the RSFSR, Winner of the Repin State Prize of the RSFSR
Casket: *The Lay of Igor's Host.* 1979
5 x 5 x 3 (2" x 2" x 1 ⅛")
Art Foundation of the RSFSR, Moscow
See note on pl. 208.

240 Boris Kiseliov. Born 1928.
People's Artist of the RSFSR, Winner of the Repin State Prize of the RSFSR
Decorative box: *The Frog Princess.* 1972
3.2 x 10 x 6.5 (1 ¼" x 3 ⅞" x 2 ½")
Folk Art Museum at the Institute of Industrial Art, Moscow
See note on pl. 211.

241 Boris Kiseliov. Born 1928.
People's Artist of the RSFSR, Winner of the Repin State Prize of the RSFSR
Casket: *Kholui.* 1980
4.4 x 7.2 x 3.6 (1 ¾" x 2 ⅞" x 1 ⅜")
Lacquered Miniature Museum, Kholui

242 Boris Kiseliov. Born 1928.
People's Artist of the RSFSR, Winner of the Repin State Prize of the RSFSR
Round box: *Suzdal.* 1964
2.4 x 8.7 (1" x 3 ⅜")
Folk Art Museum at the Institute of Industrial Art, Moscow
Suzdal is an ancient Russian city, known since 1024. In the 12th century it was the capital of the Suzdal principality.

243 Boris Kiseliov. Born 1928.
People's Artist of the RSFSR, Winner of
the Repin State Prize of the RSFSR
Casket: *Cock-fight.* 1960
6.7 x 20 x 20 (2 ⅝" x 7 ⅞" x 7 ⅞")
Lacquered Miniature Museum, Kholui

244 Valentin Krotov. 1928–1982
Decorative box: *Funeral Feast.* 1960s
4 x 10.7 x 9.4 (1 ⅝" x 4 ¼" x 3 ¾")
Lacquered Miniature Museum, Kholui
By ancient Russian custom the funeral feast
was served after the internment.

245 Alexei Kosterin. Born 1929
Decorative box: *Ivanushka.* 1967
3.5 x 6 x 10 (1 ⅜" x 2 ⅜" x 3 ⅞")
Lacquered Miniature Museum, Kholui
Ivanushka is the main character of many
Russian fairy-tales.

246 Alexei Kosterin. Born 1929
Decorative box: *Boris Godunov.* 1966
3.7 x 13 x 9 (1 ½" x 5 ⅛" x 3 ½")
Lacquered Miniature Museum, Kholui
Boris Godunov (1552–1605) was the Russian
tsar enthroned in 1598. The miniature based
on the drama of the same name by Alexander
Pushkin (1799–1837) shows the episode
when the God's fool accuses the tsar of
having murdered the legal heir to the throne
Prince Dmitry.

247 Nikolai Baburin. Born 1930.
Merited Artist of the RSFSR, Winner of
the Repin State Prize of the RSFSR
Casket: *The Tale of Tsar Saltan.* 1983
4 x 15 x 15 (1 ⅝" x 5 ⅞" x 5 ⅞")

Lacquered Miniature Museum, Kholui
See notes on pls. 171, 190. The miniature
shows Prince Guidon, transformed into a
bumble-bee, arrive in Tsar Saltan's palace.

248 Nikolai Baburin. Born 1930.
Merited Artist of the RSFSR, Winner of
the Repin State Prize of the RSFSR
Casket: *Fair in Old Kholui.* 1973
4 x 26 x 16 (1 ⅝" x 10 ¼" x 6 ¼")
All-Russia Museum of Decorative and
Folk Arts, Moscow

249 Nikolai Starikov. 1932–1974
Casket: *By a Wave of the Wand.* 1956
8.5 x 12 x 10.5 (3 ⅜" x 4 ¾" x 4 ⅛")
Folk Art Museum at the Institute of
Industrial Art, Moscow
See note on pl. 213.

250 Nikolai Shvetsov. Born 1955
Casket: *The Nose.* 1982
4 x 13 x 18 (1 ⅝" x 5 ⅛" x 7 ⅛")
Lacquered Miniature Museum, Kholui
See note on pl. 100.

251 Boris Novosiolov. Born 1946
Casket: *Guidon's Guests.* 1978
4.4 x 2.8 (1 ¾" x 1 ⅛")
All-Russia Museum of Decorative and
Folk Arts, Moscow
See notes on pls. 171, 190. The last episode of
The Tale of Tsar Saltan.

252 Boris Deviatkin. Born 1932
Round box: *Ornament.* 1969
4 x 13 x 9 (1 ⅝" x 5 ⅛" x 3 ½")
Lacquered Miniature Museum, Kholui

253 Victor Yolkin. Born 1950
Round box: *Autumn.* 1979
1.3 x 6.8 (1/2" x 2 ⅝")
Folk Art Museum at the Institute of
Industrial Art, Moscow

254 Victor Yolkin. Born 1950
Decorative box: *The Muzhik Who Kept
Two Generals.* 1982
4.7 x 11 x 9.7 (1 ⅞" x 4 ⅜" x 3 ⅞")
Lacquered Miniature Museum, Kholui
Based on the fairy-tale of the same name by
the great Russian satirist Mikhail Saltykov-
Shchedrin (1826–1889) about the diligence
and quick wit of the ordinary Russian muzhik
and the worthlessness of the tsar's generals
who lived by others' labours.

255 Victor Yolkin. Born 1950
Decorative box: *Pirosmani.* 1979
4 x 24 x 17.5 (1 ⅝" x 9 ½" x 6 ⅞")
Folk Art Museum at the Institute of
Industrial Art, Moscow
Niko Pirosmanashvili (Pirosmani, 1862?–
1918) — a self-educated Georgian primitivist
artist. The miniature shows characters from
his paintings.

256 Pavel Ivakin. 1915–1968
Decorative box: *The Flying Ship.* 1966
3.7 x 8.5 x 16.5 (1 ½" x 3 ⅜" x 6 ½")
Folk Art Museum at the Institute of
Industrial Art, Moscow
Based on the Russian fairy-tale about a
peasant's son and his friends who built a
wooden flying ship that helped the peasant's
son marry the daughter of the Tsar.